LESSONS OF
REDEMPTION

#DoRight

A MEMOIR BY KEVIN SHIRD

ISBN: 978-0-9895012-9-3

FOREWORD v

INTRODUCTION ix

WHERE IT ALL BEGAN 1

ME AND MY POPS 11

SCHOOL DAYS 19

YOU'RE IN THE GAME NOW 33

WHO KILLED ANTHONY? 59

ENTER THE DRAGON 71

BLOOD MONEY 91

WHAT'S REALLY GOING ON? 121

THE BEGINNING OF THE END 139

INSIDE THE JOINT 157

THE UNDERCOVER BROTHER 175

STEEL HOUSE ON THE MOUNTAINTOP 189

MAKING THE CHANGE 199

 GAME OVER 213

WORKING HARD FOR THE MONEY 225

INTERVENTION 241

THE CORNER 251

LETTER TO MY DAUGHTER 263

PART OF THE PROBLEM 271

ABOUT THE AUTHOR 281

FOREWORD

Whenever I'm in Washington D.C., the nation's capitol, I get a jolt of energy. I should be excited right? It's the center of the methodical universe. There are movers and shakers in every five-star restaurant in the metropolis ordering filet mignon and glasses of cognac. As my friend and mentor former U.S. Congressman Ron Dellums often puts it, "D.C. is the gateway to the entire world." When I'm here, my blood pressure rises ever so slightly and my bravado shines an extra gleam or two. My suit and tie fit immaculately and now I'm ready for an intellectual conversation with a D.C. insider. Today I'm headed to the White House compound to meet with officials from the White House Office on National Drug Control Policy (ONDCP).

The meeting is part of their 2013 ONDCP Conference on Drug Policy Reform. As I walk down 16th Street, crossing at K Street, I can see the most famous white building in the world sitting on Pennsylvania Avenue. The leaves on the trees surrounding this world-renown structure were several different shades of orange and brown. It was late November and the leaves were still holding on to the trees, but slightly. The global warming phenomenon of unseasonably warm weather had given them a few extra weeks.

On this day I've been invited here by officials to be part of the conversation on drug policy reform. I'd never been on the White House grounds before today so this is an extra special occasion. It's extra special because I never thought I could pass the security background check to get into the place, this place where only the elite of elite roam. My criminal record, which began at age nineteen, was so tainted with convictions that I assumed I could never receive a security clearance. Or so I previously thought. As I approached the security check point I could see the Secret Service agents armed with semi-automatic weapons protecting the most important home in the world: the White House. As the federal security force reviewed my identification card, I began to wonder if I might possibly meet Mr. Obama today. Could I possibly meet the first African American President of the most important country in the world? Probably not! But if I did, what would I say? What *could* I say? How would I explain my past misdeeds? How would I explain that while he was attending Harvard University preparing himself for the most important job in the world, I was selling illegal drugs to people struggling from the disease of addiction?

If given the opportunity to speak to the President during my visit to the White House on this sunny November morning, this is what I would say: "Mr. President, my life's journey, which I have chronicled in a new book, *Lessons of Redemption*, has been somewhat unorthodox. My goal, Mr. President, in writing this book was to motivate other people who've made mistakes in there lives to work harder, make better choices, and believe there is light at the end of the tunnel. Change is always possible, regardless of the negative situations you may have placed yourself in. Change starts with the complete understanding that you are truly sorry for the wrong you've done. Once you understand that you have made mistakes, believe that the strength is within you to change your behavior and believe that your Higher Power will help guide you along the way, change is possible. Nothing can stop you from becoming a positive member of society if that is what you truly desire to be. Even when it seems like your fate has been sealed and your demise is certain, a new way of life still awaits you." That's what I would say if given the chance to speak to the President of the United States during my visit to the White House.

INTRODUCTION

Spring 1992
Edmondson Village
Baltimore, Maryland

The doorknob was loose, nearly falling off the old squeaky door of the house. The paint on the windowsills was cracking and the decaying front porch creaked from repairs that remained undone. The address of the house that sat on the corner of this drug dealer's haven was 501 Normandy Avenue. Its close proximity to the illegal activities here in this failing section of Edmondson Village made this the perfect place to test our product. The constant foot traffic by the many visiting drug addicts had taken its toll on this dilapidated enclave. The door was dented from the police battering ram used in the most recent search of the house. This neighborhood shooting gallery had become an unsavory sight.

When I walked inside, Uncle Rob was standing in the middle of the living room floor, with both hands on a syringe sticking into the side of his neck. My stomach began to turn just from the sight of this awkward demonstration. His hands were trembling as he slowly pushed the plunger in. The cloudy substance from the needle eased into the veins of his neck. He took the needle from his flesh. Uncle Rob had just injected himself with two bags of heroin, heroin that the Diamond in the Raw crew had provided him.

Most of the veins in his arms and legs were already collapsed from injecting for so many years. There were only two places remaining on his body where he could continue injecting the illegal opiate. One of those places was his neck, the other was a place far too nauseating to name. This was the life of a man held captive by the disease of drug addiction, teetering on the brink of self-annihilation. Uncle Rob had been entrenched in this dreadful underworld for decades. When I needed a new product tested before it hit the streets, Uncle Rob was the man to consult. I could tell if he liked the package without asking him a single question; just watching his face was enough.

"Okay…, okay," he began mumbling just seconds after the stuff entered his bloodstream. Anthony – my confidante and mentor in "the business" – had schooled me thoroughly, before he was murdered: you mix just enough quinine and bonita with the raw to give the heroin a nice hefty boost. Using caution, Uncle Rob slowly began to walk forward, holding the syringe close. He wobbled a bit with his first few steps, but quickly righted himself. Suddenly, Uncle Rob began his slow scratch, the itch a result of the quinine, an important ingredient in this fusion of unauthorized pharmaceutical mix. This scratch was his trademark: his eyes began to flicker and his head began to nod. Then, his mouth opened and he began to drool. He loved it! When I saw Uncle Rob's scratch, I knew the package was good and the mix was right.

There were two more heroin addicts in the lobby of the shooting gallery. They had paid their two dollars and waited impatiently to be served. Uncle Rob was like the neighborhood handyman, only his fix was not the kind that would unclog your sink. I watched him "fix" Duke, the next in line.

First, he disinfected his tools with bleach. Being a heroin addict was one thing, but he definitely didn't want to transmit the HIV virus. Then, from an old but clean teacup, he drew fifty units of water into the syringe and squirted it into a bottle cap filled with dope. Fifty units of water wasn't much, but Duke liked his stuff strong. Uncle Rob held a lit match to the bottom of the cap to warm the water to dissolve the heroin. He then placed a small piece of cotton inside the cap to act as a filter. When the cotton absorbed the solution, the syringe was poked into the center of it. Uncle Rob pulled back the plunger and sucked the valuable commodity into the syringe.

Finally, Uncle Rob wrapped a belt tight around Duke's left arm, bringing his veins into plain view. You could see the anxiety in Duke's face as he anxiously awaited his rendezvous with the Asian persuasion. He was ready to be stimulated by his ten dollars' worth of euphoria in a glassine bag. Like a surgeon, Uncle Rob poked and prodded, looking for the perfect place to make the injection. Once the needle was firmly inserted into Duke's left arm, Dr. Rob pushed the plunger slowly, sending the contents coursing into the patient's blood stream. For several seconds, the room was silent. Then suddenly Duke's eyes began to roll up into his head as he dazzled in the moment.

"Goddamn, this shit is serious," he whispered with a barely–intelligible slur. His hands begin to quiver and his legs began to jerk as he reacted to the prohibited cocktail. Then came an un-controlled nod, almost tumbling Duke out of the chair. Seconds later, the room was besieged by a horrid fragrance as vomit was suddenly released by the queasy drug addict. I suddenly felt the need to exit the house for some fresh air.

WHERE IT ALL BEGAN

Baltimore was a tough place to grow up for the tall skinny kid from a section in the southwest part of the city called Edmondson Village. On the 26th day of the second month of the new year, Kevin Anthony Shird kicked down the door of this unpredictable and often hard-to-interpret scene from a Hitchcock movie we call life. The row house we lived in was no different than the others you'd find on Baltimore's landscape. I was the youngest of Brenda and Charles' four seeds planted on the earth with the intent to flourish. I had two sisters – Karen and Wanda –and an older brother named Karl. According to Karen, being the youngest kind of meant that I had more privileges than my other siblings.

Both of my parents had what could be described as conservative values. We could have mirrored the fictitious clan depicted on the popular television series *The Cosby Show* if not for the continued dysfunction and the lack of finances. And with that said there was a lot of room in-between for errors and oversight.

Being church-going people of the Christian faith, the entire family made the regular Sunday morning pilgrimage to the chapel for God's blessings, where the priest chided the

1

parishioners for their worldly sins. Just hours later, many of those who had listened to the scriptures and chanted hallelujah were back to their worldly sins, only to be back for the next Sunday morning Mass and to be chided again. For my parents, it was a constant struggle just to eat, drink, and provide shelter for us all. At the time I didn't know what *underprivileged* meant, but we were the epitome of it. Even back then I knew money was an issue for us, as I watched my parents juggle the available cash, taking what was meant for Peter in order to pay Paul. Some nights, grits or pancakes were all that was on the menu. There were times when we didn't have any food at all. Those days when my stomach was growling and that hollow pit in my breadbasket yearned to be fed still are difficult to forget.

Occasionally the water in our house would be shut off due to non-payment of the bill, prompting an excursion to a nearby relative's home to get a bath. Those were some tough days for my family and me. Did you ever see that big basket of sneakers that sat near the frozen food aisle in the grocery store? Have you ever wondered who the hell would purchase those cheap, ugly things? Of all the places to buy sneakers, my mother bought mine from Super Saver Supermarket. Even as a kid, it was humiliating to sport shoes that everyone in school knew had once sat next to the frozen waffles.

Hearing the theme song from the popular 1970s television show *Good Times* sent chills up the spine of the young skinny kid, who detested the show. *Not getting hassled, not getting hustled, keeping your head above water, making a way when you can, a temporary layoff, GOOD TIMES.* Even as a kid, the buffoonery of J. J. as he lampooned the social ills of low-income people just didn't seem entertaining to me. Many of the tough situations the Evans family endured on the show, we endured in my

2

real life. Many nights at bedtime, I would pray to God that we would hit the lottery and all of our troubles would be instantly washed away. That never happened.

My mother was a telephone operator for the local department store downtown and later began working for the federal government. My father was a corrections officer for the city jail, keeping a watchful eye on those who used to be Baltimore's Most Wanted. Neither of my parents had been able to afford to attend college. They worked hard to give us the best life they could, but having four kids made it difficult. We didn't live in the 'hood, but our community was a long way from middle class. For the most part, our neighbors, working folks like us, were content in their skin as they endured their nine-to-five jobs.

When I was very young, we got a German shepherd named George to guard the household valuables. His job of deterring the theft of our property was easy since there really wasn't anything to be stolen. It was tough to keep George clean because he didn't like getting into water, and even the lure of dog biscuits sometimes wasn't enough to get him into the tub. Once he finally did get in, he wasted no time showering his masters with massive droplets of H_2O as a way of showing his displeasure.

When we first brought George home, he was just a puppy, smaller than I was. But grew into a gigantic creature, and very quickly became bigger than this skinny 4-year-old boy. Suddenly, he was tall enough that when he stood up on his hind legs, he could easily knock me down. I definitely wasn't much competition for George and his monstrous wet tongue. I often needed to be rescued by my siblings because George would wrestle me down to the ground. I don't think he ever looked at me as being his master, but he might have thought that I was a play toy. After only a year or two, we got rid of George. I never knew the reason why.

Christmas for a kid is supposed to be a great time to live. But for many children, it's not. The additional financial burden of the holiday can be the straw that breaks the camels back of an already-struggling family. When you're a kid, you don't understand these things. The only thing that you understand is that it's Christmas and all the other kids get gifts, so why can't you?

I stayed awake every Christmas Eve night, waiting for Rudolph and the rest of the gang to land on the rooftop. On occasion I would ask my mother, "How can Santa land his sled of reindeer on our sloped roof without falling off?" I thought to myself, *this is Santa Clause, right? He's not Spiderman.* I would usually be disappointed with the gifts I received. Some Christmas mornings, I would return to my room in tears after finding out that I hadn't received one single toy that I requested. I couldn't understand why Santa Clause couldn't bring me the bike that I placed at the top of my list which was mailed directly to the North Pole. I never had gifts to brag and boast about, like all of the other kids in the neighborhood had.

I couldn't buy gifts for the others in the family, either. Often, my sister Karen and I would take things like books and clothes from around the house, gift-wrap them, and place them underneath the tree. It was the only way we could give.

Both of my grandparents were transplants from North Carolina who journeyed north for a slice of their American pie. My grandmother had long beautiful black hair – from her Cherokee mother's side of the family – that she often kept in a ponytail. My grandfather was born in the beginning of the 1900s, and life was pretty different for him during those years. In my grandparents' generation, the migration of African Americans from the southern parts of the country to the North was common. With racism and segregation running rampant in the South, blacks found refuge in the northern states. They'd try to find a home in a place with less bias and prejudice.

My grandparents would host holiday celebrations at their home every year, one of the traditions they brought with them to Baltimore. All of my relatives would attend the Christmas gathering to enjoy Grandma's good cooking. She had this humongous dining room table, which was big enough to seat probably sixteen people. She would load it up with every food imaginable. For this young boy, pig feet and chitterlings ("chit'lins," as we called them; pig intestines, for the uninformed) were never on his menu. He headed straight for the fried chicken and sweet potatoes at the far end of the table. High blood pressure and heart disease was not even a thought as we gorged ourselves with anything that could possibly clog a human artery.

Like many young kids do, I spent a lot of time hanging out at my grandparents' house. Their house was so big that I could go on an expedition for hours and hours before ever being discovered. My grandmother smoked cigarettes, so she would always send me to get them at the corner store, which she referred to as the *Chinese man's store*. I would arrive there in sixty seconds or less by going through the back alleyway, jumping Mrs. Jackson's fence, and sliding through the small breach in the garage. This young skinny kid knew the territory very well. My grandmother would select the coins – usually about a dollar – from her purse, sending me on my short journey. She'd ask for one pack of Virginia Slims, the tall lung-busters in the green-colored pack. Years later, when she would unfortunately die of lung cancer from smoking, I could still remember holding those packages of death in my hands. My grandmother's favorite beverage to go with her cigarettes was Tab soda.

The best thing about my journey to the Chinese man's store was that I could keep the change. The cigarettes were fifty cents and the soda was thirty cents, so the calculation was easy for the young kid who was good in math class to figure out how much change he got to keep. I then did some wheeling and dealing to select from everything sweet and chewy in the store. I really *was* a kid in a candy store! As I stood on the tips of my toes, I could barely see over the top of the counter to view the many choices. The colors of the candy were like a summer rainbow, stretching across the counter. When I finally made my selection, I'd dig down into my pockets in search of my coins. I'd count out my change of ten cents, just enough to pay for my colorful delectable's. What a great time this was to be a kid! I never left there without a pack of Now and Laters or a box of Lemon Heads. It was always a tough choice because everything looked irresistible. The Asian guy standing behind the Plexiglas was always frustrated by my indecisiveness. He couldn't understand why it was such a difficult decision, every time. That was the life! My grandparents were the best.

I loved playing all kinds of sports and had visions of becoming a black American sports hero. Early on, football and baseball were the sports that I enjoyed the most. I played basketball, but didn't start getting serious about it until my teenage years. Anything where I had to expend energy was excellent for this tall skinny kid with the high energy levels.

When I was about eleven, my mother volunteered me for the Boy Scouts of America. This turned out to be a real adventure. I was terrible at just about everything a Boy Scout should be good at, so I never earned any merit badges. I could never remember how to tie a slipknot. And when it came to shooting a bow and arrow, I was lucky if I hit the target.

We often took short excursions, as they tried to have us experience all things natural and ecological. This was interesting for a young metropolitan kid with an inquisitive and curious nature. I enjoyed a few of these excursions with my fellow Scouts. But for me, the worst part about being a Boy Scout was going camping. I absolutely loathed it. Sleeping in those old dirty tents with a foreign smell wasn't appealing to me in the least. The tent usually had a hole in it, so if it rained (and it always seemed to rain, no matter when we went) you would get soaked. And all of Mother Nature's little friends would also seek shelter. Waking up in the morning with a frog staring you in the face wasn't my idea of a great weekend. There were no bathrooms out in the woods, so if you had to use the toilet, you would have to find a tree, which was easy to do in a forest. I don't know why, but I sometimes forgot to pack a roll of toilet paper, so leaves from the forest bed became my second best friend. As I got older, my mother gave me a pass on my Boy Scout adventures because she finally realized that I didn't like it much. As I grew older, I realized what a sacrifice it must have been for her to have spent money on the Boy Scouts for me. Poor as we were, she was trying to give me as normal a life as any other boy would have.

Children are the most impressionable creatures on the face of the planet. Like a sponge, they absorb information and quickly turn it into action. If a child watches someone climb a rock, shortly thereafter, he'll climb it, too. A child can watch someone play the piano, and he'll start banging on the first piano he sees. This can be said for a child learning how to play baseball, chess, or do a host of other activities. The unfortunate thing is that a child can just as easily use this process to absorb negative behavior. Children imitate what they see.

One early summer day, my older sister Wanda was hanging out with some of her friends. The school year had just ended and I had just advanced to my first year of middle school. I was only twelve years old and still a huge mass of inquisitiveness. My sister and her friends were puffing away on the illegal green stuff that's occasionally brown and sometimes makes you giggle. I had no knowledge that what they were smoking was marijuana, and my curious nature got the better of me.

My sister and her friends laughed uncontrollably as they smoked their way through their Bob Marley-style smoke-a-thon. I strolled over to Big Sister, asking if I could join in the fun. She said, "Boy, you'd better get the hell out of here," just as I had expected she would. But her friends said to go ahead and give me a little hit.

My sister relented and handed me the joint.

"You had better not say anything to Mom about this," she warned. That threat was always enough to keep this kid silent.

"Okay, I won't say anything," I told her. With my first puff, I choked so bad I had to gasp for air. My nose began to run and my eyes to burn. I couldn't understand how my sister and her friends could be enjoying this so much. This was not fun.

"Hold it, hold it in," the girls directed me.

I tried a second time to inhale the illegal leaves and this time it was a little easier. I coughed, but not as much, as the cannabis slowly began to take effect. But if you practice anything, even it it's the wrong thing, you get better at it. I inhaled a third time, and then a fourth and fifth. By now, I felt like smoke was coming out of my ears as I puffed away.

In hindsight, smoking marijuana at twelve years old was definitely a dumb thing to do. I guess that was one of my first really stupid life Choices. But there would be many more to follow. Did smoking marijuana make me go out in the streets and steal someone's television set to buy more weed? Absolutely not. Did smoking weed stunt my physical and mental growth?

Probably not. But what it did do was introduce me to risk-taking. That day, I learned that even though I knew right from wrong, I didn't always have to do the right thing. I could always take a chance to dance on the other side.

ME AND MY POPS

Just before I was born, my father was a soldier in the United States Army, stationed in North Carolina, looking to do his part to protect the mainland. At that time the Vietnam War was still headlining the news, as the Asian warriors were locked into a relentless battle against their counterparts from other countries, including the U. S. My father came very close to being shipped off to the confrontation but never was. I always wondered if he had been sent overseas, would he have returned home alive. As far back as I can remember he was a corrections officer at the Baltimore City Jail, now known as the Baltimore City Detention Center. He would leave the house around ten o'clock at night to make it to the unenviable graveyard shift by eleven. To prepare for his shift, he would take a quick shot from a brown paper bag. Even when I was very young, chronic alcoholism weighed heavily on my father, with Bacardi Rum being his drink of Choice.

On my father's days off from work, he was usually home watching the television. One television set was the maximum in the homes of lower-income folks. Only a chosen few were allowed such luxuries as a color. So, of course, ours was black-and-white. The picture came in clear, as long as there was enough aluminum foil wrapped around the antenna. You also had to have a long piece of wire attached to the tip of the antenna as it hung out of the window. What a contraption that was! Of course, my father controlled what we watched. If he didn't want to watch it, we didn't get to watch it.

After I completed my homework, the evening news was usually on. Surprisingly, I began to enjoy it. I remember Walter Cronkite on the CBS Evening News giving his famous sign off, "And that's the way it is." To this day, the news is my program of *Choice*, although I prefer CNN now. I can also remember watching the 1976 presidential election, when a peanut farmer from Georgia named Jimmy Carter came out of nowhere to win the White House. This was around the same time that I became familiar with a boxer named Muhammad Ali, as he shook up the world with his verbal and physical beat downs. Watching the Saturday morning cartoons became a ritual in my house, too; *Super Friends, Fat Albert,* and *Scooby Doo* were the usual line up. So, I guess as dysfunctional as much of my life was, there were some normal days.

At a very young age, I started to realize that there was a problem with my Pops. He was not like all the other fathers in the neighborhood. The other fathers didn't stumble on the way home, holding tightly to a bottle of rum. The other fathers on the block weren't yelling and screaming out of the window all night long, like they were insane. To my knowledge, the other fathers in the neighborhood didn't physically abuse their wives. Even as a kid, I realized something was wrong with this picture that was my life.

There were times when my father and I would hang out together like a normal father and son, Dad teaching me how to do manly things, like tossing a baseball around. Those moments often ended up with the boys in blue giving us a ride home, probably more out of concern for the young skinny kid than for the man. It was probably just easier than locking him up. Plus, he would always display his prison guard badge and that gave him a pass. I can remember times when I was ten years old, trying to hold my father upright as we walked down the sidewalk toward home together. He was pretty heavy for a ten-year-old, but I couldn't just leave him on the corner. Sometimes onlookers would stop to try and help, but my father wouldn't allow their assistance. Other folks would look on in disgust as he fell to the pavement. I can remember an old lady once saying to him, "You need to get your drunken ass up and get that little boy home." She was a wise woman, but he was too smashed to even respond. I would pray that we could make it home, or just get close enough to the house so that I could run and get my mother to help.

One night, my father was walking home alone from the local bar, drunk and disoriented as usual. Some guys lurking in the darkness stopped him. During their search of my father's pockets, they found his badge and that set them off.

"Oh shit, he's the fucking police!" before they began beating him with the sawed off shotgun. A pregnant woman walking with another child stumbled across the beat down and began screaming at the top of her lungs. Swiftly the assailants fled the scene, leaving my father soaked in a pool of blood and gore. A taxi driver bought him home and my mother immediately called 911. The police had to force him into the ambulance, because he refused to go to the hospital for treatment of his wounds. He was still too drunk to be using any common sense. The beating was so bad that he almost lost his eye in the attack, but he was very fortunate. He wasn't murdered.

The only thing that little boy who I used to be wanted was a father like all the other kids in the neighborhood, but that would never happen. As I got older, one of the hardest things for me to deal with was my friends and neighbors seeing my father lying out in the middle of the street, drunk. It was mortifying. You can imagine what this could do to the self-esteem of a young child.

One day, my father was very intoxicated and he was trying to make it down the street to our house. It was a warm summer day and the entire neighborhood was out on the block, enjoying the sun. Many were out in their yards, manicuring their lawns. My friends were out in the street, playing Double-Dutch and baseball, doing what kids do in the summer. Suddenly, I looked up and there was my father stumbling down the street. I was sick to my stomach with embarrassment. I hoped that the other kids didn't notice, but of course, that was just wishful thinking. I immediately ran into the house to notify my mother of the unfolding drama.

As he weaved and wobbled his way down the block, the neighbors began to take notice. One of them decided that my father needed some help, but Pops just pushed the Good Samaritan away. He figured that he could make it on his own. Bad idea! Some of the neighbors looked on with amusement, some looked on in sadness, and others looked on in embarrassment for my mother, who had arrived on the scene. She managed to get the drunkard home, with some help from Mr. Paul who lived down the street.

For me, this had become a community event far too often. There were times when I thought that my father was making a spectacle of himself intentionally. I thought that he had more control over himself when he had been drinking than he was demonstrating. At the time, I knew nothing about the effects of alcohol abuse. There were times when I would pray, "Please, God, make him stop drinking."

One day, my mother called a family meeting that did not include my father. My siblings and I had grown weary from all of the drama on a daily basis, and it seemed our mother had, too. My father had been to several psychologists and psychiatrists regarding his alcohol abuse, but to no avail. My mother had researched alcoholism and she knew more about it than most people.

"Your father is sick with a disease called alcoholism," she told us. She went on to describe the characteristics of the disease.

"Our family, primarily on my father's side, has a history of alcoholism." I didn't know at the time, but my great-grandmother was an alcoholic, and so was my grandmother. By the time I was born, my grandmother had been sober for ten years, so I never even know she drank. Uncle Booker T., my grandmother's brother, had a very serious alcohol abuse problem himself. He'd get drunk and lie out in the street, just like my father did. I remember my other uncles carrying him home several times.

"I have a message to you from your fathers' doctor," my mother continued. The doctor asked my mother to tell us that we definitely shouldn't drink alcohol as teenagers, or even as adults. Because of our family history with alcoholism, the doctor told her, all of us could easily become alcoholics. I never forgot this conversation, even though that was over twenty-five years ago. Of course, now we know the doctor was right, and my mother was very wise to share it with us, even though we were very young. In fact, that conversation may have saved my life.

Growing up, I always worried that my pops would seriously hurt my mother one day in an alcoholic rage. When my father wasn't drinking or fighting my mother, things would be fine at home. For a moment, there would be tranquility in the household and we would resemble an ordinary, functional family. But the barometric pressure would quickly change to hurricane force winds, blowing the roof off the house, with no warning at all. I became so used to his transgressions that it got to the point where I expected something bad to happen. I developed this mentality of, "It won't be long now." That's one really messed up way to grow up, don't you think?

As I got older, my relationship with my father reached a breaking point. I was rebellious at the time, like many kids who are dealing with the growing pains of life, but I was also scared by my father's addiction. I had built up a lot of resentment over the years. I had begun to lose respect for him in a lot of ways. I guess seeing your pops lying in the middle of the street, drunk, eventually takes its toll on you.

By this time, he had lost his job as a corrections officer. He had been warned several times by his superiors about coming to work drunk. He had been reprimanded and suspended, but the administration finally had enough and took permanent action. You can't be drunk as a prison guard, you can't maintain order, and so you put all your fellow officers at risk. The union tried to fight to save his job, but even they couldn't fix the mess that he had created.

One night during a disagreement with my father, he grabbed me by the neck and began choking me. Fortunately my mother had heard the argument. Once she entered the room, he released his grip on my neck and I fell to the floor in tears of pain and confusion. I couldn't understand why he would do something like that to me.

The next morning, I woke up in physical and mental anguish. My neck was sore and I had bruises. As I got ready to go to school, my father tried to apologize. He said he was sorry for what he had done; it was just that he was under a lot of pressure because of losing his job. Then he gave me a hug, but this kid wasn't buying it. That is when I gave up my dreams of a close father-son relationship.

You would think unemployment would have been a wake-up call for him, but that's not how an alcoholic's mind works. He began to realize that it would be very difficult to fix what he had broken, and his drinking grew even worse.

Finally, when I was 15, my mother packed the rest of the family up and we moved out of the house, leaving my father behind for good. We had moved out a couple of times before, but this would be the last time. She needed to salvage the lives of her children and herself. Now it's well known how devastating growing up with an abusive, alcoholic father is to children, but my mother realized it back then. She was ahead of her time and she knew she had to save her children.

Living without my father was strange at first, because he had been around my entire life. The biggest difference now was that things were tranquil and peaceful. Some days, there was complete silence; others days you could hear the birds chirping in the distance. This wasn't what I had come to regard as normal. There was no more fighting in the middle of the night, no more yelling and screaming. My father's reign of terror over the family had ended.

Alcohol cost my father his wife, his children, his job, and his self-respect. The disease of alcoholism can be a walking prison. I can't help but wonder how his life would have turned out if he had been sober. If he had known what it would do to him, would he have ever started drinking? He was a very intelligent, proud, and decent man who loved his family very much. There is no doubt in my mind that he could have been successful at anything in the world, if he hadn't been so successful at drinking Bacardi Rum.

Though I was glad to find some peace in my day-to-day life, I was still brittle from the abuse I had experienced. Often there were times when I felt like an outcast socially. My self-esteem was in the toilet. As young as I was, I actually felt like a defeated human being. When I looked in the mirror, I saw a bum looking back at me.

The fact that my father had been the neighborhood drunk took a heavy toll on this tall skin kid. I was having a rough time. Who wants to see their father as the laughing stock of the neighborhood? I never felt that he gave a damn about me. If he did, why wouldn't he stop falling down in the middle of the street in view of all the neighbors?

When I was a kid, my father told me one night during one of his drunken fits, "If you don't straighten up in school, you're going to jail." When he told me this, I was still very young. What a hell of a thing to tell a kid, right? I wasn't selling dope back then; I was just being a kid. I didn't yearn for much, other than a sober dad to look up to. To this day, I don't understand what made him say something like that to me.

SCHOOL DAYS

The Head Start program is a place where children can use their minds to blossom into shining stars. This was where I began my education. By the time I entered the local elementary school, I was ready to make my mark in the world, especially in math. At a very young age, I had this unbridled fascination with numbers. I would actually have dreams about counting numbers. I would add, subtract, divide, and multiply numbers all night long, while lying in my small twin bed covered with Batman sheets. With the television sometimes on the blink, I'd have addition and multiplication contests with my siblings. My sister Karen lost most of the time and would get upset with the young kid who could count well. Since I was the unseasoned pup in the clan, winning at any contest against older siblings was never supposed to happen. My parents, especially my mother, were very pleased with my educational growth. She realized there was long-term potential in the kid genius.

In the fourth grade, even though I was a very smart student, I began having disciplinary problems in school. I'd lose focus very easily, which caused me to miss relevant pieces of the lesson. Other times, my thoughts would ride off into the wind, like I wasn't in the classroom at all. I began talking back to the teacher, and I'd also be fooling around with my class-mates. As I progressed through elementary school, the problem became more and more pronounced, though I remained near the top of my class academically. As the violence in my home increased, my grades began to decline. I don't know how she did it, but even though my father abused her when he was drunk, my mother never had a mark on her face. That didn't mean that she wasn't injured, because she would have scratches and bruises on her arms. She would conceal the marks by wear-ing long-sleeved clothing. I can even remember my father once hitting my brother hard enough to knock him down to the floor.

The terror my father was inflicting on my family during his alcohol binges had consumed me emotionally, which in turn, caused problems in school. Some nights, my father would be drinking and yelling until the early morning hours. Other nights, he'd be physically fighting with my mother. Some days I would come to school not being able to focus, and not under-standing why or how this problem was affecting me.

I got into one of the worst fights in the history of Rognel Heights Elementary School with a kid named Miguel. Miguel was much bigger than me and loved being a bully. He would taunt me and talk trash about everything I did. By the fourth grade, I had enough and I began plotting an attack that would rid me of Miguel's vicious taunting. First, I realized that this kid was much bigger than me, so a brawl wouldn't be in my best interest. I had to get this thing over quickly. I was working as one of the lunch tray assistants, meaning that I helped clear the trays off the tables at the end of the lunch period. It was voluntary and in those days, I volunteered for just about everything, especially when there were extra snack cakes for a job well done.

Miguel had no idea what was in store for him. As he approached the counter to drop off his lunch tray, I waited for him to say something crazy to me, because he always did.

"Kevin, what's up now, bighead? You look stupid, stupid!"

I didn't waste any time. While he was still holding onto his tray, I grabbed him by the neck and placed him in a chokehold. I got that move from watching WWF wrestling on Saturday afternoons with my brother. Holding him tightly around the neck, I rammed his head into the stainless steel table, several times, which even sounded like it hurt. Once I started, I kind of blacked out for a second from the rush of adrenaline I had never before experienced. I was winning! I had control over a bully who was much bigger than me! He screamed in horror and pain until the staff arrived to stop me. I didn't have a single scratch on me, but I couldn't say that for Miguel. To remind him of his transgressions, he had a lump on his head the size of a golf ball.

Finally, we were both escorted to the principal's office. The first thing the principal asked me was, "What did you hit him with?"

I told him that I didn't hit him with anything besides the steel table. His eyes widened in surprise as he weighed what to say and do next. This man had this look on his face as if to say to me "If you were a little bit older, I'd call the cops and send you to the jail, where you belong." (In those days, the cops never came to an elementary school for a fight.)

My mother was summoned to pick up the juvenile aggressor who had terrorized his classmate. I had been in trouble in school before, but nothing like this. This was my first fight in school and it was a really bad one. The staff discussed the situation with my mother. They couldn't believe that a fourth grader had the ability to engage in such a violent act. Little did they know, but I was getting lessons in violent acts in my home almost every day. They say that a father can teach a son almost anything and in this case, it was proved true.

Of course when I went home, my father had the audacity to beat me for getting into a fight in school. Never did he think for a minute that he might have been partly responsible for the problem. I don't think he ever realized how much of a toll his violent alcoholism was having on his children.

One particular afternoon at school, I was out in the playground during recess. Suddenly, I looked across the street and I could see my father. He was extremely drunk and staggering down the street on his way home. I was hoping that nobody paid any attention to him, but I wouldn't be so lucky. I looked on in horror as he wobbled past the playground. We lived right around the corner from school, so some of the kids had seen him before. One of them said, "Hey, Kevin, isn't that your father over there?"

There was no way that I was going to acknowledge that. I said, "No way, that guy isn't my father." I just wanted to avoid embarrassment at all cost. This ultimately got the attention of all of the other kids on the playground, and of my teacher. I was devastated as several of the kids started laughing.

I could tell that my teacher knew that I was lying. She had actually met my father once, one of the rare times he had attended a PTA meeting with my mother. But she could clearly understand why I denied being any relation to the man stumbling down the street. Later that day, I went home and told my mother about the incident. There wasn't much that she could do other than give my father a severe tongue lashing. But it wasn't like things were going to change. It wasn't like he was going to stop drinking. He would undoubtedly be intoxicated again the next day. I prayed every day that God would sober him up, but for some reason, my prayers would go unanswered. I remember many days walking home from school and wondering why God had cursed this young kid with such a life. I was only a little boy and I hadn't asked for all the drama. What had I done to deserve this?

* * * * *

Statewide testing by the school system was mandatory as a way of gauging the students' educational growth. They were also used to determine which grade levels the students would be placed in the following school year. Depending on your score, you could be placed in the class with the smartest kids in your grade, or you could be placed in the class with the kids that were having more trouble learning. This would include kids with learning difficulties and kids with behavior problems. I was always in the class with the smartest kids.

Around the end of the fifth grade, the problems at home had escalated. My father's alcoholism had reached a new level. He had even been arrested a few times for assaulting my mother, but once the police found out that he was a Baltimore City Jail guard, the charges were never filed. They probably didn't realize it at the time, but all the cops were doing was enabling his behavior.

The tests were broken down into sections and administered to students over a three-day period. On the morning of the tests this year, I had been awake early; I mean *very* early. My father had been drinking heavily and fighting with my mother. And when it looked like the fight was about to end, it began all over again, until the early morning hours. My siblings and I often stayed awake during my father's drunken tirades because we thought we might have to jump in to keep him from hurting her badly.

I got perhaps three hours of sleep before it was time to get up. Somehow I managed to get out of the bed and make my way to school, disheveled and in disarray. I was so exhausted that I couldn't focus during the tests, so I began randomly picking answers without reading the questions at all. It seemed pretty innocent at the time. I had no idea what the consequences were if I didn't perform well. But once I finished the sixth grade and left elementary school for middle school, I found out.

* * * * *

The letter I received in the mail read: "Report to the Main Auditorium at 8:45 a.m." I was now an official West Baltimore Middle School student. The auditorium was full with all of the new seventh graders, there for orientation and to be sorted into our classes. The majority of the faces that morning were new to me because this middle school pulled from several elementary schools in the city. I only recognized a couple of kids. Carlos and Ron were sitting in the front. We used to play baseball together at school. I could see my cousin Cassandra and my friend Tia sitting over on the side. We were all like immigrants entering into a foreign land. I eventually spotted Miguel, that big bully I beat up bad in the fourth grade. Seeing some of my old classmates settled my nerves a bit but it wouldn't be just like old times. Or would it?

Finally, roll call began. The assistant principal told everyone to proceed to the front of the stage when they heard their name called. All of us newly-minted seventh-graders were nervous because everything was so new to us. We all waited to find out who our new classmates and teacher would be.

First up was Ms. Myers. She was a tall, very attractive, single white woman who reminded me of the supermodel Cindy

24

Crawford, but without the mole. She had earned herself a reputation of being very cool with her students. She could be tough when it counted, but she was never unfair or overbearing. She began calling names of the twenty-five students for her new class. The only one from my old school to be placed in her class was Carlos. Next up was Ms. Jones, who reminded me of one of my aunts. She taught my sister Karen a few years earlier in the same school. Ms. Jones was a nice lady, but if you found yourself on her bad side, you'd better watch out. She would let you have it! Her favorite form of punishment was to make you write a twenty-page paper on "Why I Shouldn't Have Done What I Was Told Not to Do." Such a task was the ultimate torture. My cousin Cassandra, who was a whiz kid, was the first selected for her new class. We had begun the Head Start program together back in pre-school, blazing our trails as the young geniuses of the family.

Mr. Brooks, who had taught my brother a few years earlier, was the next teacher to call his class. Mr. Brooks was a big history buff and he always had lessons about Martin Luther King Jr. and Frederick Douglass. As more and more faculty members gathered their students and my name still had not been called, I began to worry. The kids that I had been classmates with since the beginning of my school career had already been assigned to their new teachers. I was used to being around them. But it seemed those days were over.

I turned around and saw that there were only three or four kids that I knew still remaining; everyone else was unfamiliar. For some reason, a lot of the remaining kids looked kind of strange. Later on I would understand why. Next Mr. Cunningham announced the names of his new students, and then a white man around seventy years old with a cane slowly headed toward the podium. I wasn't sure if this guy was a schoolteacher or the grandfather of a student. He was a teacher after all, and he called out the names of his students. Next was Mr. Kline.

"Edward Reynolds, Donna Robinson, Kevin Shird..." My name at last! I didn't know what to think. I had always been at the top of my class, so why was I called almost last? I began thinking that these guys don't know what they were doing. Oh, right, *now* I understood! All of the rumors about middle school staff being incompetent were true! I remember thinking that I couldn't wait to get my mother here to the school for my first PTA meeting. I could hear her scolding school administrators now.

"My son was in the Head Start Program and was first in his class all through elementary school, until he got to this place! Why is he now in the bottom of his class? I need some answers now!" My mother would talk to the principal and have this situation straightened out fast.

Finally the pedagogical auction of the seventh graders was complete as Mr. Kline collected all of the students for his new classroom. Everyone lined up at the front of the auditorium and their teachers led them to their classrooms. As I looked around at my new classmates, they still looked a little strange. Not like in unfamiliar, but like in creepy. The kids in the new class, who didn't look like them, had the same look on their faces as I did, probably thinking, "Please get me the hell out of here!"

I realized that if I couldn't fix this mess that had been caused by the school, I would be stuck with these misfits for an entire year. It wouldn't be until many years later that I realized what actually happened. It was the low scores I received on the state tests where I had guessed at the answers. That was what placed me in the very bottom of the new class in middle school.

Things started off somewhat normal, as the new kids on the block proceeded to size up their new surroundings. The room seemed just like every other new classroom I had been in. But this illusion of normalcy didn't last very long. It wasn't long before all the behavioral problems started showing up.

There was this one girl in my class named Kelly and she was the most repulsive being I had encountered up until that point. Ms. Kelly hated everyone who breathed air or had a pulse. Behind her back, my classmates labeled her the Tasmanian devil, because she looked just like the cartoon character. She used to get into fights on a daily basis with the girls in class. Kelly was just as explosive as any of the boys were. She was only around four feet tall, but her intimidation was as huge as a giant. I used to feel sorry for the other girls as they crumbled under this female gorilla. She would pick certain students to steal lunch money from and would threaten to rip off the other girls' ears or scratch out their eyeballs if they dare not comply with her demands.

There was another kid named Darryl who had this obsession with knives. He carried three knives to school with him every single day. He kept one in his jacket, another in his pants pocket, and a third in his shoe. Darryl had a couple of uncles who were in "the game," so he thought he was a young gangster. This kid was selling cocaine. In the seventh grade! I'm still not certain if he was using it, but if I had to guess, I would say he was. Darryl spent so many hours in the principal's office; some of us thought he must have employment there. This kid didn't care much about getting an education. He was just in school because he had to be.

There was another kid named Ricky, whose wardrobe was as expensive as any kid I knew. He owned as many tennis shoes as I owned socks. It was obvious that someone had been spending a lot of money on his high-priced gear. The strange thing about Ricky was that he always came to school with scratches and bruises on his face, like he had been in a fight. He would tell everyone he got them playing football on his block, but I knew better. So I guessed I wasn't the only kid in class who had an issue at home.

* * * * *

My middle school experience was a highly stressful situation for me. It seemed like half the student body had rap sheets. I had never been in a school environment as unnerving as this one. Between the madness going on at school and the madness going on at home, it was tough to even think about doing class work.

To make matters even worse, the peer pressure from school had become unbearable. Middle school began an era in my life where teenagers defined each other by the clothes they wore. Nike and Adidas ruled the landscape, swallowing up kids of all shapes and sizes who couldn't afford their pricey labels. Because of my family's economic straits, there was no way I could measure up, and I plummeted into a deep depression.

When a young teenager's self esteem is down, he or she can easily become vulnerable. Searching for something to fill that empty feeling inside, I began exploring the inner city. Unfortunately, I was looking in all the wrong places at all the wrong faces. At sixteen years old, I started hanging late at the clubs. I started just hanging out until midnight, but soon, my late night excursions extended to one o'clock in the morning. Eventually, I wouldn't return to the nest until almost sunrise the next day. My mother was irate about it, but of course, she wasn't getting any support from my father. By this time, he was drunk most days, so the young and manipulative teenager leveraged the situation in his favor.

Lured by the prospects of a good time with some good girls, my buddy from the neighborhood and I became regulars at Club Pascal's, which was located near the Park Heights section of Baltimore. Standing close to six feet tall and with puberty beginning to shape our features into adults', the two teenage boys had no problem gaining entrance to the club. Pascal's was a very popular place in Baltimore; an old gangster named Slim Butler owned it. Many of the biggest illegal drug merchants in the city held court at this club. This was where I first got a glimpse of the hustler world and its inner sanctum. When I first walked inside, I would see all the dealers dressed in their full-length fur coats and wearing their diamond rings and bracelets. The humongous gold chains, referred to in those days as Dukie ropes, were a status symbol for hustlers back then, as they represented power and ranking in the game. The generals usually wore the biggest medallions, symbolizing their leadership roles.

The tables in the booths that encircled the dance floor were often covered in a fine white residue from all the lines of cocaine and heroin that had been laid out on it. They resembled baker's tables after rolling dough. Even a small band of the female partygoers were nodding in their expensive garb as the illegal drugs stimulated and killed their brain cells, all at the same time.

This place was just like in the movies, and now I was there live, in the flesh. The many characters in this enchanted forest fascinated the young pups as they walk through this maze of glamour and glitter. Hollywood didn't have anything on these Baltimore hustlers. To me, this was better than the red carpet. To me, this was an example of what I wanted to become one day. These guys were respected and admired by everyone they came into contact with.

With my imagination running wild, I couldn't help but wonder what all the conversation was about at the tables where the hustlers sat. I could envision contracts being planned as the names and addresses of rival dealers were passed over to the killers. Deals were made over who would control the projects, and the biggest hustler with the biggest gun always won the day.

I was mesmerized by this haven for misbehaving. With the music blaring and the lights glimmering like stars of a far off galaxy, what could go wrong? I become increasingly more and more relaxed within the Pascal environment. It was starting to feel like I belonged here. But on one particular night, I learned that I did not.

An assassin lay in wait for his unknowing victim, who was enjoying the sights and the sounds. Even though there was security at the front doors, the assassin had managed to smuggle a gun in. In the midst of all the dancing to the sounds of the birth of hip-hop, a shot was heard. It was deafening as it echoed through the club. Momentarily, everyone froze in their dance steps. Then the stampede began. I could see the victim, as he lay helplessly on the floor, with blood pouring from his torso. The partygoers were frantically trying to escape, while the man who was taken down seemed oddly at peace now. The sight of the cadaver gave the young would-be street tycoon a bitter sample of "the life," as he looked on in fear. Momentarily I was paralyzed with fear.

The male patrons were scattering just as fast as the women, who were completely engulfed in terror. People were taking cover to avoid any crossfire that may erupt. In the relative darkness, everyone was frightened for their lives, as they dashed for the doors.

"Yo, Kevin, let's get the hell out of here," my taller friend yelled out to me, as we scrambled to the nearest exit.

"Try to stay together, man, and keep your head down," I yelled back, as we fled for safety. We were fortunate to have escaped without a scratch, although we did not escape the mental bruises. I had thought I was a tough guy, but I had never seen anything like this, and the fear rippled through my body.

Finally, standing outside of the club and trying to get a taxi for a safer place called home, I could see a group of guys carrying the motionless body into a car, presumably headed to the hospital. The next day on the evening news, I heard about the club patron who had become a casualty of the war. I would never feel comfortable inside a club environment again for many years. Hanging out at Pascal's for the last time certainly was creating a lot of "firsts" for me!

Eventually, the allure of the streets became too strong. With no father around to set me straight, the streets became a major player in my life. The tug of war between what was right and what was wrong became overwhelming. Was it the abuse, the poverty, or the low self-esteem that made the kid vulnerable to the streets? Or were irresponsibility and poor judgment the dominating factor? Choices.

YOU'RE IN THE GAME NOW

It was a freezing cold February night in the city of Baltimore. Your breath froze to a mist as soon as you exhaled. Naked fingertips would become numb within minutes due to the brutal night air. Even the stray dogs that roamed the alleyways sought shelter on this night. Everyone stayed inside, playing it safer from Mother Nature.

Except for me, Dajuan, and Howard. We were sitting on Howard's front porch on Linnard Street in West Baltimore, contemplating what to do next. If you were as foolish and scatterbrained as these teenagers were on this cold night, the answer was easy. I hadn't become a full-fledged criminal yet and there was still a chance for the young kid to be saved. But I was running out of dime, running out of time and still there was no sign of Super Role Model appearing in my life. We were only hanging out in the streets, despite the frigid temperatures, because we had nothing more constructive to do.

Sitting before us was a Lincoln Continental, fresh off the showroom floor and shining from bumper to bumper. I looked up and down the street to see if anyone was watching, but all was clear. The driver had run into a residence on Linnard Street, presumably to make a quick visit. He had been foolish enough to leave the car in the middle of the street, with the engine running and no one inside.

With Howard and Dajuan, acting as my lookouts I causally walked over to the car, opened the door, and climbed into the driver's seat. My heart was pumping furiously. I was relatively new to driving, being only 17 years old, so I struggled with even the simple task of getting the car out of park and into drive. As I slowly pulled away, I could hear the owner of the car yelling, "Stop, stop, stop!" In the rearview mirror, I could see him running up the street after his stolen possession. He was an older gentleman, instantly regretting his decision to leave his car with the key in the ignition.

I was having a difficult time maneuvering the huge jalopy around the corner as I drove ever so gently. It was like navigating a boat on treacherous waters. I probably hit three parked cars as I weaved and wobbled my way down the street to a destination unknown even to me. I hadn't planned this out; I was just doing it for the rush. I traveled about six city blocks before I stopped; I knew I couldn't go any farther without getting into a serious accident. I walked back around the block where my accomplices were waiting and I told them that I had parked around the corner. Howard was reluctant to participant any further – he had realized the owner of the vehicle was visiting one of his neighbors, so this was just a little too close for comfort. Dajuan returned with me to the car.

Once we got back to the object of our attention, Dajuan devised a plan. His idea was to take the valuables from the car instead of going for a joy ride. He was more experienced than I was in the art of car thievery. I told him that we had better move the car a little farther away, because we were only a few blocks from the scene of the crime.

We moved the car a few blocks away, but it was not as easy as we thought it would be. Neither one of us was excited about relocating this monstrosity. I was somehow elected driver, and, after striking another car or two, I eventually made it to our im-promptu chop shop – a deserted street corner a couple of blocks away. We were very familiar with this part of the neighborhood. If for some reason we had to make a quick getaway, the grave-yard that faced the alley was a route frequently used for this purpose. Normally, once you made it to the graveyard, you were safe because any further police pursuit was virtually impossible.

Quickly, we began removing just about everything from the vehicle that wasn't bolted or glued down. It may sound strange that two kids just looking for something to do would not only steal a brand new car, but loot it. I hadn't thought ahead to what I would do if we had found anything of value inside of the car. I think I might have just left the car there, if Dajuan hadn't devised his plan. I felt like I couldn't back down, especially since I had started the adventure. That's what can happen sometimes when a young boy grows up without a positive male image to show him how to really be a man.

We were amateurs, so removing car stereos and engine parts was out of our league. The first place we searched for valuables was the trunk, but we were disappointed, finding only a fishing rod and a couple of other inexpensive items. We then concen-trated our efforts on the interior of the car. Dajuan started with the front seats – including the glove compartment – and I began with the back. Whoever owned this car wasn't a very neat owner. The back seat was full of empty soda cans, newspaper, and all types of things that didn't belong in the back of a car.

Dajuan had completed his looting of the front seat of the car, but captured only a watch and an empty soda bottle. I was completing my part of the search when I spotted a brown paper bag on the floor. I reached inside and grabbed what felt like paper. I tilted the bag over slightly to catch a gleam of light from a nearby lamppost. All I could see was lots and lots of cash. We had hit the jackpot!

Dajuan was standing behind me when I exited the car and showed him the brown paper bag.

"What's in it?" he asked.

I calmly replied, "Money."

His eyes lit up as he looked inside. We had hit it big! The bag also contained checks and other pieces of paper. We took the bag to Dajuan's house to divide our newfound wealth.

On the way there, all kinds of thoughts rolled through my head about where the money came from. Was this money from a drug dealer or something? And if it was, since when did a drug dealer accept checks for drugs? Was this guy carrying money for the mob or had he robbed someone? What was really going on with this situation? Had we walked into the middle of someone else's deal and messed it up? With so many unanswered questions, I didn't know what to think. Taking a dealers money, or the mob's, would not go well for us. But the only thing that really mattered to me was that I could buy myself a brand new pair of sneakers.

When we arrived at his house, his entire family was home, so we went directly down to the basement and locked the door. Dajuan had some really grimy uncles and cousins living with him at the time. If they had found out that we had this money, they would have robbed us for sure.

With the basement door locked, we spread the money out on the table and began counting it. I had never seen this much money before! Close to $2,000! A large portion of the money was in one and five dollar bills. There were some checks as well, and we also noticed that the pieces of paper were actually small white envelopes with something printed on them. I could remember seeing these white envelopes when I was a little child. They were tithe envelopes used in church, and most of them were full of money. The driver of the car we had stolen was probably a pastor or deacon, and the money was probably the collection from that night's church service.

We weren't pleased when we realized that the money in our possession belonged to a church. We had intentionally committed a crime by stealing the car, but we never intended for our first robbery to be the tithes from a neighborhood church. That definitely wasn't cool.

Looking back on it, I have to say that this was a turning point in the life of the tall skinny kid from Edmondson Village. We could have returned the money. We could have just put it back in the car and left it somewhere. Nobody even needed to know it was us who had stolen it. And even if they had known it was us, I don't think they would have pressed charges if we had given it back.

But we didn't. The lure of all the goods that money could buy was just too strong for us. The next day was Saturday, and by the afternoon, we were content with the cash. Dajuan and I decided to go on a shopping spree to ease our guilt for committing such a despicable act. What else would two young teenagers have done with the money but blow it on useless material possessions? I sold my soul for two brand new pairs of Nike Air Jordan's. I wasn't used to spending money this way. Growing up financially deprived, I had never had the ability to do so, until then.

Dajuan had devised another plan for some of the money: invest it. He suggested that we buy a quarter pound of marijuana. He said that we could sell weed on his block and at school, making ourselves a fortune. At the time, marijuana was a highly sought-after commodity on the streets. Many in the city were smoking and choking on the illegal vegetation, and the guys at school selling it were making money faster than they could count it. All of these guys had cool gear, they were respected by everyone, and the girls were all over them. When you're a teenager, these seem like the most important things in the world. In just one week, I evolved from a petty car thief who just got lucky to a weed-selling knucklehead.

Dajuan's family was into just about every illegal activity you could conceive of. One of his uncles was a cocaine dealer, another sold guns, and a third was a house burglar. He had another crazy uncle who had recently headlined the evening news for shooting someone dead. It was easy for those guys to get their hands on just about anything illegal on the streets. We gave one of his uncles just enough money to buy the drugs for us to launch our illegal enterprise. I really had no idea what I was getting myself involved in.

It was three o'clock in the afternoon and school had just let out; this time of day was always a mad house. Dajuan and I were anxious to get down to his uncle's apartment because his uncle had arranged for us to get our first quarter pound. Most kids our age were waiting to get a letter in the mail admitting them to a prestigious college; we were out looking to start an illegal drug business. What a contrast in thinking.

Most kids aren't running around saying to themselves, "I want to be a drug dealer one day." The decision to travel down that road is more complicated than most people could understand. I wanted to be a football player, I wanted to be a fireman, I even thought about becoming a lawyer. I wanted to be all the things that society believed in, trusted, and admired. If I had ever said, "I want to be a drug dealer when I get older," within hearing distance of anyone in my family, I would be knocked in the head with a bag of commonsense. I've even met hustlers who would tell you, "Listen, kid, you don't want to get involved in that stuff. Become a musician, or anything else but a drug dealer." Everybody knows it's wrong. Everybody knows it isn't the career path to take.

Even in the movies, what happens? The drug dealer never rides off into the sunset. If he doesn't get killed first, someone he loves does, or something else tragic occurs. In the movie *Scarface*, what happens to Tony Montana in the end? He dies and so does everyone in his crew. In the movie *American Gangster*, what happens to Frank Lucas and his family? Just about every single one of them went to prison for years. In *New Jack City*, what happens to the hustlers as they dream of invincibility? Nino Brown and Gee Money both meet their maker shortly after saying, "I am my brother's keeper." There is never a happy ending for the street hustler who appears untouchable, but eventually is buried at the local cemetery.

Hustling weed on the street with Dajuan didn't give me the limelight that I had eagerly sought, either. I was able to keep cash in my pockets and to sustain myself financially, but I still felt empty inside. The green bud brought me a slight taste of attention, but there was something missing. Now in the game, I became even hungrier for something else. But what was it?

There was not a single adult in my life who would have said, "Hey, Kevin's making his own money now. Good for him," if they had known how ill-gotten those gains were. It doesn't take a rocket scientist to understand how a kid who grows up in a financially depressed household may irrationally begin to believe that his only way up the ladder is selling drugs in the streets. You don't have to be an extremely intelligent person to grasp this scenario, no matter how unrealistic the thought actually is. In the inner city, young kids – black, white, and Hispanic – get involved in the distribution of illegal drugs for several reasons. A lot of it is purely a matter of economics and peer pressure. They want to be a part of the crowd that's sporting the newest pair of Nike sneakers every week. Some young drug dealers support their parent(s), siblings, and other family members with this dirty money, the same way a person with a 9-to-5 job would. The absence of the male role model to supervise the young and untamed is also a major factor that can't be overlooked in this equation. Many perceive this as their only method of survival. They can't see that there is another way out. The biggest problem here is that once they start down this slippery road to nowhere, it's hard to detour. And once you go from eating peanut butter sandwiches for dinner to eating filet mignon at the finest restaurants, you don't want to go back.

● ● ● ● ●

The tug of war within me still raged as I fought a fierce battle of conflicting desires. I journeyed downtown to police headquarters to apply to become a city cop. The irony of it wasn't lost on me. But this was something that I had thought about as a child. Growing up, my father was in law enforcement. He wasn't a cop, but I was used to seeing him in a uniform and wearing a badge.

I walked around the huge glass building several times to make sure that no one I knew saw me go inside. The last thing that I wanted was to be seen by the wrong person going into Baltimore City Police Headquarters. I would have a tough time explaining that to the guys on the block. They would either have laughed or much worse, thought I was there informing on someone. Finally, I walked into the lobby, where there was an officer sitting at a huge front desk, his eye on the metal detector.

"Who are you here to see, son?" the officer asked.

"I'm here to fill out an application for police officer," I replied nervously. I attached the paper visitor's badge to my shirt and rode the elevator to the fourth floor. The young would-be-dealer-turned-would-be-cop, confused and disoriented, began to wonder, *what am I doing here in this place?*

On the fourth floor, there was another police officer sitting at another security desk. It was pretty much the same procedure as on the first floor, minus the metal detector. I couldn't help but notice the silence, which was deafening. I completed the sign-in sheet and was escorted to a very small room with no windows, located at the end of the long hallway. As I settled myself in the wooden chair, I realized the space wasn't much bigger than the bathroom at my grandmother's house.

It was several minutes before a police recruiter entered the room, holding paperwork in her hand. She was a heavy-set, older black woman with a big attitude. The kid seeking a real job was immediately intimidated by her. After sizing me up, she said, "You had better be twenty-one years old, all right." I didn't know that was the mandatory age for hiring. She took a few seconds to review the application. Up to that point, the only real job I had was delivering newspapers for a short period of time, so there wasn't much in the *Work History* section.

"Have you ever smoked marijuana before?" the woman/interviewer/interrogator asked the nervous skinny kid. I said no, but of course I was lying. This woman looked so intimidating that even if I wanted to tell the truth, I wouldn't have. She gave me this look as if to say, *Please stop bullshitting me, okay?* She said that she hoped I wasn't lying because I would eventually have to take a lie detector test. *Wow, my first lie detector test,* I thought to myself. She went on to say that if I were lying about smoking marijuana, I wouldn't be allowed to become cop. I didn't know if it was just smoking pot that would have kept this dream from becoming a reality, I thought to myself.

I'm not sure I even knew this at the time, but I had gone in there looking for someone to rescue me from the jaws of the street corner and tell me that everything was going to be all right. I wanted her to say to me, "Come on in, you're with us now," but that wasn't what happened. What happened was she told me to come back when I turned twenty-one. To this day almost no one knew that I ever tried to join the police department when I was a kid. I was only eighteen, but I still realized that I couldn't have a prolonged career in the streets. Even so, most people close to me would have been surprised to learn of my attempt to join the boys in blue. I guess all those visits by Officer Friendly to my elementary school on career day did have some influence after all, but at the end of the day, that influence wouldn't be enough.

• • • • •

I continued on the occupational bypass that would eventually seize my soul. In the twelfth grade, I dropped out of school all together. With no positive role male models in my life, the street corners become my role model. This was where I began to reshape my principles and values. This was where I began to reinvent my morals. Unfortunately, this is the case far too often for teenagers growing up in the urban centers of America with no father in their lives.

The game began to pull me in deeper and deeper. And soon I graduated from selling nickel bags of weed to selling dime bags of cocaine. The money increased, but so did the danger.

One night I was tipped off by the "Game Gods," or was it the terrible sense of double-cross and betrayal lingering in the air? Whatever the case, I was awake by a feeling, and I was ready and waiting behind the front door of the house that my family and I were living in. Suddenly, at about two o'clock in the morning, the full moon illuminated some would-be burglars at our front door. They had almost pried the door open when I opened fire with the .357 Magnum revolver I had purchased on the streets. The bullets ripped apart the door, sending small pieces of wood splattering as the varmints fled in surprise and panic. In a matter of minutes, the police were on the scene. And even though I was protecting the nest where my family lay asleep, I was handcuffed and carted off.

The white police officer that escorting me to the police transport, for no particular reason, stopped in his tracks, grabbed me by the neck, and said, "When a white man tells you to stop walking, your black ass better stop walking."

Where the hell did that come from? He didn't tell me to stop. I just looked at him in disbelief. I really didn't know how to take the cop's words, although I knew he was out of line. This was the first time in my life a white person had ever spoken to me in that way. It wasn't like this was 1965 in Selma, Alabama. This was 1988 in Baltimore, Maryland. But I guess things hadn't changed as much as many had hoped.

Looking back on the situation all I can say is, wow! What a real piece of garbage this guy was for saying that to a kid. I probably did need someone to kick my ass into shape or talk some sense into my stubborn head, but the last thing that I needed was some racist police officer getting his thing off on me. What purpose did that serve anyway? The only thing that encounter with the cop accomplished was to make me even more rebellious. This was the first legal mess I had been involved with. Although I was inside of my home protecting our property when the incident occurred, I was still in possession of an illegal firearm. For this crime I was placed on probation for one year.

Now sinking even deeper into the underworld – where the rule was, *anything goes* – I was given heroin to sell. I didn't know anything about heroin at the time and I don't think that the guy who gave it to me knew much about it, either. I didn't even know that you probably shouldn't sell heroin uncut, or raw. It's not just that you don't make much of a profit selling it that way; it's that it can potentially kill the person who uses it. I was just looking to make some money, but it quickly turned into a fiasco I would never forget.

I took the illegal opiate to my house and repackaged it in smaller glassine bags. Edmondson Village wasn't a huge drug empire, but Normandy Avenue and Franklin Street was a corner where you could make a lot of money, given the right product. I walked right up to the block and entered the fray. I made my first transaction almost instantly. The guy was back within minutes, looking for more.

"Man that is some good shit you got there, cousin. Let me get four more."

I was ecstatic. Every street merchant wants to sell the best product. It's a matter of street pride, like a good jump shot or a fine girlfriend. It's really a screwed-up mentality inside of this little world of all things screwed up.

Word quickly got out that a young skinny kid was selling some really strong dope. Suddenly, the money was rolling in faster than I could count it. When drug addicts hear that there are some really potent drugs nearby, they waste no time tracking it down.

I had no idea that I was selling an overdose waiting to happen. To make matters even worse, I accidentally placed far more heroin in the bags than any drug dealer who knew what he was doing would have ever done. Anyone who played around with this stuff could easily be on his way to the morgue. I hadn't sold this much drugs in such a short time period ever. I was excited about the money, but I really didn't completely understand what was happening.

"Let me get six bags."

"I was next. I need ten of them, homeboy."

The reaction I was getting from the buyers was intense, to say the least. Most of them didn't know how dangerous this stuff was until they injected it, and neither did Big Black.

Big Black was a regular dope head who had lived in the neighborhood for two decades or more. He knew who was selling the good stuff and who was selling the bad. He had a knack for it, like an artist knowing what types of brushes and colors to use. All of the other guys in the neighborhood viewed him as a kind of illegal drug specialist. When someone was looking to make a purchase, they would ask him for his opinion and he would direct them to the best product. The news of raw now available for ten dollars quickly made its rounds on the street. "Some new kid on the block has a bomb package that's knocking people's socks off, man."

I could see all six foot four inches of Big Black as he headed towards me. If Big Black knew about me, I must have been doing some real damage.

"What's up, kid?" I heard him growl. "What you working with?"

"I'm working with some dimes." I proudly answered.

"I heard you've got some good shit. Let me get two bags." Black gave me a twenty-dollar bill and I handed him his order to go. Of course, he had to leave me with an intimidating message just in case. "This better be the good shit that everybody else has been buying or I'm coming back."

"Don't worry, its right," I told him. Black turned and walked off.

About forty-five minutes later, the block was swarming with more buyers looking for the goods. The word got out pretty quickly that two guys had overdosed on a dime bag they had purchased from me. That just started a stampede for more of what I was selling. Now, you might think that someone almost dying would warn people away. But if you think that, you don't know heroin addicts. When addicts hear that another user has overdosed because it was good stuff, they waste no time; they want to experience the thrill for themselves. An overdose of heroin in the streets is more powerful advertising than a Super Bowl ad.

I was still only nineteen years old and I hadn't been exposed to anything like this before. The game was moving fast. Drug addicts coming out of the woodworks, yelling for me, wanting the stuff that I had. It was crazy and getting even more out of control by the minute.

Some people view addicts as being passive, but there's nothing passive about an addict when he is trying to get high. I had the good stuff and they wanted to get it, even if it was sending some guys to the hospital.

Big Black lived a few houses from the corner of Franklin Street, so I could see his house from where I was standing. There was a large group of people gathered at his backdoor. There was some yelling and pushing, but what really got my attention was that they were moving a body. As I looked closer, I saw whose body it was: Big Black. The Dope Ambassador had overdosed on the two bags of uncut heroin he purchased from me.

He was stretched out on the ground. He wasn't moving at all, not even a twitch. I thought, *oh, shit, this guy is gone.* His shirt was off and his chest was still as a board. He looked primed for the city morgue. One guy was giving him mouth-to-mouth resuscitation, while another guy was pounding on his chest, trying to bring him back around. Then I noticed something that raised my eyebrows. Another fiend had pulled down Black's pants and was dumping a bowl of ice cubes around his testicles. This was the craziest thing that I had ever seen before. I heard someone explain to another guy that they were doing it to help revive him. I had never heard anything like that before, but I thought to myself, *Okay, if it works, then whatever.* And I guess it made some sense. If someone put ice on my testicles, I could be dead and I'd still come back.

Minutes later a paramedic unit and fire engine arrived and checked Big Black's pale body for signs of life. He was lying in a pool of water, now that the ice had melted. It didn't take the paramedics long to assess the problem. Going into their black bag of tricks the paramedics pulled out their miracle drugs to save the poor soul. Using a needle as long as a ruler, they injected something into Black's left arm that revived the ailing man in a matter of seconds. Big Black's huge frame was then placed on a stretcher and into to ambulance, and sped off to the hospital. Your tax dollars at work.

Suddenly several police cars made their way to the scene of the crime. The natives immediately felt their presence. I was scared to death, realizing that the boys in blue were ready to act. Had Black died on the way to the hospital? Or were the cops there just to collect evidence? I was just standing around in a daze, attempting to evaluate the situation. My head was throbbing from everything that had just happened, when out of nowhere, I could see a group of heroin heads coming in my direction. Even with the cops nearby, they still wanted the goods. As far as they were concerned, if this stuff was powerful enough to take out Big Black, it was good enough for them. I didn't want anyone to die; I just wanted to make some cash. I was extremely nervous and I still had no idea what I was selling.

On the one side of me were the cops, looking to throw someone in jail for the sale of funk in a glassine bag. On the other side were the heroin addicts, looking at me like a lion looks at a gazelle just before breakfast. They wanted to get high and they didn't give a damn about anything else. These guys wanted the drugs! With all of the commotion going on, another drug addict from the neighborhood gave me the best piece of advice I had received all day. He walked up to me and in a low tone said, "Homeboy, you should get the hell out of here for a minute until things cool off." Why the hell didn't I think of that?

I started causally walking down the street, passing right by the police, still carrying a pocket full of evidence. I hoped nobody noticed me as I nervously passed the parked police cars, clutching my stash tightly, ready to make a run for it should the cops decide to pursue me. Walking tall but still nervous, I made my way past the crime scene.

The determined men who wanted to be medicated with the illegal prescription I was toting had me in their sights. Suddenly, these maniacs started walking behind me as I was trying to make a clean escape. They were marching like toy soldiers, as they began licking their chops for more of the good stuff. I walked about four blocks from the scene before I started running as fast as I could. The heroin heads began running as well! With every one step I took, it seemed like they were taking three. Ultimately, the legs of these addicts just weren't enough, as the young athletic kid left them all in the dust. The smell of my rubber-soled sneakers permeated the air as I made my getaway.

Off in the distance I could hear them yelling, "Hey, kid, we just want to cop a bag of dope. What are you running for?" Still running for my life, I replied, "I have to go home, I'll be back later." Quickly, I ran over to a friend's house to lay low until the dust settled. I told him about all of the commotion and he was as surprised as I was. Even then I didn't have any idea what exactly was in those glassine bags.

Later on that evening, I cautiously returned to the block. The same guy who had given me the advice to get the hell out of there was still standing on the corner, smoking a cigarette. I walked over to him and said, "What's up? Is everything cool around here now?"

"Everything is good now," he replied. "That shit you gave Big Black knocked his boots off, but he's okay."

Pleased by the positive turn of events, I said, "That's good news. I didn't want his ass to die."

"What's your name, kid?" the older man with the good advice asked.

"My name is Kevin."

"What's up? My name is Uncle Rob. Do you know what you were selling to those guys?"

Somewhat agitated by the notion that I was inexperienced in his trade, I answered, "Dope. What do you think?" I still didn't realize the true potency of my product, but I certainly didn't want told reveal any signs of my inexperience.

"Yeah, it's dope. But that shit is raw and uncut dope; that shit is serious," Rob said. "Somebody that doesn't know what they're buying could kill themselves with that shit. You didn't know that, did you?" No, I didn't. Now I understood why everyone was so hot for my stuff.

"Look, kid, I see that you're trying to get your hustle on and that's cool. But if you need some help, let me know," Uncle Rob told me. "I'll make sure your shit is right."

"Okay, that's cool," I said. Now I had someone to help me, since I really didn't know what the hell I was doing. I was still new to the hustle game and this day could have really ended up bad for me. But luckily, it didn't.

"Anthony is my nephew, so you know I'm on the up and up. You know my nephew, right?" Noticing my bewilderment, Rob elaborated, "The guy that drives that blue convertible Corvette." He must have been talking about that guy who I heard was making a lot of money on the streets.

"One day when you got some time, I'll introduce you to him," Uncle Rob said. Since I was trying to make moves in the game, this guy Anthony was definitely someone I needed to meet. "If you need some help getting rid of the rest of your package, let me know, all right?" Uncle Rob said. "The next time, you are going to want somebody to test that shit out first. I live right across the street at 501 Normandy Avenue."

●　●　●　●　●

Back in the early 90s, when roller skating was very popular, there was a skating rink in the city called Shake and Bake. Saturday night was the biggest night of the week for the young music maniacs to roller skate 'til early in the morning.

Every weekend I'd spot Taiwan there alone, either on skates or strolling around the dance area. We were both very young then – I was just a pup of 20 years – but I remember it like it was just yesterday. Taiwan used to wear her signature denim jacket with the Looney Tunes cartoon characters imprinted on the back of it. In those days, that was a really popular piece of gear. The jacket and the fact the she was very pretty always caught my attention. Taiwan was tall, slim, and had long black hair. She was like a young Tyra Banks, forehead and all. Other than just seeing her around the skating rink, I had never said a word to her at all. Still, the shy skinny kid from Edmondson Village was contemplating when to make my move.

Late one night I was leaving Shake and Bake with my friend Sean, when a friend of his requested a ride home. Melanie was a very pretty and sexy girl, plus she was really cool as hell. Even though I really didn't know her at the time, she was okay with some other guys that I knew very well. Melanie was wearing this expensive fur jacket that assured everyone that she was the girl-friend of a hustler. As we began walking toward Sean's truck, Melanie stopped and said, "Wait a minute, I have to find my girlfriend first. She's going home, too."

As we sat in the SUV waiting for Melanie to return, I could see Melanie and her friend walking toward us. As she got closer, I could see that her friend was the same girl that I always saw inside the skating rink, wearing the jacket with the Looney Tunes Cartoon characters on it! She looked really good.

Taiwan and Melanie climbed into the back seat and we sped off. On the way to dropping them home, I was quiet, as I contemplated how to proceed. Melanie was very outgoing, so she was busy bantering away with Sean. Taiwan was pretty laid back and low key, so she didn't say much. Maybe this was my opportunity to make some progress with her. I realized that before I could ask her for her number, I had to try to engage in some casual conversation first. That was how a real player would approach the situation, right?

"So, Sean, what is your friend's name?" Melanie said, referring to me. Suddenly, I realized that maybe this wouldn't be as difficult as I expected.

"Oh, that's my homeboy, Kevin," Sean replied. I looked back at Melanie and Taiwan and said, "How are you doing?" When they said hello to me, Taiwan was so pretty that I couldn't look directly into her eyes.

The girls didn't live far from Pennsylvania Avenue, so it only took us a few minutes to arrive at their home near Druid Hill. As we pulled up to the front door, you can imagine what was running through my mind. Of course, there was absolutely no way I was going to let the sexy sister get away without getting her number. But I had not managed any conversation with her. She was just too pretty. Briefly, I wondered to myself whether or not she was dating anyone – after all, she was the prettiest girl in the city.

As I jumped out of the vehicle, I had to get myself into position to accomplish my goal. I took a quick glance into the truck's mirror to make sure that my gear was in order. After all, my view was that you can't get the digits if your clothes were out of whack, right? I looked down at my feet to check my sneakers for any signs of disarray. The Adidas were fine and there was no damage after a long night of hip-hoppin' with friends. Finally, I tilted the baseball cap slightly to the side, completing my quick self-inspection. Sean and Melanie both jumped out on the other side of the vehicle, where they continued their banter. I realized I could now make my move on Taiwan, while they were distracted.

Taiwan was the last person to exit and as I opened the door for her, I struggled to keep my composure. Getting out of the SUV, it was almost like she was moving in slow motion, as her hair began to shift in the light breeze. Her caramel skin was gleaming from the moonlight as she stepped onto the ground.

My strategy was to use small talk as a way to generate the more important conversation. The first thing I managed to say to her was, "Did you have fun tonight?"

"Yes, we had a great time!" she answered. "My legs are sore from skating all night long, but I'm cool. Did you skate tonight? Because I didn't see you on the floor."

"No, I didn't skate," I answered. "I was just chilling. I haven't skated in a long time." The truth was that I wouldn't be caught dead on a pair of skates. Falling down on your face wasn't cool.

"When are you going back to the rink?" I asked her.

"I'll be going back next weekend," she answered. Suddenly I realized I was running out of time. I had to make my move now if I was going to make it at all. I couldn't wait until next weekend. That would have been an entire seven-day away that the young playa wasn't at all interested in. As the conversation continued, I could feel myself getting more and more anxious. My heart began palpitating, as the sweat in the palm of my hands evolved into a real annoyance. To make matters worse, the young hustler began stuttering a bit, as he fought to put together sophisticated words and phrases. I finally got the courage.

"So, how can I get in touch with you?" I blurted out.

A second seemed like a minute and a minute seemed like an hour as her pause continued. What was the holdup? If she said yes, I had it all planned out. We were going to Friendly's Restaurant for dinner and fudge sundae, and then after that, a good movie. *Do the Right Thing* was still causing controversy on the silver screen as Spike Lee's claim to fame. If Taiwan said no, that would be a problem. But how could she say no to the kid, right? That definitely wasn't going to happen.

Finally, she turned to me with those big beautiful eyes and said, "I can't give you my number." Befuddled, I wasn't sure what she had just said. I thought she said, "I can't give you my number," but I had to be mistaken. I knew that she didn't just diss the tall skinny kid!

"I have a boyfriend," she explained. "But we can be friends."

We can be friends reverberated through my head; *we can be friends!* Where had I heard that line before? Even though the chips didn't fall in my favor, Taiwan had really been nice throughout the whole situation. Maybe another time or place, things would have been different. That was just my luck; I meet the prettiest girl in Baltimore and she has a boyfriend.

Sean and I jumped back into his SUV and headed up Reisterstown Road, toward home. My bubble was burst, but only for a short time. So, Taiwan had boyfriend. Okay, it wasn't that serious, was it? I would be in the club tomorrow night, getting my groove on, looking to meet some girls. There were a lot of nice honeys in the streets in those days; they came a dime a dozen. But who was I kidding? There was something very special about Taiwan that I just couldn't resist. She was different from all the rest of the girls I had met. It wasn't just that she was so pretty; it was something attractive about her personality that intensified the allure.

A few months later I spotted Taiwan in the city, but this wasn't such a pleasant moment. On this particular day it was raining and cold. It was one of those ugly winter days when you just want to lie in the bed and sleep all day. By this time I was working my way through the hustle game and moving up the

YOU'RE IN THE GAME NOW

ladder. Still young and wet behind the ears, I thought I had it going on. Driving down Gwynn Falls Parkway on my way to dropping of a package in East Baltimore, I spotted the Looney Tunes jacket off in the distance. A bell began to ring in my head. I realized that it had to be her. It couldn't be anyone else! As I got closer, I confirmed what my eyes had assumed: it was Taiwan.

I hadn't seen her since the night we dropped off her and Melanie months ago, but this time something was wrong. Again with Melanie, they were standing on the corner as I approached the red light. My plan was to pull over and give them a ride to wherever they were going, but as I approached, I could see that they were both crying hysterically. They looked like they had really gotten some bad news. Taiwan had her arm around Melanie and Melanie was doing the same. They were consoling each other over something bad. Once the red light changed, they began walking across the street. Impeded by other drivers, I got stuck in traffic and couldn't pull my car over to them. I was somewhat hesitant to interfere anyway, because it seemed they were having a really personal moment. Weighing the situation, I continued on my way, hoping that whatever was happening with them would be okay.

A few days later I found out that Taiwan and Melanie had been friends with a hustler named Glen from the Westside. Glen had been murdered a few days before I had seen them on that rainy day. When I found this out, I understood why they were crying their hearts out on that corner. I had not noticed this at the time because all I could see was Taiwan, but they had been standing in front of the funeral home where Glen's body was being viewed prior to his funeral. Glen and his partner, Fats, had a heroin operation on North Avenue and Pulaski Streets. They were making about $15,000 a day, based on the rumors at the time. Glen died after he was shot in the back of the head, execution-style. The word in the streets was that Linwood "Rudy" Williams and some guys in his crew killed him, although Rudy had never been charged. He was supplying Glen and half the Westside around that time. The story was that Glen had bad mouthed Rudy behind his back, so Rudy decided to take him out. It was a surprise to hear that Glen had died, but it wasn't a surprise to hear who supposedly killed him. This guy Rudy wasn't someone that you fooled around with. With him you had to watch every step you made. I guess Glen found that out a little too late.

Almost one year later, I spotted Taiwan in Mondawmin Mall, while she was involved in that obligatory pastime for women called "shopping." She was alone again; similar to when I used to see her at the skating rink. In the course of two and a half years, we had both matured. I hadn't seen her for a while and she still looked ravishing. She still had those long, sexy legs with the light, caramel-colored complexion of an Egyptian goddess. I still haven't met a woman with legs as beautiful as hers. She was so sensual and seductive that it was unbelievable, because just one look in her eyes made me melt. I walked over to her and we began a casual conversation. Still intrigued by the beautiful vixen, I asked her for her telephone number again, but this time her answer was different. This time she said yes.

Our first night hanging out together on the town was at a restaurant downtown in Little Italy, where we had a great time. In just in a brief period of time, it seemed like we had known each other for years. I discovered that she was a very caring and genuine person. I found out that not only was she very attractive, but she was also very intelligent as well. She was one of the few women who I could actually describe at the time as an intellectual. She actually encouraged me to broaden my horizons beyond the streets, at a time when I actually thought the streets were all that mattered.

We would stay good friends over the course of many years. I still believe that she was one of very few women in the world who really understood me. She knew what type of lifestyle I was involved in, but she also understood that my lifestyle didn't define who I really was. I can remember one day, having a bouquet of roses delivered to her for Valentine's Day. The deliveryman told me that she was so touched and surprised that she began crying. I never understood why she cried, but I guess it was something only a woman could completely understand. Our friendship would sometimes become complicated, but it was nothing that couldn't be fixed. She probably never knew it, but one of the main reasons why I appreciated her so much in my life was the fact that she never disrespected me in any way, not one single time. We never got into arguments where we would say degrading or disparaging things to one another. We would have disagreements, but we would never have any disrespectful arguments. As a man, the fact that she respected me so much meant the world to me.

WHO KILLED ANTHONY?

"I'm going to kill him one day, man, I swear, I'm going to kill him. He thinks I've forgot, but I haven't forgotten at all."

This kind of babble continued for almost five years, so after a while, it went in one ear and right out of the other. For some people, hearing a menacing statement like that one could set off some alarm bells, but not here. If I had a donut for every time I heard someone in the streets telling me that they were going to kill someone else, I probably could open a bakery. In an attempt at bravado, a lot of guys in the streets blow smoke like that without starting a fire. Usually, by the end of the day, they've forgotten all about their urge to commit a homicide. But in some instances, well, you just never know.

"You punks better get the hell from in front of my grand-mother's house selling that garbage." Anthony would always give the local street hustlers grief for selling drugs in front of his grand-mother's home. He felt like any good grandson would, that this was disrespectful to the elderly woman, who only wanted to live in peace. But wasn't that ironic, coming from one of Baltimore's most infamous movers and shakers in the drug business?

Anthony was one of the sleekest hustlers I've ever known to pound the pavements of Baltimore. It was almost like he invented this game. Anthony was more like a businessman, like a Donald Trump, but without the blondes hanging around. Often, he would be dressed in a business suit as he surveyed his illegal empire. He never wore any attention-getting gold chains or watches, no *New Jack City* bravado or anything like that. Don't get me wrong, he was a little flashy, but in a very different way. People either loved him or hated him; there wasn't much in between. But either way you sliced it, he was well respected throughout the city.

He was different from all of the other hustlers. Most of the guys in the game were loud, flashy, and not very bright; plus many of them got high on their own supply. Anthony was the complete opposite. He had class rarely seen in guys from the street. Place him in the boardroom of any Fortune 500 company and he'd fit right in. He had the kind of personality that could motivate people into action. The problem was that the tasks Anthony motivated people to engage in, more often than not, were illegal.

Still wet behind the ears, I looked at Anthony the way a young kid would look at an older brother. Unfortunately, some of the skills the elder passed along weren't useful in any other arena. When I was nineteen years old, Anthony provided me the knowledge of how to cut and package heroin. He was a master at this; I used to refer to him as "the chemist." This was when I came to the conclusion that a man could become very wealthy selling heroin on the streets. I guarantee you; Anthony netted at least a million dollars during his career. Boats, motor homes, and motorcycles were just some of his toys. He always navigated through the streets of Baltimore in his navy blue convertible Corvette. This was just one of the reasons I thought Anthony was so different from the other guys in the game. But it wasn't just the material things that made him different, it was his entire approach.

Anthony was the proud owner of three huge dogs that were anything but man's best friend. They were vicious and ready to attack in the blink of an eye. Two of them were Rottweiler's and the other was a giant pit-bull terrier with a beautiful white coat of fur. Getting too close to them was not a good idea, not if you wanted to keep your limbs functioning properly. He had a kennel built on the side of his grandmother's house to secure the massive beasts. He didn't approve of dog fighting, even though his could have ripped a man's throat out. He loved these dogs far too much to turn them into killers. Anthony spent thousands of dollars caring for these mammoth beings he regarded as pets. For a small fee, Uncle Rob used to take care of them when Anthony was out of town on business. When the pit bull had her litter, Anthony sold me one of the pups, a snow white male with a dash of brown on the tip of its tail and both ears. I named the pup Al Capone. Al briefly became my best friend, as he rode shotgun through the city with me in my new sports car. Stories on the evening news of vicious pit bulls motivated one of my neighbors to inform the leasing office of my little guest. With their "No Dogs Allowed" sign in hand, representatives from management told me, "The dog leaves the apartment, or you leave!" The choice was no choice at all, and my best friend had to go.

In 1990, the feds made two colossal federal drug sweeps in Baltimore. Both of these occurred in the early months of the year and created chaos on all drug corners. There were two major federal grand jury indictments were handed down, one involving a dealer named Rob Downey and his crew, and the other involving Rudy Williams. Both of these men had been labeled drug kingpins by the U. S. Attorney's office. Both of these cases became infamous, as they graced the front pages of the local newspapers for several weeks. All of the members of these organizations were arrested and convicted of conspiracy to distribute hundreds of pounds of heroin and cocaine in Baltimore. At the time, these two organizations ran the city with an iron fist, using violence when they decided it was necessary, with no sense of remorse. Nothing happened on the street corner without someone from one of these two syndicates profiting from it. At the end of the day, more than fifty of them were sentenced to long prison terms. From then on, they roamed different avenues: the corridors of federal penitentiaries all over the United States.

Unfortunately for Anthony, he was drawn into this massive investigation. The half million-dollar bail was no problem for Anthony. He intended to mount a strong defense, too. But it would be tough. The feds had pictures of him meeting with Rob Downey, the main target in one of their investigations. The feds also had recordings of him talking to Rob on the phone. They had so much evidence against Rob; he eventually caved and turned government witness. That testimony added to the mound of evidence they already had against Anthony, he hardly had a chance, even if he could afford the best legal defense available.

It was around eleven o'clock in the morning and I was driving up Edmondson Avenue, when my pager rang. This was before the days of frequent cell phone and text messaging use. I saw that it was my girlfriend. I made an abrupt turn off of Edmondson Avenue and on to Normandy Avenue, where I knew there was a pay phone. The phone was directly across the street from Anthony's grandmother's house. When I parked my car, I could see Anthony's nephew Dante standing in front of the house, looking distressed. That didn't set off any alarm bells for me; I assumed he was just having a bad day. But while dialing my girlfriend's number, I could see Uncle Rob walking across the street towards me. The receiver was at my ear when he told me the bad news.

"Did you hear what happened to Anthony last night?" the dejected man mumbled. Immediately, I assumed Anthony had gotten into some ridiculous fight with someone, or maybe he got arrested again for driving on his suspended license. I was not prepared for what Rob would eventually say.

"Somebody killed Anthony last night." The phone dropped out of my hand and for a split second, I became numb.

I stood there, in disbelief, staring across the street at Dante, who hadn't moved. After briefly consoling Uncle Rob, I got back into my car and sped away. I never did make that call to my girlfriend.

For almost forty-five minutes, I drove through the city streets, wracking my head for clues as to who could have slain my friend and mentor. I was shattered; the pain rippled through me in waves. The clouds in the sky seemed grayer and the light of the day was dim, mirroring the gloom of the moment. The man that I had admired was now gone forever. *Why? Why?* Kept going through my brain, as I tried to make sense of the senseless. I realized Anthony had been in the game for years and probably had plenty of enemies. There were many individuals who may have wanted to dethrone my friend. The fact that Anthony was out on federal bond could have also made him the target of assassination. Someone could have assumed that he was going to turn informant and reveal their secrets. But then, I thought of Mike.

Could Mike have done this? *Would* he have done it? Could he have rationalized killing Anthony in revenge? In reality, the theory made no sense whatsoever, but in the streets, reality can often be like a far off galaxy: unreachable.

I considered the deadly incident that had occurred years earlier that had set Mike into this murderous need for vengeance. In 1986, Anthony's nephew Miguel shot Mike's brother Tony in the head. It was a stupid, meaningless argument; both men were high on drugs. Tony died in the hospital that same evening. Anthony and Tony were close friends at the time, but for some reason, Miguel hated Tony. I never knew exactly why there was this bad blood between them, but I did know that Mike was devastated by the death of his older brother and vowed to exact revenge on the killer.

For years after Miguel murdered his brother, Mike would periodically tell me that he was going to kill Anthony. I didn't put a lot of stock in his vicious threats. Mike was only around seventeen years old when Tony died. Anthony hadn't killed him, but I guess Mike felt that Anthony could have stopped his nephew; realistically speaking, it all happened so fast, there wasn't much Anthony could have done. But as I have said, reality often seems unreachable in the streets.

I think that Mike really wanted to kill Miguel, but Miguel was out of reach, as he was now serving a twenty-year sentence for the murder. I also think that Mike just needed to exact his revenge on somebody and his fury fell on Anthony.

But I still didn't really believe Mike had killed Anthony. The only thing I knew for sure was that Anthony had let his guard down with someone. I knew that the street tycoon was far too intelligent to let someone he had a problem with get that close. I also knew that he was under a lot of pressure with his legal problems. He was still out on bond and facing twenty-five years in prison. Even though he was trying to take it all in stride, the reality was that it was a heavy burden. The government had seized his cars, cash, and just about everything else when they arrested him. His high-priced legal, team with fees of $350 an hour was running up an incredible bill. The man was understandably stressed, so he was more vulnerable.

Both Mike and Anthony were my friends. Mike and I attended the same high school and pounded the pavements together in the neighborhood. He blocked my shot a few times during basketball games as I drove to the hoop. Clubs and parties were a weekly event for the two homeboys who often hung out together. I also knew his mother well who tried her best to keep Mike in line. Mike and I were very close at one point, but we eventually began to drift apart as time went on. I believe he began to harbor resentment of my success in the game. Mike hustled in the streets too, but he was in the game more to impress the women and not for the success and advancement. In my opinion, he was never as hungry as I was to prosper in the business.

I had come to rely on Anthony more than I realized. He was someone that I trusted for advice and for a swift kick when I did something stupid. He was my personal consigliore, and I could talk to him about anything. I can remember him scolding me one night because I had a few drinks. He was of the opinion that your head had to be clear at all times to play the game safely.

Still uncertain how my comrade became a victim of homicide, I decided to at least look into the matter. I wanted to know if Mike had followed through with the outrageous threats he'd made over the years. Feeling uneasy, I drove over to his apartment. He invited me in and when I entered, I could see that he was holding a nine-millimeter handgun in his left hand. I knew something was very wrong.

I sat down in the living room and told him about Anthony being murdered. After a brief pause, he said yeah, he already knew about that. Then, he confirmed my belief.

"I killed him," he said. He looked strangely lethargic, as though doing the unforgivable had drained him. He had just killed someone! He had just killed my friend.

I just sat there and stared at him for about a minute, with my heart bleeding for Anthony. I struggled to gather my thoughts. This was like a bad dream. But it was real. As I stared at my once-close friend and thought about what he had done, part of me wanted to return the favor and kill him.

Finally, I spoke. More like, I yelled.

"Man, do you realize what the hell you've done?! You fucking killed this man for no damn reason at all! Why would you do something so fucking stupid? What sense did it make to kill Anthony?"

"You know why I killed him!" Mike shot back. "I killed him because of Tony!" At that point, I realized that Mike's irrational thoughts were dominating any common sense he had left.

Mike just kept saying, "You know why I did it, you know why I did it." To me, this was unimaginable. This guy's brother had been dead for five years and it wasn't Anthony who had killed him, and in Mike's mind, he could still rationalize killing Anthony.

Mike was totally paranoid and scared out of his mind that he would be discovered. I asked him why he would think the police were looking for him so soon, but he didn't have an answer. He should have been terrified of a death sentence because this was premeditated murder.

He described to me how he lured Anthony to his grave. Anthony was a very smart guy and had never looked at Mike as a threat. Anthony didn't make many mistakes, but he only needed to make one. Mike had given him a phony story about having a large amount of cocaine and needing help disposing of it. Anthony was a businessman, so he took the bait. He was in financial trouble too, since the feds had shut down his cash, and he needed to make sure his lawyer's fees got paid. This was how Mike was able to trick Anthony into the last business deal he would ever make.

Mike drove him to an apartment complex under the pretext of taking him to inspect the merchandise. Once they arrived, Mike led Anthony to the rear of the building. He then pulled the weapon out of his waistband and told Anthony he was going to rob him.

Anthony yelled, "Rob me for what? You've got the fucking drugs, not me!" Mike told him to turn around and then pushed him to the ground. Then he put the revolver to the back of his head and slowly pulled the trigger. Anthony's skull exploded, showering blood and brain matter into Mike's face. He stood over Anthony's lifeless body and shot him once again, in the back, just for insurance. The whole thing was over in a matter of seconds. It's amazing how little time it takes to remove someone from this world. Anthony never suspected that Mike was up to anything because he never knew Mike held a grudge against him for so long. Who could have ever known?

All those years of Mike saying he was going to kill Anthony, I never took him seriously. I never believed he'd actually do it. If he was going to do it, he would have by now, instead of just talking about it, I reasoned. Mike had no history of violence and he sure hadn't ever killed anyone, so why would I take him seriously? It occurred to me a few times to tell Anthony what Mike had said, but I really didn't think he was serious. And I was afraid Anthony would have killed Mike for nothing more than having a big mouth. And he wouldn't have waited five years to do it, either. So, I didn't tell him.

What could I have done to prevent this? How could I have fixed this thing before it erupted into the destruction of life? I had thought I was doing the right thing by ignoring Mike, but I was mistaken. And now I felt just as responsible for my friend's death as Mike was. I had good intentions, but in the end, someone was still dead.

Just a few days after the assassination of my compadre, I was standing on the corner of Normandy and Franklin Streets, across from Anthony's grandmother's house. Staring at the empty parking space where Anthony used to park his Corvette, I began thinking about how Anthony would always one-up me when I started talking trash. I'd be trying to prove what a hot shot I was, but Anthony really was a hot shot, and he kept putting me in my place. I could never gain ground with him by way of the verbal jab, since Anthony was quick with his wit. His absence made my heart heavy, as the mourning process began.

Anthony's funeral was a tough pill to swallow, for me and everyone else who shared in his life. Now I can't remember where the funeral was located, even though I was there. I was in a daze through the entire service. I do remember that Anthony's mother and sister were sitting in the front row of the chapel, as I entered through the stained glass doors. I can remember leaning over the railing to hug his mother and almost tumbling over. As I walked past Anthony's casket, I placed cash by the side of his still body. I'm not exactly sure why I chose this gesture to make my final salute to him, but I felt like it was something he wouldn't mind me doing. He did love money. At the conclusion of the service, Anthony's casket was slowly closed, as many in the chapel released tears they had fought to conceal. This was when it really hit me, that I would never see him again.

This was the first and last funeral that I attended for a fallen comrade and confidante. The entire situation had left me shaken, as I tried to make sense of it all. After the funeral, I sought the calm quiet of my apartment so I could think. I was drained by Anthony's death and by my feelings of responsibility in it. I had a very difficult time sleeping that night, as my brain struggled to understand what had just happened. When I closed my eyes, the images of Anthony lying in the casket were vivid in my mind. This wasn't my first time losing a colleague in this battle for the streets, but in the past, I didn't feel it so deeply. My constant tossing and turning eventually woke my girlfriend, as she lay next to me in bed. As she turned to me, she could see a single tear slowly rolling down my face.

"Kevin, please talk to me. What is going on?" she finally asked. "I know Anthony was your friend, but something else is going on, isn't it?"

"I don't want to talk about it. I can't," I told her. "I don't want to talk about it." She left me alone, but she was still watching my face closely. Finally, I told her.

"I know who killed Anthony." This shocked her, I could tell, but she remained calm.

"Who?" she asked. "Who killed him?"

My soul was torn between the desire to keep her protected from my street life and my need to tell somebody.

"A friend of mine," I said. "And I couldn't stop him," I answered. But no matter how much I needed to unburden myself, I would not put her in danger, so I never told her who it was. That was the first and last time I ever had such a conversation with her regarding Anthony.

It might not make any sense to you that I didn't turn in my once close friend for the murder of my comrade and mentor.

And I understand that. Looking back on it now, I wonder the same thing. All I can tell you now is that that is not the way things work in the streets.

Following his death, I had become very close with his mother, Ms. Alternease, who reminded me of my grandmother. She was one of the sweetest women I have ever met. Ms. Alternease would do almost anything she could to help another person in their time of need. She gained satisfaction from assisting other people and wanted nothing in return except to see the person smile. For some reason, she had really taken to me after Anthony was gone. Maybe I reminded her of him.

Ms. Alternease was a skilled chef and loved to prepare her Southern-style dishes. She knew that I lived alone and it had become obvious to her that my life did not lend itself to healthy eating. Whenever she saw me, the first thing she would say was, "Have you eaten today?" She regularly gave me huge plates of fried chicken and her delicious sweet potato pie to take home. I could always get a good home-cooked meal as long as Ms. Alternease was around. She took care of me kind of like she had taken care of Anthony. She would always tell me stories about the good deeds he had done in his short life. The stories always put a smile on her face. Even though her son was a drug dealer and she didn't approve of drugs, he was still her son, and she didn't love him any less for it.

ENTER THE DRAGON

Now that Anthony was gone, what else could I do but plow ahead? Who would I turn to now for advice, in a business where deceit, treachery, and foul play were the norm? With thoughts of arriving at the morgue through the wrong entrance constantly on my mind, the new name of the game was *Watch Your Back*. Trust was now a rare commodity, and I dare not lend it to many. The murder of my companion had sharpened my wit, but also hardened my soul. I realized that I couldn't lower my guard to anyone if I had the desire to live to see another day. This up-and-coming young hustler was still trying to find his way through the maze. I was handling my business on the streets in a more thorough way now. No more fooling around. No taking chances.

Donald had brought the scheme to me, wanting my stamp of approval. "Fayette and Mount Street, that's where it's at, home-boy; that's where we need to be, man." Donald and I were really cool, and I looked at him like he was my little brother. Donald had been my number two guy in Edmondson Village, selling dime bags of cocaine for me. We weren't accumulating a huge amount of cash, but we were a formidable duo. Donald was like a young pup, wet behind the ears, but hungry for money and mayhem. His biggest downside was that he enjoyed the women a little too much. If he had $100 in his pocket, ninety-nine bucks would go to the ladies in all the wrong ways. He had a big problem holding on to his earnings.

"Kevin, I'm telling you, man, I got this block down in West Baltimore where we can get rich. Man, they're selling dope down there like it's going out of style." I believed him, but the problem was, I didn't believe *in* him.

I was skeptical about Donald because I knew it was tough for him to stay focused, especially with his propensity to turn his attention to the ladies at any given moment. A move like this was somewhat dangerous because the guy's downtown where these blocks were located played for keeps. But it wasn't unfamiliar territory for me; I knew the neighborhood very well. My grandmother and my aunt had lived there since I was a little kid. Once, when my mother left my father for a brief period of time, we lived there with my grandmother. My sister and her husband had a grocery store a few blocks away, on the corner of Lexington and Smallwood Streets, and I was in the area almost every day. I was already cool with a couple of guys who were hustling down there, so I knew it was a good opportunity.

I was still undecided, but Donald was hitting me every day with the same old line. "Kevin, what's up, man? I'm telling you, man, you need to make this move. The real money is downtown, bro, the money's on Mount Street."

He had a good point and I knew that it was time to make a move to expand my business; I just wanted to make sure it was the right move. I didn't want to move and then have the situation blow up in my face. Making bad decisions in the streets is an easy way for you to get yourself exterminated. Everybody in the game knew that if you really wanted to make some money selling heroin, the closer you got to the projects, the better. The guys down at Lexington Terrace and Murphy Homes projects were raking it in faster than the clouds made rain. One crew was bringing in $35,000 a day.

After an intense due diligence process, I decided that we could make it happen. The only heroin on Mount Street was named "Brown Bags," distributed by a crew of guys from New York City. They were selling some outrageous amounts for a few years on that block, but they had big problems. They had just gotten raided by the cops and most of their crew was in jail. Weighed down by drug and murder charges, they would be out of commission for a while. Even if they beat the case, they would be sitting on the sideline for several quarters, giving this rookie time to score. Just a few blocks away from our intended target were the Boyd and Pulaski Street area. The guys who ran this Baltimore version of *New Jack City* would be our closest competitors. Boyd and Pulaski were practically owned and operated by members of another New York crew. The neighborhood was on out of control, so I knew it was just a matter of time before the police would be back. Far too many violent incidents were making the evening news.

There were a lot of guys moving in from New York to Baltimore in those days, to secure drug spots all over the city. The main reason these illegal traveling salesmen landed here was quite simple: profit margin. Drugs wholesaled for much less in New York, so they'd buy it there and sell it in Baltimore, which guaranteed them a bigger profit. ; If they weren't murdered first. It sometimes wasn't so easy to just walk in and open shop on another guy's terrain.

Eventually, the deal to move forward was hatched and we were ready to venture into uncharted waters. But first we needed product, and it had better be good to compete on these streets!

A friend of mine named Ears had an extensive inventory of heroin from his Nigerian connection. The Nigerian worked with a well-organized drug importation ring out of Miami, who shipped the heroin to Baltimore, concealed inside of watermelons. The heroin was then distributed wholesale to the clandestine hands of Baltimore and DC dealers. Most of the dope Ears was receiving was being issued to his own workers in Southwest area of Baltimore. So, I made Ears an offer he just couldn't refuse. Since he had just lost one of his operations and several of his crew to a recent police raid, he needed an additional source of cash flow. I told him that I was going to open shop on Mount Street. With a handshake and four ounces of uncut raw heroin the deal between him and I was sealed.

The next morning, Donald and I journeyed over to the record shop on Garrison Boulevard in search of the supplies we needed. The record shop didn't just sell CDs and audio equipment; this was the primary location in Baltimore to invest in drug paraphernalia. These guys sold everything you could think of for preparing, packaging, and consuming the illegal substance. They were making almost as much money selling valves, cut, and glassine bags as the hustlers on the street corners were making selling heroin and crack. The difference was that their business was legal, at the time.

We were in need of quinine and bonita, two ingredients used to cut raw heroin. We also got yellow glassine bags, since no one had claimed that color. The color of the bags was how the different drug operations were distinguished from one another. It was a primitive way of marketing the product, but it was effective.

Back at my apartment in the upper Park Heights section of the city, we went to work packaging the drugs. On a glass table,

I weighed a small amount of the tan-colored heroin, using a digital scale to ensure accuracy. Then I mixed together the quinine and the bonita, and measured it out. The quinine boosted the potency of the heroin and the bonita was like a preservative. Using what Anthony taught me, the cutting process was simple. The competition in this new haven was fierce, so our product had to be strong. If we wanted to make any money at all, I had to cut the heroin with less quinine and bonita. It would slice into my profit margins, but there was no other way to break into this area where so many dealers were already established. I would cut one gram of heroin with five grams of quinine and bonita mix. That was far less cut than most drug dealers were using at the time. So, you can understand why the uncut (raw) stuff I was selling in Edmondson Village a few years earlier caused Big Black to overdose.

The next morning, I gave Donald about two thousand dollars' worth for his first day on this new job. He quickly employed local fiends to be his eyes and ears on the street when he began selling the drugs. By afternoon, he was paging me for a refill. I was pleasantly surprised because the commodity didn't move this quickly in our previous location.

"Yo, I told you, man, I told you," Donald said. "We're going to get rich fucking with this shit, Yo. These motherfuckers love it. They *love* it."

Our move into West Baltimore was a success. In a few months, we had established a strong presence in the neighborhood and the yellow bags became highly sought-after. By this time, the other dealers on the block had their eyes on us and they were not happy. As far as I was concerned, there was more than enough business for everyone, but not everyone agreed with my rationale. I could feel the tension surging through the air as a few of the regular dealers in the area felt they had been intruded upon.

There was one crew in particular that had a big problem with our success. The Blue Thunder crew, led by a fellow named Chucky, was furious because they began to lose their grip on their once-secure market. Not only that, prior to coming onboard with me, Donald had worked with them briefly, so they felt that he had double-crossed them.

Fayette and Mount Street was an unpredictable and vicious area, a Mecca for everything unholy. The street soldiers that dwelt there didn't care about life or limb. The cocaine and heroin addicts would rob your grandmother for two dollars to get high and the hustlers would slice your throat if you got in their way. This place was a jungle, where only the strong survived. You had two *Choices* down there if you wanted to see the sun rise in the morning. You could rule the jungle like a lion, or you could run away like a gazelle. This was the reality.

I was on the block with Donald a few days a week, making sure he played his position. Business had really picked up and everyone knew about it. I hired a few more guys to keep up with the demand. But as Donald's financial status improved, so did his number of female companions.

One morning I came down to the block to check on things. There were a couple of loyal customers waiting for us as usual, but something was up. They were waiting for us, but not to make a purchase. They had been burned the night before and wanted to talk to someone about their unpleasant experience. One of them was a woman who was very thin and frail. She looked like the average neighborhood drug addict, track marks and all. Her approach was very timid and I sensed that she didn't want any trouble. Most addicts don't; they just want their high.

"Can I talk to you for a minute please?" For the most part, I tried to stay cordial with our clientele.

"What's up?"

"I was down here last night about nine o'clock and I bought a bag of dope from one of your people. He sold me a bag filled with sugar." At first I thought she was playing, trying to get a free bag of heroin from us. But as I looked closely at the woman, I could see the trepidation in her eyes and I saw that her hands trembled. There was no doubt in my mind that this lady was sincere. To make matters even worse, there were five other customers waiting to tell me the same story. Donald had allowed this to take place on his watch, right under his nose. He was supposed to be taking care of things like this, but he had allowed himself to be distracted.

The burned customers kept showing up. We always closed up shop at around seven o'clock in the evening. But these people were all saying that they were coming through the block at around nine o'clock, looking for yellow bags, and they had been getting them. That could only mean that one of our people had been coming back out and running his own hustle. But who? I needed to know because I had to put a stop to this. You could get killed playing that kind of game on the streets.

I asked them to describe the guy who had been selling the fake merchandise and they all described the same person. It was one of my new guys, Terry. He was coming back out on the block after we had closed. Everybody assumed it was the good stuff because they saw the yellow bags, but Terry was just filling them with sugar. The thing I could not get myself to comprehend was how he thought he could get away with it.

I could see him standing down at the other end of Vincent Street, smoking a cigarette, and I was furious. This piece of garbage was hanging around, as if nothing wrong had taken place. My blood began to boil as I weighed how to deal with the matter in the correct way. I couldn't believe this guy had the balls to pull a stupid scam like this. What the hell made him think that these people wouldn't be coming back for a refund after injecting a bag of sugar? I was almost as upset with Donald for missing it. He was supposed to have more control over the guys that worked the street. But Donald was so busy chasing the women that he didn't see what was happening right under his nose.

We were only in for about five hundred bucks at this point, and I gave them all full refunds. It wasn't the money I was concerned about; it was our reputation. This kind of news travels very fast in the streets. On top of that, you might end up selling a burn bag to someone who may come back looking to blow your brains out. When a hardcore addict has scratched and scraped all day long to get ten bucks to get high, you never know what he might do if he gets screwed. Terry must have thought that the entire world was stupid and that he was the only smart guy in town.

Donald was man enough to take full responsibility for falling asleep at the switch. He wanted to make it right. Donald yelled down the street, "Yo, Terry, we need to see you for a minute."

Terry stood up and started walking towards us. Standing there with us were the people who had purchased the burn bags from him the night before. I wanted to see how he would react to seeing all of his accusers standing there together.

"Yo, were you out on the block last night?" Donald asked.

"No, I wasn't out," Terry claimed. "I left the block when we closed down at seven." Donald was looking at me to get a reaction, but I didn't say a word. I wanted to see how he handled it.

"These guys said that you sold them some bullshit last night after we closed shop," Donald pressed. "They said that you sold them some burn bags filled with sugar."

"That's bullshit; I didn't sell them a damn thing," Terry lied. Each one of the individuals that had accused Terry was still standing around as he stated his innocence. I knew that he was lying, but I needed confirmation. The frail woman was standing next to me.

"Is that the guy who sold you the shit?"

"Yes, that is him."

"You sure?"

"I don't have to lie about something like this," she answered. I could see a tear in her eye. I took over the interview of the burn bag suspect from there on.

"Look, man, all of these people ain't lying on you," I told him. "You know that you did this shit, so let's stop playing games." I was getting hot because this guy was trying to make me look like a fool in front of our customers.

"I didn't give them shit!" Terry yelled. That was it. He didn't give a damn about the people that he had burned or anyone else. Any one of them could have blown my head off if they thought I had known about his idiotic plot.

During all of this, I had been drinking a bottle of orange juice. Aggravated I smashed the glass bottle over the top of Terry's bald head. He was dazed and discombobulated as he struggled to stay on his feet. For a split second, he was out of it because his eyes rolled up into his head and his knees wobbled a bit. I hit him again landing three more punches to his face. With the rest of the block looking on, I had to set an example for the next genius who thought he could get away with this. Everyone watching would know that my crew was reliable and didn't cheat its clientele, and that I would hand out consequences to any one of my crew who tried to.

As I continued to explode fists of fury on him, he attempted to flee the scene, making a run for the other end of Vincent Street, but I wasn't finished. Right on his heels, I was able to get in one last blow to the side of his temple, knocking him weary. He stumbled up against the brick wall of a vacant storefront before finally making his escape.

As I made my way back to the block, the perpetrator was gone and a feeling of liberation abounded through the crowd. There would be no more sugar-bag play in the area for months to come. But I had not escaped unscathed. It was an older drug addict named Shirley who spotted the blood on me.

"Baby, you've got blood on the side of your face," she told me. I wiped my hand across my face and looked down at the blood in my palm. I was sure that it belonged to the loser of the match. The staggering thief hadn't gotten a lick on me. Or had he? I bent down to take a look in the mirror of a parked car. The crook had done some damage after all. There was a three-inch gash on my left cheek.

"This motherfucker stabbed me in the fucking face!"

I never felt it, but the guy must have had a razor in his hand and he definitely made contact. I drove myself to the hospital, where thankfully, an experienced plastic surgeon was on duty. She did a masterful job of repairing the souvenir that my disgruntled employee had given me.

A few days later, I was back on the block, overseeing the company profits once again. The neighborhood had been reassured by my performance that I wasn't having any games in my business. Only the real deal would exchange hands out on the block as long as I had anything to do with it. Walking down the street, I could see Drac and Sweet Pea – two of the regulars in the area – regulating their small crew of crack cocaine hustlers. When I first started in the neighborhood, I assumed that these guys would be a force to be reckoned with. But I was wrong. They sold crack cocaine and we were selling heroin, so they didn't worry about us squeezing their revenue.

"Yo, what's up, Sweet Pea. What's up, Drac"? I said.

"What's up with you Kev? We heard you had to demonstrate on Terry for fucking around with your peoples."

"Yeah, he was on some bullshit," I said.

"You couldn't let him get away with that shit," Drac said, "because he would've just kept on doing it."

"You should've killed his ass," Sweet Pea chimed in. But sending someone off to heaven, or hell, is a pretty serious thing.

Drac and Sweet Pea were street soldiers who you didn't want to have any problems with. Like Batman and Robin, where you saw one of them, you saw the other. They were as dangerous as they come if you made the foolish mistake of crossing them out on the streets. I realized that early on, after watching them bring the pain to one sad soul who may or may not have asked for it.

● ● ● ● ●

It was an average day in the concrete jungle down on Vincent Street. This block had become like a sidebar to the more infamous Fayette and Mount Street Empire a block away, which ruled the neighborhood. The local drug trade was like a snapshot back to a time when outdoor food markets were jammed with people bartering for lamb, wine, and produce. The only difference now was the commodities being exchanged.

Sitting on the stoop with my back up against the wall, I could observe all of the movers and shakers, my nine-millimeter close by. It was always a good idea to have a clear view of my surroundings because you just never knew. The temperature on the block could go from cold to hot in just seconds. I had lookout men at each end of the street, keeping an eye out for trouble, sounding the alarm – "Five-0!" – at the sight of the imperial forces. The runners (or touters, as they're called, by those from the old school) were collecting the currency at a fierce pace.

From my post, I could evaluate that it was the same old hustle and bustle, with every man and woman enthusiastic about getting high. Suddenly, I spotted Drac and Sweet Pea marching down the middle of the street. The block cleared a path for the two men, like the parting of the Red Sea. These guys were in gangster mode. As they approached, they whispered to me, "Lay low for a minute; it's getting ready to go down."

Drac sat down close to where I was sitting, as his partner implemented the premeditated attack. Sweet Pea slowly crept his way over to his unknowing victim; the poor soul never saw it coming. Suddenly, everything slowed down and seemed to turn into an old black-and-white movie. The scene was eerie, and there was a tension that could only mean a show of violence was imminent.

The .357 Magnum was long and it seemed as if it took minutes instead of seconds for the attacker to remove the weapon from his waistband. Both hands tightly gripped the handle of the revolver. His knees were bent slightly, as he moved with the grace of a character in *The Matrix*, inching closer and closer to his prey. With the victim's back facing him, Sweet Pea placed the huge cannon to the side of the man's skull, his finger on the trigger. The man had no idea he was breathing his last breath. With a slight squeeze from his index finger, the hand-held canon exploded one round of death into the man's head. The sound ripped through the block like thunder, startling the natives, their intoxication momentarily interrupted by fear. The body hit the concrete with an eerie sound that rattled everyone within feeling distance. Everyone scattered like bugs, quickly removing themselves from the scene of the crime. Within seconds, the block was empty of all human life with, the exception of the bleeding victim who was just barely hanging on. None of the witnesses wanted to spend the next twenty hours explaining to the cops why they witnessed nothing at all. I was never to know the violation of the dead man. But just as everyone knew you did not sell sugar to my clientele, everyone now knew you do not mess with Sweet Pea and Drac.

As time went on, my operation grew, which created more responsibilities, more pressure, and more problems. I had finally begun to reconcile the fact that Donald wasn't ready for prime time. He was more of a street soldier and less of a leader of the pack. I needed a general who could give orders and make demands.

Case in point: We had been working out of the same stash house on Fairmount Avenue for a couple of weeks straight. If you stay put for longer than that, the police can catch your scent, so I told Donald it was time to move to another house. But obviously, he didn't think so. I was trying to lay back and let him handle the situation. I told him, time and again, that he shouldn't keep using the same location.

"Switch to another house, that's all you have to do, Donald," I urged. "That would keep you a step ahead of the cops." He would say to me the same old line:

"I'm working on it."

Just a few days later, all hell broke loose, as the cavalry from the Western District Narcotics Unit kicked in the door to the stash house.

I was walking down Baltimore Street on a warm sunny afternoon, on the way to pick up the cash for the day from Donald, when my progress was suddenly impeded by one of the runners who regularly worked the corner.

"What are you doing down here?" she asked. I looked at her like she had been using more of the stuff than she normally sold.

"What are you talking about?" I said.

"You haven't heard what happen today? You didn't hear that the house got raided by the cops this morning? Donald and a couple other people got locked up when the cops kicked the door in."

I still thought she was enjoying too much of her own product. "What are you talking about, Debbie?"

"That house he uses over on Fairmount Avenue."

I couldn't believe what I was hearing. During the raid, police had seized $10,000-worth of heroin and cash. By the time I got Donald and the other guys out of jail, I had spent another ten grand. I wanted to choke this guy. Not only was he costing me money, but he was risking my freedom along with his. And I *told* him this might happen! I had warned him many times. I liked Donald a lot, but like I said, he wasn't a good leader.

About three weeks later, we ended up doing the same thing again. Donald was selling heroin out of the hottest house in the entire neighborhood, making the crew sitting ducks for trouble. He was so busy trying to sex every young lady in West Baltimore that he again lost focus and forgot the mission. The door of the stash house was kicked in again and, just as before, guys were hauled off, wearing metal bracelets, courtesy of the Baltimore City

Police. And just as before, we were spending a lot of unnecessary money to bail our workers out. Every time someone went to jail, we were putting our entire operation at risk, but Donald couldn't comprehend that. He couldn't understand that we had no way of knowing what these guys may have been saying to the cops behind closed doors.

Finally I lost confidence in Donald altogether. You may wonder why I didn't do this sooner, when it was obvious he was more interested in the ladies than in doing his job, and when he would never listen to what I was telling him. All I can tell you is that he was my friend. On the streets, you stand by each other and you watch each others' backs. I guess I just kept hoping he'd wise up. But it was clear that his priorities were in disarray, and I couldn't gamble on him any longer.

"Yo, you're spending so much time chasing girls, you're going to end up sending both of us to prison," I told him. "Yo, this shit ain't a joke. You're bullshittin' around too much and not focusing on business the way you're supposed to be. We keep having problems down here because you're not handling your business, man."

Donald could not seem to understand that there were heavy consequences for mistakes in the game, and that they could cause people to die or go to prison for a long stretch. Eventually, the situation between Donald and me got heated. Since it was his idea to open up the operation on Mount Street in the first place, he felt that I was indebted to him. He felt like this was some type of partnership between us. When I leveled with the young brother about the reality that *he* worked for *me*, and it wasn't the other way around, he didn't like it.

"Yo, just chill for a while and we'll straighten this shit out us later," I told him. I was upset with him for screwing up, but he was still my homie, but he just wouldn't listen.

After a couple of weeks, I pulled in a couple of new guys to work with me. I felt bad severing ties with Donald, but I had to move on before he sent me to the pen forever. I couldn't put my neck on the line with him any longer.

After we both moved on, Donald began doing his thing again with another crew. I wanted everything to work out for him, but he was still upset over our split. Unnecessarily, he created a problem with one of the new guys, which almost led to Donald's downfall.

Ronnie didn't have any problem with Donald. "Yo, look, I ain't got no beef with you, okay? I'm just out here trying to get some money." Donald turned around to Ronnie and said, "Fuck you." Donald was still feeling double-crossed, but Ronnie didn't want to fuel his fire. Donald hadn't realized that he had got a pass. Ronnie was a very dangerous guy, but Donald couldn't understand that. He had just started a very bad situation that couldn't possibly end well for him.

I could see Donald standing there at the corner of Fayette and Gilmore, arguing with Ronnie once again. Suddenly, I saw Ronnie place a gun to the side of Donald's temple. CLICK, CLICK, and CLICK. The revolver resounded as Ronnie pulled the trigger. My heart skipped a beat, as thoughts of my friend and former worker leaking blood on the streets filled my head. The poor guy didn't have a chance. But suddenly, all was well. The pistol had misfired and spared the life of the shaken but stirred young man. With a burst of speed I had not known he was capable of, Donald ran up Fayette Street toward the nearest toilet to relieve his discomfort. I was certain he needed a private moment after that ordeal.

There were twenty people standing on the streets, in broad daylight, for the attempted execution. I couldn't tell if Ronnie was trying to commit murder or suicide with his actions. Ronnie could have been going to prison for the rest of his life if that gun had not misfired. At least four out of the twenty people standing on the streets that day would've been sitting on the witness stand. The difficulty I was having with Donald wasn't severe enough for someone to lose his life. There was no need for murder. But that's how fast the climate in the jungle can burst into flames.

One Sunday evening, after spending all day recuperating from a long Saturday night of fun, I left my apartment in the suburbs and headed to the city. The ride was unusually short because of the light traffic, so I made it within 30 minutes. When I arrived at Cold Spring Lane, the yellow lettering of the McDonald's sign was a sight for sore eyes. The convenience of Mickey D's was always a benefit, so I turned in its direction to get a bite to eat, a *Choice* that almost proved deadly. The plan was to grab a quick shake and some fries and continue on, but plans don't always work out.

I badly needed to make my way over to the stash house to prepare a new package of heroin for the morning inventory. I also had the responsibility of collecting the cash from the guys from the day's receipts. The unruly Druid Hill Park crowd, who regularly migrated to the lot adjacent to McDonald's after Druid Hill Park closed, had settled in for the next few hours. This had been a Sunday evening ritual in Baltimore for many years, as every motorcycle rider and every sports car club member in town made their presence known. Hundreds of girls and local guys flocked to the lot to relax and mingle with friends.

I usually tried to avoid places like this, places where the dealers in the city go to see and be seen. There was a lot of competition on the street corners back then. Something bad could start at any time, putting you in a compromising position. In a huge, unpredictable crowd, it's difficult to see who's a friend and who's a foe. Plus, if you were a Sunday regular on the scene and you had a beef with someone, they could easily locate you there.

Even though I knew all of this, I stopped at the McDonald's anyway. I thought I would just jump in the drive thru, get my food, and be on my way. As I sat waiting to order, I felt very uneasy. I was getting a bad vibe from something, but the source of that uneasiness was unknown to me. Because of that, I reached inside the glove compartment for my nine millimeter and placed the weapon on my lap. If something happened, I would be ready and waiting, with a vengeance. I still couldn't explain the feeling that I was having, but I knew that it was real.

Out of nowhere, I was startled by a hard knock on the passenger door window. I gripped the pistol tightly, readying myself, but quickly I realized it was only Erkie. Erkie was a guy from Monroe and Ridgehill Avenue who worked for my associate Ronald. He jumped in my car and started talking.

"Kevin, what's up, man?"

Though Erkie worked for Ronald, the relationship between the two had slowly begun to sour. Ronald was even playing him at a distance because everyone thought that Erkie was smoking crack on the low.

"Yo, Kevin, when are you going to give me a shot? Ronald is over there fucking up, man, and you know it."

Erkie did have a good point. I knew that things weren't going well with Ronald. Besides, he still owed money to me for a package. But I wasn't interested in doing business with Erkie, so I just brushed it off. During this entire conversation with Erkie, I was wondering whether or not the negative energy I was feeling was coming from him. I told him that I would talk to him later and that I needed to get out of there. Erkie said okay and got out of my car.

Just as Erkie closed the car door, the shots began to blaze. Pop! Pop! Pop! Pop! My ears were ringing from the blast as I struggled to stay focused and stay alive! I floored the gas and sped past the drive thru of the fast food restaurant. Luckily for me, there were no cars in my way. I was like Ali on the ropes, dodging every bullet thrown at me. As I bobbed and weaved my way through traffic, I realized one thing: I was still alive. Flying past the other cars in the parking lot, I headed north on Reisterstown Road in search of a safer place. With my wheels screeching, I made a quick right turn and never looked back.

Driving up the street, I performed a quick inventory of my upper torso, checking for bullet wounds. I finally crossed Woodland Avenue, only a few blocks away from the scene of the shooting, when I pulled over to the side of the street for a more in-depth evaluation. My ears were still ringing from the sound of the shots. After inspecting my person, I got out of the car, looking for damage to the vehicle. The glass had not been shattered and there were no bullet holes visible. *What the fuck just happened?* I asked myself. *Was somebody trying to kill me, or was I just in the wrong place at the wrong time?* I continued to scratch my head in dismay. Was someone trying to shoot Erkie? And since the triggerman was standing nearby, why wasn't I hit? Whoever these guys were, they must have had the worst aim in the world. Or they were aiming for someone else. Had Erkie tried to set me up by coming over to my car to distract me? There were so many questions, but very few answers.

LL Cool J was playing on my car radio during the drive to West Baltimore, as I continued my deep thought over the matter. I had no idea what to make of the situation because my wrong-place-wrong-time theory began not to make sense. *This was intended for me*, I concluded, after ruling out everything else. Almost becoming the lead story on the evening news wasn't what I had in mind that morning when I awoke. By the time I made it across town, my pager was lighting up with calls. I grabbed the pager out of my pocket and I recognized the number. It was my man Ronald from Monroe Street. At the time I thought that he was calling about the money that he owed me.

"Yo, what's up, Ronald?

"Yo, man, you alright"?

"Yeah, I'm cool. What's up"?

"Erkie said those motherfucker's from over your way was shooting at you at the lot," Ronald told me. "After they fired at you, Erkie said they ran and jumped back in that blue truck." He was referring to Chucky from the Blue Thunder crew.

"Erkie saw the whole thing, man," Ronald continued. "He thought they got you."

Without Erkie, there was the possibility that I would have never known what really happened. Also without him, there was the possibility that I could have been murdered that day. I believed that Chucky and his brother were on their way to my car to shoot me, when they stumbled across Erkie getting out of my car. The assassins probably believed they had been spotted, causing them to begin shooting sooner than they originally wanted. By shooting at Erkie first as he exited my car, instead of shooting at me, they gave me just enough time to make an escape. Never did they realize we were both completely clueless to their very presence before the barrage of bullets erupted. We never saw them coming at all. Nevertheless, there would have to be a price to pay for their attempt on my life. When the time was right, these wannabe killers would get what they had coming. But it would happen on my terms. And I wouldn't miss.

BLOOD MONEY

"Diamond in the Raw, right here in the hole, Diamond in the Raw, right here in the hole," was the mantra of the day. This wasn't an auction up in the Hamptons of New York, where the finest paintings, vases, and sculptures were being sold to the highest bidders in a glamorous setting. This was the concrete jungle, where people died and got high. This was the "hole" at the corner of Fayette and Mount Street, where poison and mayhem were sold for ten dollars in a glassine bag filled with the heat of a fire breathing dragon: heroin.

"Stay in line and keep your fucking hands out your pockets," the men in the alley holding the nine-millimeter handguns snarled at potential buyers. Order and control wasn't optional, but a prerequisite to sales, as a glassine bag filled with funk was sold to each and every buyer who displayed cash. This maddening scene was rarely a picture of calm and tranquility. This scramble for illegal drug purchases was often interrupted by violence, as the crew sought to regain control of the situation. The lines stretched around the corner, like a Barack Obama rally, but "change" wasn't the serum these unregistered voters yearned for.

Like the crystal gems scattered throughout the rivers of the bush in Sierra Leone, these diamonds were viciously sought after. This open-air market, nestled away on the mainland of West Baltimore, resembled an ATM. But instead of drawing cash out, they were depositing it, right into the hands of the man with the best product. Usually, the Diamond in the Raw brand, marketed to every intravenous needle concierge within driving distance of the "hole," was selected.

The Baltimore heroin epidemic was rising at a fierce pace, as the crisis turned into opportunity for those willing to ignore the law. I had arrived at the pinnacle of the illegal trade as the leader of the crew with a devastating product named Diamond in the Raw. The bank notes were being collected at a rate of $21,000 a day during the peak of our Fayette and Mount Street sales. That was an enormous amount of money generated by this felonious factory, no matter how you sliced it. Another branch of the operation sold heroin wholesale to a couple other crews from Lexington Terrace projects and other hot spots around the city. They were grossing another $65,000 a week. Nobody could touch us. As far as the money was concerned, everything was going well...for now.

The source of our supply of Asian persuasion, which was based in New York City, was very happy with the way we were handling our business. Straight from the Cali Cartel of Colombia, South America, Fernando was the name of our contact. He had a dark complexion, which was often the case for Hispanics from Cali, a city in southern Colombia. These guys had access to any illegal substance desired on the streets. The Cali Cartel was known for being a violent bunch, but as long as the bills got paid, the relationship was secure. But if these guys weren't paid on time – it didn't matter if it was by error, neglect, or intention – you may have had to relocate your family to a safer place.

With our Colombian friends, we could get our hands on just about anything we needed, whenever we needed it. On top of that, the quality of the merchandise was always the best. Every ten days or so, like clockwork, Fernando and a couple of guys from his crew would drive down from New York to Baltimore to pick up their money. At around $250,000 per trip, their excursion was well worth it. Usually tucked away in the false compartment of their Chevrolet was our refill supply, produced in the jungles of Burma, sometimes accompanied with a few kilograms of cocaine. Just from the heroin sales alone, we were grossing three quarters of a million dollars a month.

The drug epidemic had devastated the entire area, but the heroin trade was dominating the illegal activities of this once pristine neighborhood. Nowadays, you could buy and sell everything from cocaine and heroin to guns and bullet proof vests on the block. This wasn't anything like the old days on turf like Pennsylvania Avenue in West Baltimore, or in places like Harlem. In the old days, you had to pay a percentage of what you made to the number one guy who controlled the territory. Even the Mafia was offered a slice of the pie in those days, just to keep the peace. That was when there was order and governance in the streets. That was when a guy could become a millionaire in a matter of weeks, just from selling dope. Those days were long gone and nowadays, it was every gorilla in the jungle for himself.

We would be ready to conduct business at 9:00 a.m. sharp. I had made the decision to run the operation like any legitimate business, even though our wares were illegal. How would you feel if you walked over to your local 7-Eleven in the morning for a cup of coffee and it was closed? That's just bad business. And it was also bad business for the addicts to look for you and you were not there. I insisted that we have a regular schedule and for the most part, it worked.

Guns were always in the stash house, sitting on the table, ready to protect the valuable commodity. If anyone got some crazy ideas – and sometimes they did – there would be hell to pay. The regular early-morning customers were gathered in the alleyway, waiting to buy. Some would be ill due to the early morning illness from withdrawal symptoms, which a bag of dope could temporarily cure. At the beginning of the day's business, we distributed, free of charge, what we call on the streets "testers." Ten to fifteen bags of heroin were given away as free samples to ensure our clientele that the product was up to par. This was the hustler's version of marketing and promotions. This would spread the word on the streets that Diamond in the Raw had the good product for yet another consecutive day.

The addicts would be lined up outside of this de facto drug store, ready to fill their prescriptions for more pain and less gain. These guys didn't give a damn about the cops that patrolled the area, who were frustrated by this market they never could shut down. With eager anticipation, forty to fifty individuals were sometimes waiting for us to open our imaginary doors.

By noon on an average day, the cash register was bursting at the seams, with $12,000 in cash; no checks or IOUs. Our mixture of gloom and doom was selling like wildfire. Most of the other dealers in the area could only sit with their hands folded and watch as we raked in the money. After we closed down for the day, the other hustlers could commence operation. But once the latecomers realized that they couldn't purchase Diamond in the Raw, they were extremely disappointed with the next best thing. And the other dealers were extremely disappointed as well, once the disgruntled customers requested their cash back.

Stuffy and I were business partners and we split everything right down the middle. We shared in all the work and shared in all the profits. We also shared in something else: the stress of avoiding a kingpin charge, which carried the maximum penalty in the courts. He and I had been friends since peewee football, when all the kids wanted to be a Dallas Cowboy. But now we were cowboys of a different sort. After the fiasco with Donald, I needed someone who I didn't have to babysit. I needed a right-hand man to help me keep up with the daily grind of the game, and Stuffy was one of the best business *Choices* I made.

Our business plan was simple enough – sell the best dope on the streets and let the drug addicts decide who ran the show. A free market society works on the streets as much as in the board room. Since we knew that we were being supplied with more heroin than any of the other crews on the block, we could afford to put less cut on the drugs. That meant it would be the most potent stuff out there and we still would make a substantial profit. None of the other crews could afford to add as little cut as we did, because if they did, their profits would have been obliterated. For us, this formula worked like a charm. We were bringing in the money faster than we could count it. The drug business is just like any other business seeking to corner the market. If you keep the customer happy, he or she is almost guaranteed to be back for more.

Having the best product was also my way of sending the rest of the dealers in the neighborhood off to new careers. I never believed in fighting over territory, anyhow. I learned that from Anthony, long before he died. That just draws unnecessary attention and problems, adding to a laundry list of other issues. Anthony's philosophy was that if you don't want anyone making money on your block, sell the best dope. Put out a better product for the same price and the customers will come. Anyhow, turf war usually end with someone dying and the police shutting down everything on the street. But just because I didn't believe in getting into beefs and gunfights didn't mean I didn't still have trouble.

Smith and Ronnie were our lieutenants, who oversaw the Fayette and Mount Street empire. We assigned all products and services to these guys, while they managed the operation. David, Nate, and Harvey were the other soldiers in the crew, itching to unleash havoc on any misguided fool who requested it. They made sure that things ran smoothly out on the street corners, which sometimes meant distributing a free lump or two to the rowdy and rambunctious. Together, these five guys controlled every bag of heroin that moved within an inch of the hole. On a typical day, they organized ten to fifteen other guys, who worked with them in different capacities, to move the drugs from hand to hand. Over time, this turned into a much larger operation than any of us had ever anticipated. According to the critics who taste-tested every glassine bag of pain in town, our crew was retailing the best illegal narcotics in Baltimore.

The corner of Fayette and Mount Street was a thorn in the side of every law enforce official on the west side of town who was paid to preserve order. There was one Baltimore police officer in particular who had a real hard on for our crew. With dreams of making detective dancing in his head, this guy wanted to bust this case wide open, by any means necessary. This cop was tall and skinny, with a peanut-shaped head, so I gave him the nickname Peanut head; to me, he resembled the guy on the Planters peanut jar.

Occasionally, I made the trek out to the center of the action, just to check the pulse of the natives. One day I was telling one of my runners to look out for that cagey cop, who was often invading our space. He seemed to be sharpening his investigative techniques throughout the neighborhood and was going to great lengths to get information about our operation.

"There are a lot of cops running around the block," the runner reminded me. "Which cop are you talking about?"

"You know the one I am talking about," I answered. "The one with the peanut-shaped head." The very next day, I stopped by one of the stash houses to pick up the cash. As I was leaving the house, one of the runners said to me, "Be careful when you walk outside because that cop with the peanut head is out on the block." The next thing that I knew, other runners began referring to the patrolman as Peanut Head. Soon the entire neighborhood was calling him this unfaltering name. I was later told that when he discovered that half the criminal suspects in West Baltimore were referring to him as Peanut Head he really didn't like it very much.

This guy was an idiot, in my opinion, and that assessment had nothing to do with him being a law enforcement official and trying to do his job. He would drag heroin addicts into alleyways or abandoned houses and begin beating on them for no reason, even when he had no evidence they had committed any crime.

"Get the fuck out of here and don't let me see you again today," he'd tell his victims, after his unprovoked and downright criminal assault. The fact that he was black made no difference because he handed out equal injustice to all. In my book, no one gets points for kicking around some weary drug addict who weighs ninety pounds soaking wet. Most people can't understand that most addicts are out on the corners buying dope because they suffer from the disease of addiction. It's not because they have this uncontrolled urge to commit a felony. In my opinion this particular cop's strategy in his War on Drugs was to humiliate and assault one drug addict at a time.

When a drug addict receives what amounts to assault from a police officer, he or she can't really do anything but suck it up. Who does the addict have to complain to? The cop who broke his nose? It's an unjust situation because no one is going to take the word of a fiend over that of a boy in blue, even if it was Peanut Head. And if they complain too much, they'll probably end up in jail on some bogus charge, like loitering or disturbing the peace. Its one thing to do your job as a police officer, but it's another thing altogether when you're violating the laws that you're supposed to upholding. Once this line in the sand is crossed, who exactly is the criminal?

Late one night, Stuffy and I were driving through downtown Baltimore after a long day of controlling the ills that the game can conjure up. Suddenly, a police cruiser pulled out of nowhere for what appeared to be a traffic stop. I knew that I hadn't violated any traffic regulations, so I was concerned as to why the cop wanted to stop me. I assumed right away that this was some idiot cop, looking to bust my balls because he was having a bad day. I didn't have a clue what this guy wanted, but I knew it couldn't be good.

The first thing the cop said to me when he approached the car was, "Kevin, what the hell you been up to, man?" When I saw the face of the law enforcement official shoving his head into my window, I almost fell out of the car and onto the ground, laughing. It was an old buddy of mine, now in a city police officer's uniform. Who would have thought he'd be upholding the law now instead of breaking it? I guess I wasn't the only one who thought of joining the department.

We had actually been classmates in middle school, when we got into a fight in gym class over a basketball game. After that we became good friends in high school, where we began selling weed together for a short period of time. He made the traffic stop because he saw that it was me driving by. I had heard a rumor that he had joined the police force, but this was my first time seeing him in uniform. To me, he looked odd standing there wearing a badge.

"How in the hell did you get a job on the police force?" That was the first thing I could think of to say to him. I had known this guy pretty well, and I knew that he had been involved in some real dirt at one time. There was a possibility that he had changed, but who knows?

"I got a break when my mother started dating a lieutenant downtown at headquarters," he said. As our conversation progressed, he hinted that he wasn't exactly unaware of my new occupation.

"I heard that you guys were making a lot of money in the streets." Then he told me something that really didn't surprise me very much.

"You two guys and your entire crew are under investigation by narcotics. I saw your names and pictures posted on a bulletin board inside a conference room at the station." He said that the display had been labeled Diamond in the Raw Crew. I tried to press him for more information, but he shut down. He was willing to give a little information to an old compadre, but I guess he really was a cop now.

I knew that it was only a matter of time before there was an official investigation launched on us, which would probably include the feds. We were making too much money and making too much noise to go unnoticed by the downtown brass. The second best thing that came out of this traffic stop was the fact that our beliefs were now confirmed. The first was that I saw my old friend again.

Usually, when you're moving drugs in the quantities that we were in a particular neighborhood, cops carry out a raid or two on a couple of houses, in search of the drugs. The cops know you're not keeping all of this stuff in your pockets, so you've got to be keeping it somewhere. We were selling far too much dope to simply keep it stashed in the alley or the bushes. You'd be asking for a lot trouble if you tried that. There's no question that some genius would try to make a move on you only inviting you to send him off to a better place.

The runners needed a safe haven to drop off the cash and pick up the dope for the waiting customers. There were always at least two guys in our stash house, guns cocked and ready. Their job was to watch the money, watch the dope, and watch out for the stick-up kids. The customers never came anywhere near the stash house and most of the time, didn't know its exact location. We had about ten different stash houses spread throughout the neighborhood and every couple of days, we would move to another house. One day we would use a house over on Fairmount Street, and then a few days later we'd be using one over on Lexington. Just now, we were using a house over on Boyd Street, and then a couple of days after that we'd be over on Lombard. This kept the cops guessing. We knew it took time for the cops to get a search warrant from a judge once they actually locked down our location. By the time they got it for one house, we were no longer there.

One day, we were playing our usual hide and seek routine with the police, when the situation got sticky. We had two stash houses located on Bruce Street, which looked more like an alley and less like a narrow street. The two houses were in the middle of the block and sat side by side. Things were rolling along just as they had for many days before, as this carnival of crime played on. The money was falling out of the sky. Around eleven o'clock in the morning, three unmarked police cars swarmed onto Bruce Street. The officers jumped out of their vehicles, just like in a scene from *Law & Order*, itching to give a bad guy a bad day. The lead officer in the raid was Sgt. Brown, who had worked this area of the city for years. With the battering ram in hand, the cops slammed the flimsy front door completely off its hinges as they made their way inside. With pistols drawn, they began yelling at the top of their lungs, "Everyone on the floor! Get the fuck on the floor!" They were serving a no-knock warrant, which gave them the green light to search for illegal narcotics without first letting the residents know they were even there. All of the occupants in the dwelling quickly complied with the officers' demands. With this raid, the cops must have hit the jackpot…or had they?

The officers secured the first floor and all its occupants, and then proceeded to the upper levels. All of the folks on the second floor were placed in plastic flex cuffs and herded down to the living room with the rest of the unhappy residents. As the cops continued their inspection of the house, no kilograms were located, nor were any weapons found. They had a drug-sniffing police dog, and as the dog made its rounds throughout the house, there still seemed to be something wrong. Still, there wasn't any discovery of illegal drugs, not even a bag of weed. But the cops were certain something was there.

The warrant clearly read: "Search and Seizure Warrant for *15* Bruce Street" but on this day, Diamond in the Raw was running the operation out of *13* Bruce Street, next door. We had decided to use that house to give the other location a rest for that day. Stuffy was in the real stash house, and he said he could hear the entire situation through the walls as it unfolded. He was sitting in the kitchen, with $20,000 worth of heroin on the table, when the cops smashed in the door of the neighboring house. When he heard the commotion next door, he ran upstairs to the toilet, ready to flush the entire package. By that time, he realized that the police were raiding the wrong house. When he told me the story, I wasn't amused in the least, because this was as close as it gets. If the cops had kicked in the door at 13 Bruce Street, it would have been all over for him.

Sometimes, the decisions that keep you afloat in the game are made from instinct. You can feel when something bad is getting ready to happen, the same way I could feel when my pops was just getting ready to go ballistic at home when I was a kid. When you get that feeling, you have to go with it. If you're wrong, you're wrong. But if you're right, you may have just saved your rear end. In everyday life, it works the same way, especially when you're living on the edge.

One warm summer evening, Ronnie and Nate were sitting on the steps at Fayette Street, keeping a sharp eye on everything that moved. Out of nowhere, four detectives from the homicide unit drove up Fayette Street and grabbed them both off the stoop and threw them separately in the back of two unmarked Chevys.

"What the hell is going on?" the captives asked the angry officers. There was no response, and the drive down to Central District police station was silent. At the district, the homicide detectives told their prisoners,

"We have an informant who has given us a very serious piece of information." The cops told them they had information that we had placed a hit on Officer Peanut Head. The informant told them that Peanut Head had been putting a lot of pressure on Diamond in the Raw, so we wanted him dead, like in the movies. Irritated by the foolish accusations, Ronnie told the detectives, "I don't know where you got this information from, but its bullshit."

It's a common thing for police officers to sometimes receive inaccurate and erroneous intelligence from informants on the streets. Sometimes the salacious scoop is wrong to intentionally mislead the cops. Or the informant may have a vendetta against the target the information is centered around and could be doing this on purpose. Other times the informant has the whole story wrong, or may not even have the whole story, but thinks he's providing accurate information. At the end of the day, officers are sometimes acting on bad intelligence, which could put an innocent man in prison. It doesn't happen as often now because DNA evidence can clear some wrongly accused individuals. In a situation like this, nobody benefits—not the criminals, not the authorities, and definitely not the public.

Ronnie told the detectives that he wasn't stupid; he would never put a contract on a cop for any reason at all, which was true. The detectives listened to Ronnie and Nate as they pleaded their case. Fortunately, they were released after a couple of hours, with no charges being filed. But the sting of the situation was lasting. I was almost certain that the cops knew this was a bullshit accusation, but I wasn't completely sure. Were the detectives busting our balls because they had nothing concrete on us? Was this something to be concerned about?

Putting a contract out on a police officer would have been suicide. If you lived long enough, there's not a police department in the country that wouldn't pull out all the stops to make sure you got the maximum penalty allowed for your stupidity. Right after this incident, Stuffy and I decided that Ronny and Nate should stay out of sight for a while, because none of us really knew how far this thing would go. We were definitely feeling the heat. Sometimes when you're having problems in the streets, it's in your best interest to back off.

On the block, there's always some type of situation to deal with; often it just comes out of nowhere. If it's not the cops, it's the addicts. If it's not the addicts, it's the stick-up kids, and if it's not the stick-up kids, it's some mother's son that wants to play tough guy. Chucky and his brother B were running the Blue Thunder Crew on Fayette and Mount Street. It had been almost a year since they tried to take me out in the drive thru at McDonald's. I had many chances since then to exact revenge on these guys, but I decided to give them a pass. I felt like time was on my side and I was in no hurry. For some reason, these fools thought they could just muscle us out of the way. What they didn't realize was that those tactics only works in the movies. In real life, when someone tries to make a move like that, somebody usually dies.

The reason the Blue Thunder Crew couldn't sell their dope was that it was poor quality. The heroin addicts in the area called it garbage and vowed to never purchase another bag from them as long as they used drugs. This unofficial beef had been going on for a long time and it didn't look like it was going to go away anytime soon. I tried to avoid extinguishing people over problems which developed in the street because at the end of the day, it wasn't worth it. I didn't need some mother's dead son on my conscience. Eventually, that type of stuff catches up to you, in one form or the other. The more I tried to avoid the madness with these guys, the more they just didn't get it.

One cold February afternoon, I was walking down Fayette Street, looking for the guys in my crew. Usually I stayed off the block because I didn't want the locals or the heroin heads becoming too familiar with my face. I didn't want to be known as "the man." I learned from all the guys before me that you can't be a superstar in the game. The superstars of the streets go down and they go down hard. I could see that business was doing well because there were about thirty customers standing near Vincent Street, hoping to make a purchase. You could always tell when drug addicts are trying to buy a bag of something to service the soul because their attempt to look inconspicuous just makes them all the more noticeable. I could see Nate standing farther down Fayette, at the corner of Gilmore, directing the buyers down the alley, like a traffic cop. As I headed toward Nate, I could see one of the guys from the Blue Thunder Crew standing at the opening in the alley, talking with our customers.

"What the fuck are these guys doing back out here today?" I asked Nate. Even though it had been almost a year since they tried to cancel my Christmas, my loathing at the very sight of them was still fresh. I never looked at them as a threat to our business because I knew they didn't have the resources to compete, but the chance they took at taking my life would never be forgotten.

While talking with Nate, I was also keeping track of everything else that was going on around me, like any good street hustler hoping to live another day. At the mouth of the alley, I spotted Chucky walking in our direction with a nine millimeter in his hand, barrel shinning in the afternoon sun. My pistol was in my waistband, locked and loaded as always, but I realized it would be difficult to reach it in time. Chucky had his gun ready in his hand, anticipating work to be done. I wasn't sure why he chose this day to turn into Rambo but it was his decision.

I pushed Nate out of harm's way and launched myself across Fayette Street, hoping to buy time for me to draw my weapon. Suddenly, Chucky began unloading his entire clip in my direction. Not ready to see my friend Anthony again so soon, I ducked behind a parked car, trying to elude the gun blasts. As I dove for cover, I struck my head on the lamppost, drawing a small drop of blood from my forehead. At the same time my head hit the metal object, my gun, which was now in my hand, hit the ground, releasing the ammunition clip onto the pavement. As bullets continued to punch holes into the parked vehicle that shielded me, shattering glass began to rain down on me. As I struggled to reload my weapon, my survival instincts began to take over. Still dazed but fighting to stay alive, the tall skinny kid from Edmondson Village wasn't ready to die.

As I came up from behind the parked car, gun now back in my hand and reloaded, I emptied the entire clip in the direction of my attacker. I must have been channeling the character of Tony Montana from the movie *Scarface*. "Say hello to my little friend," I thought, as I fired off fifteen rounds of death to even the score. Surprised by the fact that I was still alive and daunted by now being out of bullets, Chucky began to run in the other direction. My desperate attempt to leave a stain of red on the back of my target wouldn't be realized on this day. Ultimately, the fact that neither of the two urban cowboys could shoot straight allowed everyone to live.

Breathing heavily and running up Fayette Street, I checked my torso for any leaking plasma as a result of the melee. Delighted to be alive and well, the man who could have died on this day mumbled a gentle "Hallelujah." It all happened so quickly, it was almost like it never even happened at all. If it hadn't been for the smell of the gunpowder in the air, I probably would have thought it was all a bad dream.

They make it look easy on television and in movies. Two guys pull out guns, start squeezing the triggers, and one falls victim within the first couple of rounds. But it's not easy to hit a moving target, especially if you are not used to firing a gun, which is the case for most guys in the street life. They carry guns mostly to intimidate anyone who might try to inflict harm on them. If they do have occasion to use it, it's usually very close range and the victim is standing still. Most of the time, in a turf war like this, there's a lot of noise and a lot of smoke, but not a lot of damage done to your perceived enemy.

It is the unwitting bystanders who are most likely to fall victim to a bullet. Incidents like these get innocent people killed in the concrete jungle all the time. The lead story on the eleven o'clock news explains how two fools sent some mother's eight-year-old child, who was playing in the street, off to heaven. I hated guns, but I felt that I needed one because the guy standing next to me probably was packing. This was a crazy and irrational way to survive, but that's how the game goes.

Smith, my lieutenant, was standing at the corner of Fayette and Mount, watching helplessly as the battle unfolded. There wasn't much else he could have done, except possibly get murdered himself. As soon as the dust settled, he began running down the street to see if I was okay.

"Yo, you good?" he yelled as he approached me. He was happy with the fact that no damage had been done, but he was furious for obvious reasons. "I thought you got hit when I saw you down on the ground."

We ran together up through the alley, to 13 Bruce Street, where the rest of crew had been working. As I burst through the door of the stash house, gasping for breath, I was ready to annihilate anything in my way. My adrenaline was still skyrocketing from Chucky's failed attempt to turn me into a vegetable. I wanted to kill this guy and anyone who got in my way. I couldn't believe that he had tried to pull this! I had made my best attempt to let the situation go for almost an entire year. I had given these guys a pass on many occasions, but now it was my turn!

There was no way that I could let this situation go now. I was left with no Choice; now I had to retaliate. My entire crew was looking at me to see what I would do. There was no way that I could show any sign of weakness. That would have sent a bad signal and I knew it. I realized that I had to react, and I had to react soon.

Sometimes in the street, you're put in a situation where your hands are tied and you don't have a lot of good options. This was one of those situations for me. Looking at the options at hand, none of them seem satisfying. It's just like a game of chess, the only difference is that this wasn't a game; people die and things happen at lightening fast speed. I was left with no Choice – the Blue Thunder Crew had to pay a price.

Just that quickly, Ronnie heard about the fierce shootout between Chucky and me. Seconds after the first shots where fired he grabbed the tech-nine sitting on the table in the stash house and sprinted to the scene. He didn't know the shootout was already over. Inflamed about the matter, he went on a hunt for anyone he could find from the Blue Thunder Crew. As Ronnie made his way down Fairmount Avenue, he spotted Chucky and his brothers trying to make an escape. They were piling in a white Honda Accord when they saw Ronnie coming down the street with the Tech-Nine, ready for war. Driving fast in reverse, they were making a desperate attempt at a clean exit.

"You motherfuckers are dead!" Ronnie screamed at them, as he opened fire. The muzzle of his semi-automatic weapon oozed with smoke and fire as it ejected the empty bullet casings onto the pavement. With their wheels screeching, they were running for dear life. Glass and debris was flying everywhere, as the car somehow made its way out of the tiny one-way street towards safety. Not knowing whether or not there had been any casualties in the car, Ronnie made a brisk return to 13 Bruce Street.

Down in the basement, I directed anyone who was not part of the inner sanctum of our crew to exit, including the residents of the house. Now the game had changed. I had to look like a leader; I had to look presidential. I was being tested by the Game Gods. The Game Gods wanted to see how I would react, and so did my crew.

"Look, we're at war now with these motherfuckers," I said. "I ain't playing around with these clowns anymore. They gotta go and I don't want to see these guys around here no more; this is it. If they want a beef, we're going to give them a beef. No more talking, no more bullshitting around. They have fucked up."

Everybody in the room knew that I was serious about the situation; you could hear a pin drop after I stopped talking. Most of them had welcomed the beef because they wanted to see these guys gone a long time ago. The reason they hadn't done anything before was that they were waiting for me to give the green light. The Blue Thunder Crew had crossed the line for the second time, and there definitely wouldn't be a third. They wouldn't be alive long enough for that.

"We're going to hit them and hit them hard!" I fumed, while still breathing flames. We had known for a long time now where Chucky lived, because he wasn't the smartest hustler in town. In fact, we had actually followed him home one night, with thoughts of putting him out of his misery. We could have easily brought the pain to his front doorstep, but I put that deal on the shelf because I didn't want the possible fallout. Before you act on anything, you have to consider the negative after-effects. Business had been going really well for us up to that point and I didn't want to disrupt it. I wasn't ready to give up Fayette and Mount, but I wasn't ready to die, either.

Four weeks had passed since the shootout and everything was quiet. Business was pretty good and Diamond in the Raw was still the best selling pain reliever in town. We had our ears to the ground, listening very intently, but there were still no signs of Chucky or his crew. These guys had gone completely underground, almost like they never existed at all. I couldn't keep from wondering whether or not they were planning something. We had inquired with many of our contacts around the city to see if they had heard any noise, but everything was silent. Chucky's crew hadn't returned to Mount Street that was for sure. Like the mob guys used to say, "They have gone to the mattresses."

Late one Saturday afternoon, the situation would go from cold to hot very quickly. Once again, I made a stop on the block to check on the crew. The corner had only been rocking for a couple of hours now and things seemed normal. Ronnie and Smith were out on the corner, running the show, as usual. The stash house on Lexington Street was the meeting place for the day, as we flipped and flopped through the neighborhood, maneuvering around the boys in blue. As I walked in the front door, it was just like another day on the job. The owners of the home had already been paid their $200 for the day, and the crew was down in the basement, counting the cash. Two knocks on the basement door meant that a touter had a sale or two, or maybe even ten. Lying on the table was around $12,000, meaning that business had been good so far. The cops had been heavily patrolling the area, but no one in the crew had been arrested, which was always a good thing.

Suddenly, Ronnie ran through the door, excited and breathing heavy.

"Yo, what's wrong?" I asked.

Finally he spit out, "One of the runners just told me that Chucky and his brother are over on North Avenue! They opened shop selling that Blue Thunder garbage!"

Silence filled the room. Everybody realized this was the chance we had all been waiting for. Deep inside, I was actually hoping that these guys had just disappeared, but I realized they wouldn't go away unless I gave them a good reason to.

"Let's go take care of this shit," Smith said.

Smith and I each grabbed one of the two nine millimeters that were lying on the table and Ronnie grabbed the tech-nine semi-automatic weapon. Having more than enough firepower, we made a mad dash for the door, hoping to see some action. The runner told Ronnie that Chucky had been working on North Avenue and Longwood Street for the past four days. It didn't even matter to me that they hadn't come back to our block. As far as I was concerned, they had tried to kill me and I wasn't going to let them sell a dime bag of Kool-Aid anywhere in Baltimore.

As we made our way over to North Avenue, I was nervous, but I would never show it. None of us knew actually what to expect once we arrived, but the plan was to do some serious bodily damage. Once we reached North and Longwood Streets, we circled the block several times to get the lay of the land. We were driving a rental car, so we wouldn't be easily recognized. As we scoped out the area, we could see that someone was selling something on the block. The wheeling and dealing of narcotics activities was alive and in full swing when suddenly, we hit the jackpot! The white Honda Accord was parked in the middle of the block. This was the same car Chucky and his crew was driving when Ronnie opened fire on them on Fairmount Avenue.

"This is it!" I said to the guys. "I told you that these guys were stupid! Why would they drive the same car that you shot up?" This was a clear giveaway that these guys were close by. Eventually, they would have to come back to the white Honda Accord, and we would be waiting.

We circled the block a few more times and then Ronnie said, "We should park about a block down the street from the Honda."

"Good idea," I replied. As we parked, we had a clear view of the white Honda. If someone tried to get in it, we would be all over him within seconds. Then, Chucky and a guy from his crew began walking out of a house in the middle of the block. They were like little lambs and we were the wolves waiting to devour them. They would have had no idea what hit them, until it was too late.

Gripping the steering wheel tightly, I was ready for the confrontation. Smith and Ronnie were on the passenger side, one in the front and one in the back, preparing their weapons to do battle. They rolled down the windows to make sure they had a clear shot at our target. I had this feeling in my stomach that some mother's son was getting ready to meet his maker at the hands of the young skinny kid from Edmondson Village. Was this something I really wanted? This hadn't been what I asked for, but these guys had backed me into a corner. But little did they know, they had backed themselves into a corner, too. There was no room for them to squeeze out of this mess they created for themselves. Choices.

I started the engine of the rental car as the scent of revenge filled the air. We could see them as they walked across the street toward the Honda. We let them enter the car first. Chucky entered through the driver's side as his partner got in on the passenger side of the vehicle. Gently, I began a slow creep up the street in their direction. "Slowly, slowly," Smith mumbled, as we edged closer to the prey. Just when we realized that they were totally boxed in with no escape, the gunshots began. Pop! Pop! Pop! Pop! I still didn't want to kill anyone, but the situation had reached a boiling point. Even though these guys had done something really stupid and foolish, should they die for it? Pop! Pop! Pop! Pop! The gunfire crackled as the massacre continued.

Just inches away from their mobile tomb, I could smell gunpowder and I could see glass shattering all over the place. The sound had been deafening as the gun muzzle flashed. We had just raked the parked Honda with a stream of bullets from a tech-nine semi automatic weapon. I thought for sure that those inside had been de-activated.

We could hear the two men screaming at the top of their lungs during the episode. This had been ironic, because these same guys, who had tried to take my life weeks earlier, were now crying in fear. Even with all of the stress they had caused me over the past year with their two failed attempts on my life, I couldn't find it in me to escort them to the gates of hell. I couldn't find it in myself to bring our car to a complete stop right next to theirs. If I had, Ronnie and Smith would have turned them into Swiss cheese.

Finally, as the dust settled on the destruction, an example had been made for others to reflect upon. I floored the car up the street, pleased that this battle had come to an end. There had been twelve or more people running to the corner to witness the action-packed adventure after hearing the gunfire. In my rearview mirror, I could see one of the casualties exiting the passenger side of the car and stumbling into the street. My first thought was that he was going to take a couple shots at our get-away car, but that wasn't the case at all. He was actually waving at someone for help, because in the blaze of bullets, their fearful leader Chucky was down.

"Go! Go! Go!" Smith shouted, as we weaved our way through the back streets of Leakin Park, headed for a safer place. My adrenaline flowed rapidly and I was excited, numb, and nervous as hell, all at the same time. I just wanted to get as far from the scene of the crime as I possibly could. Our faces had been covered and there really weren't any witnesses. As of that moment, it appeared to be a job well done.

Heading toward the county line was the nearest escape route I could envision. Realizing that the city and county police didn't communicate directly, we began driving into another jurisdiction. It could be a while before they put it all together and by then, we would be home free. It was a Saturday afternoon, so the traffic on Windsor Mill Road was moderate to heavy. There were enough cars out driving around on this sunny day to give us plenty of cover. The farther we traveled from the scene, the more comfortable I felt. Smith had a girlfriend who lived near Liberty Road, so we decided to go there to lay low. He suggested that we switch cars with her, ridding ourselves of the only outward sign that could tie us to the crime.

The prospect of spending the next thirty years in prison suddenly loomed large, when, out of nowhere, a county police cruiser abruptly swung right behind us. Everyone in the car became anxious because we all knew what the consequences were if we were to get pulled over. With three young black males looking as guilty as hell, the cops would undoubtedly want to search the car. Under the circumstances, finding evidence that might send all of us to prison was extremely likely. Ronnie was sitting in the back seat with the tech-nine and it was still simmering hot. Smith was also still in possession of his weapon and I was still carrying mine. This would have been an open-and-shut case for any state prosecutor looking to solve the drive-by shooting. We wouldn't have had a chance with the twelve men and women in the jury box during a trial. Quickly, we had to come up with a plan fast, just in case things got ugly.

"If the cop pulls me over, get out and run like hell," I told my two accomplices, as we tried to think of a strategy that might get us out of this mess. "I'll stay with the car, okay?" Hopefully, they could get away with all three guns, which would at least give us a chance.

The police car had been traveling directly behind us for several blocks and we had no idea what he was doing back there. The officer could have been calling in the license plate or just getting a closer look before he made his move. Regardless, we were ready. We weren't going down without a fight. Anxious, I decided to test the waters. He had been behind us far too long without making a move, so we had to make our move first. Holding my breath, I carefully made a right turn onto a side street, expecting the cop to follow. He did no such thing, and just continued cruising down Windsor Mill Road. What I had not realized was that my "escape route" had taken us directly in front of a police station. The cop was only behind us because he had just left the station.

Finally, we made it to Smith's girlfriend's house. There we switched cars and made our way back to the Fayette and Mount Street in victory. On the way, Smith questioned me about why I didn't stop the car fully during the ambush.

"What do you mean, why didn't I stop?"

"If you would've stopped the car completely next to Chucky," Smith answered, "we could have dusted him off easily."

"I didn't want to stop because I didn't know if they would be shooting back at us," I said. "That's why it's called a drive-by, homeboy. What the fuck you talking about?"

At that point, everyone began to laugh, but for me, the humor was not there. I was just trying to cover my true motives. I didn't stop the car because I didn't want anybody to die, but I couldn't tell them that. When it really came down to it, I didn't have the appetite for murder. Sure, I got into a gunfight with the guy, but I wasn't a cold-blooded killer. On the outside I had to keep up the façade that I was the man, but on the inside, I was just a twenty-three-year-old kid trying to find his way through the maze.

Then it hit me. I just wanted the financial rewards the game afforded and not all the other things that came along with it. What I still hadn't fully accepted was that you can't have the money without all the problems.

A few days later, we discovered that our intended victims had not yet received a one way ticket to the morgue. Chucky was still alive and breathing, although shaken and stirred by the event. He could have easily met his maker on that day and he was well aware of that. After that situation, we never had a problem out of them again. Actually, they sent a peace delegate down to Mount and Fayette to squash the extended beef. Still high from our victory, we wanted no part of their declaration of surrender. I informed the peacekeeper that he could go to hell.

"Listen, you guys started this shit, so it won't be over until we say it's over." I told them that there would be no peace talk. Like the decades-old battle for Gaza in the Middle East, the war would continue. The distressed messenger walked off into the sunset to deliver the bad news to the rest of his team. We had these guys on the run and as soon as we applied a little pressure, they would break like a number two pencil. In reality, I wanted this thing to be over with, but I couldn't tell them that. I knew that my entire crew and everyone else were watching me. I had to appear to be a murderous tyrant, capable of homicide at the drop of a hat. Our crew was selling more Asian persuasion on the streets of West Baltimore than anyone, so our demise was highly sought after. The scent of weakness would have exposed us to every stick-up kid, slayer, exterminator, and assassin within the city limits.

I learned a valuable lesson dealing with this situation. I could have easily fallen for the bait, but I resisted the enticing lure. I could have easily murdered these guys, but I chose not to. In the end, I understood that regardless of how tough these guys may have imagined themselves to be or regardless of the idiotic moves they made, it wasn't worth giving them a one-way ticket to a graveyard. In the beginning these guys wanted war, but at the end of the day, they wanted to sit down and talk about it. Regardless of how far another man may push you, murder is a big deal. And once it's done, it's done. There is no turning back.

As the dust began to settle from the Blue Thunder debacle, other wolves disguised as sheep began to make their rounds. Watching my back was a 24/7 task that was starting to make me paranoid. I had no idea who to trust. The cops wanted me shut down. The feds were undoubtedly waiting in the shadows for the tall skinny kid to slip and fall, so what could I do and where could I go? I had to deal with the constant worry that someone might kidnap my sister or my girlfriend, or in some other way, seek to hurt me. Suddenly, my enemies wanted to be my friends and my friends were acting like enemies. In the jungle, it's usually not the guy across the street that wants to get you, or the guy around the corner. It's usually the guy that's standing right next to you, smiling in your face.

One day I received a page from Stuffy. He asked me to meet him downtown in front of Lexington Market because he had something very important to discuss with me. Meeting him downtown was no big deal. You could never know if there was a wiretap on the line, so we didn't take any chances. A face-to-face meeting was always safer than rolling the dice on the telephone, even if it was a pay phone. We'd seen the feds tap pay phones.

It was a clear and mild Saturday evening, the August sun had begun to retreat, and the downtown traffic was light. When I arrived across the street from Lexington Market, Stuffy and Smith were sitting in Stuffy's expensive white Lexus. Smith was as loyal as they came. He was right on top of our operation and he was running it well. Smith didn't need a babysitter; he didn't need us looking over his shoulder to make sure he was doing his job. It may have been an illegal job, but he still viewed it as employment. The money was always correct and that was the most important thing.

"We're not standing out here ducking bullets for free," I often told the guys. "We're here for the money, so the money is what matters."

I parked my car and walked over to Stuffy and Smith. They both had this very intense look on their faces.

"It's Ronnie," Stuffy said. "I'm not sure what's going on with him."

I was really baffled. Ronnie had been with us early on, since the beginning of Diamond in the Raw. We had been through a couple of skirmishes together and he always had my back. What I also knew was that Ronnie had a short fuse. Then Smith chimed in with some news that was *very* troublesome.

"Yo, Ronnie approached me with a plot to rob you and Stuffy of all the dope and money," Smith said. "I don't know what made him think that I would be in on some shit like that." I wasn't completely shocked, because I had become used to people looking to cross me. I had actually begun to expect it would happen within the crew sooner or later, but not with Ronnie.

"We've done a lot to help him, but this is how he repays us," Stuffy stated. Smith said that Ronnie was unhappy with the money that he had been receiving from us and he wanted more. He had been with Diamond in the Raw from day one, so he felt he deserved a bigger slice of the profits. When Ronnie brought the proposed heist to his attention, Smith told him that he would think about it and get back to him later. But what he did was immediately call Stuffy.

Betrayal is a despicable act that sometimes can't be forgiven. By the time I got to Lexington Market to meet with my partner and lieutenant, their minds were fixed on annihilation. They were taking this double-cross extremely hard.

"I'll take the contract myself," Smith said. He wanted to kill Ronnie personally, which really took me by surprise, because he and Ronnie were close. "For $20,000, I could easily kill him for you and no one would have a clue." Smith was set in his position on this matter. We had been very good to Ronnie and we never had any problems. Smith felt he should be dealt with in the most severe way.

"Let's get rid of him now," Smith said. He thought that Ronnie had made his own bed and should now sleep in it. Smith believed that this situation had completely tainted any possible business relationship we could have with Ronnie from that point on.

I wasn't so sure and decided to take the high road. I had learned by then that, even when it seemed like it's the only *Choice*, murder is never the only *Choice*. I knew Ronnie's family very well. They were good people who were never involved in the streets. I didn't want his execution on my conscience and I wasn't so sure about Smith's story. I also thought that we didn't need a murder investigation swirling in the wind. A couple of guys had been killed near Mount and Fayette Streets that no one in our crew had anything to do with. The unfortunate part for us was that since we were basically running the neighborhood, we were the prime suspects. Everyone thought that we had something to do with these murders, but we didn't. The cops and everyone else had it all wrong. But trying not to commit murder, while still running an efficient drug operation is a delicate balance. *Choices*

In this jungle we call the streets, there's no telling what type of web you may find yourself trying to wiggle your way out of. Deceit, betrayal, or attempts to extinguish your light can be a second away. You can also place yourself in some tough situations by making bad decisions. It can be as simple as making a right turn or left turn at the intersection. Some decisions don't have a significant impact on your life and future. Unfortunately, some bad decisions can send you to prison forever, and some can leave you crippled or breathing impaired. There's a lot of money on the streets, but there's always a cost.

WHAT'S REALLY GOING ON?

Anthony had a way of communicating the unvarnished truth like no other guy I knew. His calm, cool approach to making his statements crystal clear was surpassed by no one.

"This shit is deadly, kid, so stay away from it." "Don't ever let me see you messing with this stuff. If *it* doesn't kill you, I will."

One of the things that Anthony stressed to me very early in my deals with him was to never, ever, under any circumstances, use drugs, especially heroin. As a general on the front lines of a conflict, he saw the devastating effects up-close and personal. He sold the stuff for years and, like many others, he had family members who dabbled in its use. There were no doubts in his mind that heroin had the power to rip the soul right out of a man's chest. One iota of the stuff could turn a human being's world into a living hell.

Anthony's message to me was a valuable one that I never forgot. It remained at the front of my mind throughout my time in the streets. Little did he know that a few years before his warning, my curiosity had gotten the better of me. I realized at a very young age that getting high wasn't something I had a lot of interest in, but at one point I experimented with recreational drug use during my teenage years. Quickly, I realized I didn't enjoy getting high. What I disliked the most was the fact that the next day I felt like trash. It was a dumb thing for me to be fooling around with, considering that I am the son of a chronic alcoholic. The odds of my getting hooked on drugs were definitely very high.

I always knew that drug use could do something bad to me. I had the examples right in front of my face each every day in the streets, so what more of a deterrent did I need? Eventually, I began to look at the drug addicts around me, especially the ones that I sold to, and I despised getting high. As time went on, it began to seem despicable; I developed a disdain for it. But what a real hypocrite I was to develop this opposition to drugs at a time when I was making money off the people who were hooked. Heroin is one of the most highly addictive drugs on the face of the earth. There have been many people – some famous, but most not so famous – who have walked this slippery slope, only to slide down it and never return.

There was a long period where Stuffy and I were cutting and packaging huge amounts of heroin on a daily basis, just to keep our crew on the streets supplied. This process of packaging was just as tedious a job as selling the stuff on the corner. We had to put together about 2,500 individual bags of heroin daily just to keep up. It was a very difficult task to package this much, of anything. But to make matters even worse, heroin has a horrible smell and for some reason, God decided that he would give me a very fickle stomach. On several occasions, after preparing a package for distribution on the streets, I would be nauseous and I would often have headaches. It happened to Stuffy sometimes, too. We both knew this task was taking a toll on us, but we thought it was a small price to pay for the financial reward we were reaping from it. We tried all kinds of breathing filters, from dust masks and paint masks to military-style gas masks, just to avoid the fumes. (Can you just imagine a guy standing there with an Army gas mask on his face, cutting heroin?) We tried just about anything to avoid breathing them in, but none of these devices were designed to help someone with the task of cutting heroin. The military ones worked, but it was very difficult to see and breathe wearing one for several hours at a time. We did anything we could think of to offset the side effects of the unpleasant fumes, but the only thing that seemed to work for me was participating in a lot of basketball with a lot of sweating. We both got memberships to the local gym and spent a considerable amount of time there.

Stuffy and I had been friends since childhood. We kind of thought alike and had the same kind of ideology when it came to most issues. I considered him my best friend. But I was soon to learn that that does not always count for much in the drug game. The number one rule – and we both felt strongly about this – was to never get high. As a hustler, getting high was the sin of all sins. Heroin has the ability to destroy a person and turn a man into a zombie. And that was what happened to my best friend and partner, for a brief period of time. The game got the best of his.

There had been rumors floating around for a while that Stuffy had been getting high. I had always dismissed them as false. I knew neither one of us would ever do something that stupid. I figured that I knew him better than anyone else, so if he was getting high, I definitely would have known.

But soon, incidents began to occur that would raise my eyebrows about my business partner. In hindsight, I can see that I was in denial. I just didn't want to believe it. But eventually, I began to see the effects of drug use on him. It showed on him physically and in his business dealings.

Late one night, Stuffy was driving down Edmondson Avenue. Business had been going very well for us at the time and he had just purchased a brand new car. A Baltimore City police officer decided to pull him over for what the officer described as a routine traffic stop; which turned out to be anything besides routine. The officer pulled behind Stuffy, alerting him with his signal lights and siren to pull over in his expensive vehicle. He walked up to Stuffy's car, requesting the usual documentation from him. He found a discrepancy in the registration of the new vehicle. This gave the officer probable cause to search the car. Prior to him conducting the search, he called for backup and suddenly about six police cars were on the scene.

The officers removed Stuffy from the car, handcuffed him, and began their search with the trunk. Their search of the trunk revealed a large brown shopping bag. Inside that bag was $12,480 in cash, part of the proceeds for the day from the guys in our crew. The officers' search of the interior of the car also turned up a Glock nine-millimeter handgun. But the curious portion of this arrest, the part that really bothered me, was the folded dollar bill containing a small amount of cocaine they found in Stuffy's pocket. He was then transported to the police station, where he was charged and booked.

Early the next morning I called a bail bondsman, who contacted the police station. Stuffy's bail was $20,000, meaning that he would need $2,000 cash from me to make bail. In the car on the way back to his house, he and I had a discussion about how he got arrested. He stated that the police officer who pulled him over just got lucky.

I wasn't worrying about why he was arrested, because that was no big deal. In the game, things happen; you know at one point you're going to be arrested for something. You just hope it's not something big. My main concern was the cocaine. I told him to give Leslie Stein a call around midday. Leslie was a popular lawyer in Baltimore who knew his way around the downtown courthouse very well. I thought he could beat the case since the officer had no legitimate reason to pull his car over in the first place, so the search of his car may have been illegal.

We continued to talk about business and where things stood with the crew down on Mount and Fayette Streets. He told me everything was okay in that regard.

"By the way, the bail bondsman said that the police charged you for the gun and with possession of cocaine," I said. "He said that they arrested you with a half gram of coke wrapped in a dollar bill. How did that happen?"

"Man, that was some bullshit," Stuffy said. "They put that shit on me. I didn't have any fucking cocaine on me."

At that point I wasn't sure what to believe, but I was more then willing to give him the benefit of the doubt. We had been business partners for a long time and things had always been on the up and up with us; plus, I still considered him to be my best friend.

As time went on, we were still cutting a lot of heroin almost every single day. Eventually, we began paying someone else to package the drugs, which kept us from having to inhale the fumes for such long periods. Even with being around the dope for less time now, Stuffy was still looking sick and nauseated. I was feeling sick sometimes as well, but far less than before. Since someone else was packaging the drugs for us now, we both should have been feeling better.

A few months after that arrest, he was arrested once again. It was around two o'clock in the morning. I almost never hung out in the streets after midnight, because for a guy who is in the game, not a whole lot of good things happen in the streets at that time of night. I wasn't into the strip clubs and bar scenes, either, so to be home in bed by eleven o'clock was normal.

My girlfriend and I were sound asleep when suddenly the phone rang. My girlfriend rolled over to answer the phone.

"Hello?" she murmured. *Whoever this was calling must have something very important to talk about,* I thought to myself.

"How are you doing?" I heard my girlfriend ask. "Kevin? He's right here. Let me wake him up." She handed me the phone and whispered in my ear, "It's Nikki."

Nikki was Stuffy's girlfriend. They had been together for almost a decade. Nikki would never call me at this hour unless it was an absolute emergency, so I took the phone.

"Kevin, this is Nikki. Can you stop past my house for a minute? I need to talk to you about something."

Thoughts started racing through my mind a million miles a second before I headed over to her house. I didn't know what to think. I knew Nikki very well and I knew she was very intelligent. I realized this must have been serious and I realized that she definitely wouldn't tell me about it over the telephone; she knew someone could be listening.

The ride from Randallstown to Edmondson Village was normally twenty minutes, but I traveled the route in less than ten. I pulled up in front of Nikki's house, not knowing what to expect. *Is Stuffy still alive?* I wondered. *Has he been kidnapped by another crew? Are they demanding ransom money?* Still nervous, I got out of the car, my hand on my nine millimeter, just in case. I didn't know what to expect. We had been friends since peewee football and I sure hoped it wouldn't end like this.

Nikki started out by telling me that Stuffy had called her from the police station. To me that was a slight relief, because at least nothing tragic had happened, but still this was not good. She said that Stuffy had been arrested at a hotel in the city and that he called and instructed her to contact me. She didn't have any details, except that he had called from the Southwestern District Police Station. I immediately called the station to get more information.

"Southwestern District, can I help you?" the voice on the other end of the line asked. The officer informed me that Stuffy was there. He also told me that it would be a few hours before he would see the commissioner and could receive a bond for release.

I wanted to know what he had been charged with. The officer replied that Stuffy had been charged with attempted conspiracy to distribute heroin and he had also been charged with possession of cocaine. We weren't selling any cocaine at that time, so I couldn't understand why he continued to be arrested with the drug on him.

But still, I was somewhat relieved to hear this because the charges weren't as serious as they could have been. The attempted distribution of heroin charge made sense to me, but the separate possession of cocaine charge made no sense at all. Possession charges are usually received by drug addicts or persons possessing small amounts of drugs, usually only enough for them to get high. It's very unusual for a guy selling large amounts of drugs in the city, like Stuffy, to be charged with possession. More often than not, when guys like him are arrested with drugs, they usually have far too much on their person to justify a simple possession charge.

Nikki was pretty upset, but she remained in control of her emotions. I told her that it wasn't that serious and that I would get him out soon. As we sat there in her kitchen, she told me there was something else she needed to talk to me about regarding Stuffy.

She told me that Stuffy was using drugs.

"Kevin, I don't have anyone else to talk to about this. This has been worrying me for a while now." Nikki said that while on their vacation in Las Vegas a few weeks earlier, she found a folded dollar bill in the bathroom of their hotel suite containing white powder, probably cocaine. When she confronted Stuffy with it, he tried to brush it off. He told her that he was handling some business matters while in Las Vegas and that was where the small amount of drugs came from. Nikki wasn't stupid. Her uncle had a drug problem in the past, so she knew some of the signs. Stuffy's behavior in the last few months had become very strange. She said that he was sleeping a lot, he was very angry at times, and his overall mood was often erratic.

I was glad to finally have a real answer, even though I didn't know what to do with it. I had been reluctant to ask him if he were using because he was my best friend. But now I had to do something. I was torn between acting as a business partner and acting as a friend. From a business partner perspective, the answer was simple—our business relationship was over and I would move on. But that is not how you treat a friend.

All of a sudden, I was angry. This was a betrayal! Stuffy had betrayed me. I had felt a sense of sadness first, and then sorrow, but now it was just complete rage.

I can't believe this shit, I kept repeating to myself. I had been out in the streets defending him against the rumors, but at end of the day, they were all true. I felt like he had stabbed me in the back.

At the police station I sat in the car while the bondsman was inside taking care of the paperwork. When Stuffy came out, I drove him back to Nikki's house. Now I was beginning to wonder what else he had been lying to me about. Had he been honest with me throughout our business dealings? Or was he doing something else behind my back?

I began to question what he was doing at the hotel in the first place and what had brought the police there. He told me that he had been arrested dealing with a Nigerian supplier that we had previously met together. The Nigerians were importing a lot of heroin into the country during this period. We both agreed that we wouldn't do any business with this Nigerian until we got more information about who he was. Somebody had to vouch for this guy before we did anything with him. During our first meeting with the African smuggler, he seemed a little shaky and I didn't like the vibe he was sending. All of the Nigerians I have met in the drug game were very crafty, so you had to keep both eyes on them at all times. For some reason, they assumed that they were the best bullshitters in the world. I couldn't tell if this guy was trying to hustle us or if he was working with the cops. I felt like if I had to guess which side this guy was on, then it was probably better not to deal with him at all.

Stuffy completely went against everything we had agreed upon regarding this situation. In this instance he definitely wasn't thinking. This new arrest started to shed light on the fact that his drug use had been taking a toll on his judgment. He had been arrested twice now in the last few months on cases that he could have easily avoided. There was no way he should have been arrested in the hotel with this guy. Later, I found out that the partner of this Nigerian guy Stuffy had been arrested with was nabbed earlier that night in downtown Baltimore getting off an Amtrak train. He was carrying three hundred grams of heroin stashed in a briefcase. Once he got caught, he wasted no time giving up his partner and Stuffy. The cops persuaded him to lure them to the hotel and were waiting when they arrived.

Pulling up in front of Nikki's house, I asked him to come back outside after he finished talking with her. I said that there was something that I wanted to discuss with him. His latest arrest showed me that he was now putting my freedom in jeopardy as well as his own. Once Stuffy returned, I wasted no time getting down to the important matter.

"Look, man, I know you have a problem," I began.

He actually thought that I was referring to his most recent arrest, but I told him that I was referring to his drug use.

"What are you talking about?" he said.

I told him that I knew he had a drug problem and that he was getting high. He attempted to deny the facts again, but I pressed on, this time I pressed a little bit more aggressively. When he heard my tone, I think that was when he started to understand that I knew more than he earlier realized.

I told him that we would do whatever we had to do to get him some help, regardless of what it was. I told him that even if he had to go to a rehab in California or wherever, it didn't matter; we would work this out. At that point, he broke and stopped trying to deceive me. I saw he was holding back tears. I had never seen him like that before, and that is when the reality started to sink in: My peewee football partner and best friend was addicted.

He told me that he regretted lying to me and began explaining how he got in this trouble in the first place. He said it was the fumes during the cutting and packaging process that got him hooked and then things suddenly got out of control.

On the one hand, I was relieved to have everything out in the open. There were no more lies and no more games to be played. On the other hand, I was angry because he had let some powder get the better of him. He had risked everything both he and I had tried to accomplish; he had gone against everything that we both felt strongly about. We had made a pact all the way back when we were playing Dallas Cowboy's when we were kids to watch each other's back.

Now I had to apologize to other friends because I didn't believe them when they told me about Stuffy. I originally believed they were trying to drive a wedge between us, but I was completely wrong. Stuffy and I had never been in a situation like this before.

In the game, you learn to stay alive by not trusting people because that's the only defense you really have. When you've got a partner in anything, you've got to be able to depend on him. You've got to believe that your partner is going to be honest with you, no matter what. Those rules apply to any type of partnership. The most painful part of this was that I couldn't understand why he would get high. He saw first hand what it does to a person and their lives. It's like shooting yourself in the foot and then watching you bleed to death without trying to stop it.

It seemed like everyone was having some type of personal problem back in those days. Dave was a real soldier in our crew, but he had serious issues. I knew he could be a hot head at times, so I had to keep an eye on him. Dave was a very different character. He was a mild-mannered type of guy, but once he got ticked off, it was a wrap. He was a black belt in karate, so if you messed around with him, he had the ability to really hurt you. He also had a background in the military and knew all about making bombs and stuff like that. In the streets, you didn't meet too many guys like him hanging out on the block.

His job in our crew was to watch the runners and keep order in the streets. If someone wanted to get stupid, it was his job to persuade them to think twice. Dave was our muscle on Mount and Fayette Streets, and if there was a problem, he was right on top of it. Every now and then, the stick-up kids would ride through looking for easy prey, but when they saw Dave, they kept right on moving. I watched him drop a few guys on their heads on several occasions. I remember him kicking a guy in the chest for talking trash and the guy couldn't breathe for a minute or two. People feared Dave for several very good reasons.

In the beginning, Dave was very reliable and if we needed him for anything, he was always there. That was the reason his absence became so noticeable. Dave began to disappear from his post for days at a time. We wouldn't see the guy sometimes for three days and then he would suddenly reappear. This new pattern of his came out of nowhere.

Whenever I suspected that any of the guys were having an issue, I would always discuss it with Smith. Since Smith was spending more time with them than I was, he had more of an inside track on things. One day I called Smith and I told him to meet me on Baltimore Street at the barbershop where we often met. I still didn't fully know what was going on with Dave but I knew it was something bad.

Smith pulled up in his new BMW at the same time I was parking my car. "Yo, what the hell is going on with Dave?" I asked. Smith paused for a second. That was when I knew something was up.

"Dave has fucked up, Kev," Smith answered. "Dave is smoking fucking crack, man. I don't know what the fuck he was thinking about."

Smith was disgusted with the whole Dave situation. They had been very close around this time and I could see that the situation was weighing heavily on Smith. He had introduced

Dave to Stuffy and I just before he started working with us on Fayette Street. He probably thought that he was betraying Dave by telling me about his problem. On the other hand, he knew if he wasn't truthful with me, he would be betraying the trust that he and I had built.

So, even though he was reluctant to do so, Smith explained everything to me. Dave told Smith that he had begun smoking crack with his new girlfriend. I remembered meeting Sharon a few times when I was with Dave. She was actually very attractive. Somehow she used her charm to persuade Dave to take a hit from a crack pipe. That first hit was all it took to lock him in and from that point on, my man was finished.

I simply told Smith that Dave couldn't work with us any longer. I liked Dave very much, but he was smoking crack, so I couldn't do business with him. At any moment, he could turn on us because addiction is unpredictable. I was already sleeping with one eye open, but this was too much to deal with. It wasn't anything personal and after I explained my position to Smith, he agreed with me.

A few days later, we had a meeting with the entire crew except Dave, who was, of course, the topic of conversation. Everyone agreed with my decision. We then sat down with Dave and had a long talk with him, which was difficult because I liked him. He was more upset with himself than he was with us for letting him go because he realized he created the mess. This wasn't something that he had planned, but it happened. Dave was a standup guy, but crack took him down with ease.

Eventually Dave was able to rid himself of his crack addiction and then a few years later, he began running his own operation with some other guys. Unfortunately, his life would come to an end sooner than anyone expected. Dave had gotten into a deadly beef with someone over a drug deal that went very bad. He was shot dead on the front lawn of his house, as members of his family looked on in horror.

As the Diamond in the Raw crew continued to spread the drug of Choice, I grew closer to Smith. Ronnie had introduced him to Stuffy and me when he first got out of prison. Smith had only been home from the penitentiary a week when he first started working with us. It took him a minute or two to get back in his zone, but once he did, he was off to the races. Smith had been a straight shooter and that was one of the things that I appreciated about him. More importantly, I didn't feel like I had to look over my shoulder with him. He had displayed his loyalty to us on many occasions, but the story about Ronnie had me a little confused.

I noticed that he was drinking a lot, which was odd for him. Now every time we met to conduct business, he had an alcoholic beverage in his hand. Most nights now when Stuffy or I went to his place to pick up the day's receipts, he would be drunk. Subsequently, I noticed that in the mornings when I dropped off the package to him, he would be hung over from the night before. As this occurred more and more frequently, a red flag popped up in my head. Since my father was an alcoholic, I was more observant of the signs than others would be.

I confronted Smith about the situation because I thought that I could talk straight with him. That was the type of relationship I assumed we had at the time. I told him that he might want to think about not consuming so much alcohol. He agreed with me, but he also said something surprising. Smith confided in me that he had also been smoking weed. I asked him why he would want to smoke weed with all of the responsibilities he had with Diamond in the Raw. To me, this didn't make any sense.

He didn't know what to say, but gave me this look like, "I'm really fucking up, right?"

I had previously gone through the same type of ordeal with Stuffy, so my antennae were up. I watched his behavior very closely during our meetings and whatever he was doing was beginning to show. I wasn't sure what to do because I couldn't supervise the life of a grown man. As long as the money kept flowing, I shouldn't have had any complaints, should I?

I always felt uneasy about working with a guy that used drugs. Smith had all of our lives in his hands. If he got himself into a bad situation because of his drinking, it had the potential to send each and every one of us to jail. There was never a problem with the money, not one single dollar. But I realized that his problem could create bigger issues for everyone in the long run.

Early one morning, something big did happen. Smith was hung over from the night before and never saw it coming. The police were waiting for him when he pulled on to the block. I'm not sure if they had been tipped off or what, but it was that cop Peanut Head, and he had finally gotten the case he had been looking for. There were two thousand bags of heroin stashed inside the trunk of Smith's car, the entire package for that day. With the cops in pursuit, he tried to run, but he didn't make it far. The police easily caught him in the alley and beat him down pretty bad. He was dragged off to the station and charged with attempted distribution of heroin. I was at my girlfriend's house when I heard about the arrest and I remember the incident like it happened yesterday. It was the lead story on the six o'clock evening news as I sat watching television and eating my dinner. Very quickly, my appetite vanished.

We lost $20,000-worth of product during the arrest. We also had to pay $25,000 cash to bail him out. On top of that, we had to shell out more than $30,000 in attorney's fees, even though there wasn't much the attorney could do. Smith had been caught red handed. If he went to trial, he would have been looking at a forty-five-year prison sentence, so a plea bargain was his only option. He had some leverage because the probable cause issue for the cops searching the car was shaky. His attorney was able to work out a deal and he was sentenced to ten years in state prison. I later found out that it wasn't just alcohol or weed that Smith was medicating himself with. He was also sniffing the same heroin that he was supposed to be selling for us.

While serving his time, Smith's addiction became progressively worse. He was being held at the Maryland House of Correction. This facility had become notorious for its raging drug problem. Drugs were so accessible there that it was almost like being out on the streets. Smith became even more dependant on drugs while in prison. Just a few months after his release, he was shot dead in the street while trying to steal drugs from another dealer. What an ugly and depressing way this was to go out.

The drug addiction is an insatiable beast that can only be tamed with total abstinence. It had tempted almost everyone that I knew, including a member of my own family. It had even bitten my older sister. How ironic was that? The poisoner was now being poisoned himself, but not directly by the drugs. He was being poisoned by the same misery that he had been serving to the loved ones of others. Now that other street dealers were selling crack to someone in my family, I was furious, but I couldn't stop it.

It was hard on my family to watch my sister go through this complete transformation. She and I had been very close, but once she started using, our relationship became really strained.

To see my sister out on the streets, buying drugs, tore the life out of me and I felt helpless to fix the mess. Finally, with the help of drug treatment and counseling, she made the progress we all had hoped for and she never turned back.

THE BEGINNING OF THE END

On this cold winter morning, the skies were gray and the clouds were thick. During the month of February, four to five inches of snow was likely on any given day, usually accompanied by subfreezing temperatures. The winter months in Baltimore can be grossly unpredictable. I have always been an early riser and this morning would be no different. Often I stayed the night at my girlfriend's house because she lived in the city and because she was about four months pregnant with our daughter. After a long day of trying to tame a world that was virtually untamable, family life, even for a short period, felt good.

I was excited about the prospect of becoming the newest father on the block. My girlfriend was having morning sickness very often. She was attending a local university that was only a ten-minute ride from her house, majoring in journalism and had several early morning classes. She was very smart and had aspirations of delivering the six o'clock news from behind the anchor desk. We had become accustomed to leaving the house together in the mornings, then going our separate ways for the day.

On this particular morning, I was going to follow her to the gas station to fill up a rental car she had been driving. I had placed her car in the repair shop, which was there for a couple of days. I didn't want her to have any problems while she was driving around alone. A pregnant woman in a disabled vehicle could be a recipe for trouble. I told the mechanic to fix anything and everything that he could find wrong with the car.

Women are notorious for taking a long time to get dressed, but imagine how long a pregnant woman takes. You could be sitting for hours, waiting for the mother-to-be to assemble her attire.

"Are you ready yet to get out of here? You're going to be late for your class," I said. I knew it was important to be patient, but I finally had to get going.

"I'll be waiting for you up at the gas station, okay?" She lived only about three minutes from there. We hadn't realized that we had let the gas level down to just about empty. In those days, when the gas needle was on empty, that meant you had about two minutes'-worth of gas left before you were in big trouble.

I drove up to the Exxon station and waited several minutes for her to arrive, but she never showed up. I had just assumed that she was still in the house, making that all-important wardrobe decision. I did realize that she was moving a bit slow because of being pregnant, but this was taking much longer than usual.

I drove back to the house to see if she was still there, but she was gone, along with the rental car. I was baffled because there was no way she could have just driven right past me without me seeing her. I turned my car around and drove back to the station a second time, but still there was no sign of her. I didn't know what was going on, but I also didn't have any real reason to worry at that point. I started to get a little angry because she knew I had things to do this morning. I assumed that she may have made a quick stop at one of the neighbor's houses for some reason. I left the gas station again to scour the area, but there was still no sign of her. Then I remembered that there was another route to the gas station, so I decide to check it out.

As I drove up the street, I began fooling around with the new state-of-the-art audio sound system I had paid a few thousand bucks to have installed. I loved the new device because the music was ridiculously clear. There was a twelve-disc CD player and two heavy bass speakers in the trunk. This would have been one of my favorite little toys except that I could not figure out how to use it. Programming the system was difficult because it had so many dials and buttons to operate, so I pulled over to the curb to adjust the sound. As I was setting the dials on the console, I looked up to see my girlfriend frantically running up the street toward me in complete distress.

She had no coat on and she was yelling, with this terrified look on her face. I was struggling to find the button to lower the volume. When I finally found it, I could hear her yelling, "They robbed me, they robbed me!"

"Who robbed you?" I didn't understand what was going on.

"They pulled a gun on me and took my coat and purse!" she cried. I couldn't believe what I was hearing. That fast, my girlfriend had been robbed. Two thugs had snatched her purse and coat.

Her rental car had completely run out of gas while she was on her way to the gas station to meet me and she was stalled in the middle of the street. She was walking back home when some guys pulled up in an SUV and began asking her for her telephone number. As she politely said no and continued walking, they pulled the SUV over and stopped her. The next thing you know, they have guns out telling her to take off her coat and hand over her purse.

I was furious! I told her to jump in the car. I was going to find these guys! I always kept a nine-millimeter on me, just for occasions like this. All I wanted to do was stick my gun in their faces, the way they did to an innocent woman, just to see what they had to say. My girlfriend knew me and she was well aware that I wasn't going to let these guys do something like this to her and get away with it.

"No, just let them go," she urged me. Wanting to go after these guys may not have been the smartest thing to do, but I was responding out of anger and not out of common sense. My girlfriend was still upset that someone had just pointed a gun at her. It pained me to see her in that state.

"Get in!" I ordered her. "I'm gonna get these motherfuckers!" I was incensed and I wanted revenge.

"No, no, let them go!" she repeated, and refused to get into the car with me. I asked her to describe what they were driving and she said it was a burgundy Ford Explorer. By this time, one of her neighbors who were taking out the trash overheard the conversation between us. I asked him to take care of her until I got back and I sped off in pursuit of the two armed bandits.

I could see the rental car parked over to the side. I continued up the street, turning at the next block, traveling at least sixty miles an hour through the neighborhood. I needed to give these guys a taste of their own medicine. I wanted to get my hands on them for just two seconds. Once I caught up to them, they wouldn't know what hit them.

I looked all over the place but there was no sight of them. These guys had disappeared. When I calmed down, I realized that it was probably good I couldn't find them. At the end of the day, they would get what they had coming and it didn't necessarily have to come from me. You don't have good luck pulling out guns on women, especially pregnant women. The Game Gods would deal with them when they least expected it.

I returned to my girlfriend's house to find three police cars parked outside the door. The police were taking a report, but by now, there wasn't much that they could do. She had given them a description of the vehicle and the guys, but she didn't have a license plate. I was convinced that the cops would never find them, but if this made my girlfriend feel better, I was okay with that. For months after that, every burgundy Ford Explorer that drove by received extra attention.

She had been really shaken up by the episode. To see someone you love in such anguish is heart-wrenching. You want to do whatever you can to make them feel better. She later told me that she asked them not to hurt her because she was pregnant. The coat that she was wearing was very expensive, but she could always get another one. The only thing to do now was for her to get to her college class.

Later that night I got a call from the hospital. "We need you here quickly, there is a problem." It was my girlfriend's mother. She had rushed her to the hospital after she had complained of strong stomach pains.

"We hope it's not a miscarriage from all that stuff earlier today, but we don't know." I was worried because she was already having a tough pregnancy. She had been hospitalized twice because of the severe morning sickness that made it hard for her to hold down food. The doctors had placed her on intravenous feeding because they were concerned that the baby wasn't getting enough nutrition.

I was with my crew when I got the call. I immediately jumped into my car, weaving my way in and out of traffic, on the way to the hospital. My mind was racing a million miles a second. I had heard about women having miscarriages after a stressful experience. Was this what was happening now? Could my dream to have a beautiful daughter one day have been shattered that fast? A few months earlier there was a sonogram to check the health of the baby. That was when we found out that we were having a girl and that she was the picture of health. I had been carrying the photo from the sonogram around in my wallet for weeks, showing it to anyone who would look or listen.

By the time I reached the hospital, the doctors had concluded that the stomach pains that she was having weren't from a miscarriage at all. The pain was actually a pulled muscle in her lower abdomen. She had injured herself running up the street after being robbed. This had been a drama-filled day from dusk to dawn. A day that seemed to start off normal, ended up so bizarre. By the time we returned home later that night, we were both exhausted.

As I continued to play my position in the game, I sometimes felt like I was losing my mind. The pressure was intense, as every day was another issue. Paranoia began to set in and I didn't know who I could trust. If you pay too much attention to the fear, it can drive you nuts; but if you ignore it too much, it could cost you your life. I was sure there were people who wanted to send me to prison or stuff me in a garbage bag and drop me in the Baltimore Harbor. While driving home, I stayed glued to the rearview mirror to make sure I wasn't being followed. One set of headlights behind me for too long and my daredevil driving maneuvers would kick in.

Every night when I pulled into the parking lot of my complex, I observed very carefully to see if anyone was waiting in the shadows. I'd get out of the car with the gun in my hand, covered with my coat or something else. It was a foolish thing

to do because I could have shot one of the neighbors by accident. When you're anxious and you're worried about someone
sending you to the morgue in a plastic bag, all kinds of irrational
thoughts run through your mind. Under the immense pressure,
you don't know what to think.

I often walked into the house checking the windows to
make sure no one had broken in and was lying in wait there.
You couldn't be too careful in those days. If you let your guard
down just once, that could be all it took to end your career. The
stick-up boys were regularly targeting hustlers throughout the
city. For some guys, their full-time job was to rob deals that were
making money out on the street corners. I remember hearing
how some stick-up kid had broken into the house where a hustler lived with his wife. He wrapped them both in duct tape and
robbed them just before committing the double homicide. This
was a crazy way to live, period. But for some, it was the only way
they knew how to live. I no longer understood if this was the
life that I had chosen or if this life had chosen me. Either way I
sliced it, I wasn't too happy.

I began having thoughts of departing Baltimore in search
of peace and sanity. My girlfriend had family living in Ohio that
she always spoke about. She suggested that we escape the mayhem for a while, maybe even for good. Ohio seemed like a nice
place to live, but what would I do there in the Buckeye State?
The game was all I thought I knew. I was bringing in $20,000 a
day on the streets. What kind of job could I get to replace that
kind of income? I needed to do some serious thinking to re-eval-
uate my life and the future of my soon-to-be new daughter.

Maybe a short vacation, some fun in the sun, would be
just what I needed. I had never taken a real vacation before. I
had traveled on business many times, but that was different. I

had never taken time off just to rest my mind and reinvigorate my soul. My girlfriend was five months pregnant and she was just about to enter into the stage of pregnancy where her doctor would prohibit her from flying. So if we were going to do it, it would have to be now.

I was steadily feeling the pressure; every corner I turned seemed to have an urgent matter waiting. I felt like the weight of the world was on my shoulders. The game was taking its toll on me and it was well past time to take a break from the madness. My girlfriend had spring break coming up and there was a travel agency in Mondawmin Mall where I could get information, so I had no more excuses not to.

The older guy with the gray hair sitting behind the desk inside the travel office was named Herb. When I first walked in, I had absolutely no clue where I wanted to go. There were posters of exotic tropical islands all over the walls of the office. I was like that kid in the candy store back at my grandmother's, only Herb wasn't as impatient with me as the Chinese man had been.

He asked me questions as to what I was looking for.

"Do you want to go to an island?" he asked.

"No, I don't think that I want to go to an island."

"Where do you want to go to? Mexico?"

"I don't think that I want to go Mexico, I don't speak Spanish." In the end, Herb sent me on a twenty-one day trip to Florida. I would spend two weeks in Orlando and seven days in Clearwater. It was a low-key vacation, where I could relax. My girlfriend would be with me for part of the trip, but she had to return for school.

The sun was intense in the skies of Orlando, as the heat massaged the brow of the tourist from the north. The tantalizing breeze that whispered in the wind provided relief from the stress. The tropical flowers I had never seen before gave picturesque views of beautiful colors. The tall palm trees and the white clouds that sprinkled the backdrop completed the scene. With the stick-up kids and the rival Fayette Street crews a far-off thought, peace and harmony were finally within my grasp.

After hanging out in Orlando for two weeks, I headed over to Clearwater, on the west coast of Florida. There I chilled on the white sand beaches that stretched for miles and miles. The blue waters that rolled in from the Gulf of Mexico produced a feeling of tranquility in the young businessman on his first Florida vacation.

The time I spent in Florida was an excellent way to soothe the soul, but it was abruptly interrupted by bad news at home. While I was out of town, I regularly called Stuffy to check on the status of the operation and on my girlfriend's condition when she was back in Baltimore. An admitted workaholic, I couldn't be fully at ease until I was assured that things there were okay. Just before I left town, there had been a few fires that we needed to extinguish and I wanted to make sure they hadn't sparked again. Also, Stuffy would stop by my girlfriend's house every couple of days to make sure she was doing well.

I paged Stuffy from the hotel pay phone in the lobby, where he always returned my calls.

"Yo, what's going on up there?" I asked, as I answered the phone. "Is everything good with the rest of the guys?"

"Everything is okay. A few minor things, but nothing serious," Stuffy said. "Things have been slow 'because the cops have been hot around the way. Alex sent down another key of raw and we put another two-hundred thousand on our bill with him." I was relieved to hear that, but I was starting to get anxious about returning home.

"I should be back in town next week," I told him. "I'm in Clearwater now, near Tampa."

At the end of our phone conversation he said to me, "Look, I almost forgot to tell you something." I just assumed that whatever he had to tell me wasn't that important, but I was very wrong.

"Mike got shot last night," Stuffy said. This was the same Mike who had killed Anthony a few years earlier. In spite of the heartache Anthony's death caused me, Mike and I had continued to be friends. But this news stunned me.

"Mike was shot nine times while he was going into his apartment," Stuffy continued. "Someone had been waiting for him in the hallway when he got home the other night. The MediVac transport helicopter flew him to the hospital and I heard he might not make it."

I called my girlfriend to tell her what had happened with Mike and to tell her that I was coming home. She desperately pleaded with me not to get involved in whatever was going on with Mike. I packed my bags and grabbed a taxi to the airport. I'm still not even sure why I went back so abruptly because there wasn't much that I could do for Mike. But I considered the guy a friend and he was in trouble, so I would definitely try to be there. I guess that was the number one reason I hurried back to the city. Even after what he did to Anthony, I still considered him a friend and I wasn't sure why.

When I arrived at BWI Airport that evening, it was snowing lightly and I was having a tough time locating my car in the airport parking lot. I stopped at a pay phone just to call the hospital, to tell Mike's wife, Kim, that I would be arriving shortly. I knew that visiting hours would be ending soon and I didn't want any problems, so I asked her to notify the front desk I was coming.

When I finally made it to the trauma unit, Kim took me to the floor where Mike was. Standing in the hallway were three homicide detectives who were investigating the shooting. There were some other guys there who were friends of Mike's. They wanted to go out and shoot anyone they thought was involved in Mike getting shot, without even taking the time to find out who actually shot him. I heard one of them muttering, "Let's kill them all, anybody that knows anything." I made an attempt to talk some sense into them because no one knew exactly what was going on, but my tolerance for stupidity was low and I realized that these guys were thinking out of their rear ends. And I was pretty sure it was just talk, I didn't think they'd actually do anything. Of course, I had been wrong about that in the past.

I followed Kim as she escorted me into the back to see her husband. This was a really eerie scene for me. It was almost ghostly because I could see several of the trauma patients and they were in really bad shape. There were people there who looked like they had fallen out of the top floor of buildings. This place was grim. Once we finally made it to Mike, I could see that he was in terrible shape. His face was so swollen I could barely recognize him.

"Yo, hang in there, man, hang in there," I urged my gravely wounded homeboy, who was fighting for his life. One bullet had grazed his chest, right over his heart. He had a few bullet wounds in his legs as well, and bullet wounds to the abdomen. One bullet had struck his testicles and one of the doctors told him that he would never be able to have another child.

He had tubes everywhere on his body that were pumping blood or medication or some other type of fluid. I had never before visited anyone that close to being on their deathbed. Nine metal foreign objects had entered and exited or were still lodged in Mike's body. That was an incredible amount of damage for one person to sustain and still be alive. Even the doctors were telling him, "Young man, you are very, very lucky to still be with us." These doctors worked in the shock trauma unit for many years, so imagine how many people they've seen die as a result of Baltimore's murderous machine. God was really watching over Mike on this day, as he walked the fine line between life and death.

When someone in the game gets shot or killed, the rumors and misinformation spread like wildfire through the streets. And the same way these types of rumors reverberate through the cracks and crevices of the concrete jungle, at some point, that information will reach the curious ears of law enforcement. The sad thing is that these rumors are incorrect a great portion of the time, but the cops still have to act on them. In Mike's case, the rumor was that I had put a contract out on him because he refused to pay money he owed for a package of cocaine. This was a ridiculous accusation, but there wasn't anything that I could do about it.

Who, what, and why, were all the questions everyone wanted answered, but only Mike and the shooter knew what had gone down. Maybe it was a simple case of what goes around was now coming back around. Maybe it was the Game Gods balancing things out. Maybe it was something else entirely, but I didn't have a clue.

About two weeks later, I found out that a few days before Mike was shot, he and his wife had a violent fight. Mike told me that he slapped her in the face when he discovered that she was cheating on him. Her cheating on him wasn't a big surprise to me. Mike had been caught cheating on her several times before, so he had to expect this. You can't do that to a woman and not expect something bad in return. The suspicion was that Mike's wife's lover was upset that he had assaulted her. The guy may have wanted to kill Mike for that reason, as well as to get Mike out of the way so that he could be with his wife permanently. The entire situation turned into a real soap opera. The writers from *The Young and the Restless* couldn't have written a more intriguing script than this.

In the end, no one, not even Mike, knew exactly who shot him. The police were still investigating, Mike only had suspicions with no real facts, and I definitely didn't have any idea. I was out of town when the whole thing went down, even though some would later say that was the perfect alibi for me. I began to wonder if somehow someone had found out that Mike had killed Anthony and was now seeking vengeance. The bottom line was that someone wanted him dead. If someone is going to wait for you in the hallway as you enter your apartment in the middle of the night and shoot you nine times at close range, he wants you dead.

Roughly one year later, Mike was hanging out in his neighborhood, selling crack, when an unknown assailant blazed him. Supposedly, a stick-up kid walked up to Mike and some local guys as they stood on the corner, pulled out a gun, and demanded their goods. Mike wasn't having it and began to panic. It had only been one year since he was lying in shock trauma and he wasn't ready to give this guy an easy opportunity. As the armed gunman made his way through the small group, removing their money and valuables from their pockets, Mike thought he saw an opening and made a run for it. The assailant wasn't prepared to let him off the hook that easily and opened fire.

The crowd dispersed in all directions as bullets were blazing: POP! POP! POP! POP! Mike thought he had made a clean getaway, but he was mistaken. He was struck four times. In search of help, he made it to a hair salon down the street, owned by a friend. The salon was full of customers when he burst through the door, bleeding profusely. He fell down on the floor.

"Please help me," he begged the patrons in the shop. "I don't want to die." The alarming scene horrified them. They were only there for grooming and to hear the latest gossip, not to become witnesses to such horror. One of the stylists quickly called 911. Mike had the great luck to survive this second attempt on his life.

Rumors again began to make their way around the city that someone had a contract on his life and I didn't know what to make of it. Either he was blessed or he was cursed. He had been shot multiple times on two separate occasions and lived to tell about it. I began to wonder whether or not he was being punished by a higher power for what he had done to Anthony.

All of the drama swirling around me made it clear that I had some big decisions to make. With my child on the way, plans for her future were a top priority for me. If something happened to me, how would my child be taken care of? I definitely didn't want her to grow up like her father did. I didn't want her to end up looking to the streets for admiration and acceptance. I also had to think about my own future. I was starting to realize that my days in the game were numbered. The Feds were on the heels of just about every hustler in the city who was raking in heavy cash and my name had to be on the list. Guys were being herded off to prison before the ink on the wiretap transcripts was even dry. I didn't want to be like them. I wanted to be one of the very few who retired from the game before the game retired me.

I started looking for a legitimate business to purchase where I could pursue calmer days. There was this Israeli fellow with a heavy Mediterranean ancient whom I admired for his style and wit. I had known the guy for several years, all the way back to my days of hustling nickel bags on the street corners. He was the number one workaholic in Mondawmin Mall, as he operated three businesses in this popular urban shopping Mecca. For some reason, my Israeli friend often disguised himself as an Italian fashion guru. One day he told me that he was selling one of his businesses. He was selling a flower shop, which I wasn't too excited about, but the prospect of going legit was very attractive to me. When my long-nosed friend offered to sell me the business for $100,000, I took it. A handshake sealed the deal, which was cemented by a Nike shoebox filled with the cash, handed across the table, just like in the movies.

"You're going to love going into business for yourself, Kevin. This is a good move for you," he said.

"Yeah, it's time for me to do things a little different now, man. I got a kid on the way."

A *florist*.... *Wow,* I said to myself. I was now faced with the challenge of pitching red roses and carnations, wrapped in a box and tied with a bow. It wasn't that I adored flowers or anything like that, but I was taking advantage of what I believed to be a good opportunity. Later on, I found out that the business I purchased was really worth something closer to $20,000, but by then it was too late. My Israeli comrade must have seen a big sign on my forehead that read "DUMMY," but the deal was done. I could have made a phone call to remedy the situation, but I didn't. It wasn't his fault I thought I knew what I was getting into and didn't bother to evaluate it more. And this was still my opportunity to back away from the streets.

When I told the rest my crew that I bought a flower shop, they thought I was crazy, even though they didn't say it at the time. Most guys in the game that were looking for a way to legitimize their foul play, recognized hair salons and barber-shops as the easy way to cross over to a legit business. But as long as the money kept flowing, I really didn't care what business I was in. I was a practical man, and selling flowers for a living was as practical as it gets.

Running a legitimate business was nothing like hustling on the streets. The fundamentals are somewhat the same, because I ran Diamond in the Raw like a business; but really, it's like night and day. I hired my sister Karen and my aunt because I was clearly exposed. They in turn hired other family members, and in no time, we were off and running. But with no formal training in the management of a business, we were still teetering on the brink.

I was inside the shop, putting together a horrible version of a flower arrangement, when I got the call from my girlfriend.

"Kevin, my water just broke and I'm on my way to the hospital." Our new baby, named Brooke, was on her way. Brooke's mother was in labor for a few hours, but it didn't seem that long. I guess that was because I wasn't the one in labor. We moved from the labor room to delivery room. I had no idea there were two separate rooms for that.

We were only in delivery for a brief moment before the doctor ran in, assessed the situation and then yelled, "Push!" It looked just like in the movies. A minute or two later, I could see the top of my daughter's head.

This was an incredible experience. I was looking at my daughter and I was stunned. I know there was a lot of noise going on around me because this was a hospital, but to me, it seemed like everything was suddenly silent. All I could do was mumble, "Oh, my God!" If you've witnessed the birth of a child, you know what I'm talking about. If you haven't, there's no way I can explain it to you. All I can tell you was that this was the moment that I realized everything I had been doing to get out of the drug business was the right thing to do. I was responsible for someone else's life now; I was responsible for a baby girl named Brooke. All of the decisions that I made from here on out had to revolve around her.

After the experience of her birth, I was hypnotized by the prospect of living the American dream and walking my daughter to her first day of school. The possibility of seeing her off to the Girl Scouts to sell Thin Mints and then off to her senior prom was now real. My appetite for destruction was soon to be only a memory.

But it was already too late.

It was a warm summer day in 1992. I was downtown, grabbing a shrimp salad sandwich from Lexington Market, when my sister paged me, using the 911 code.

"I just got a call from Aunt Connie," Karen told me when I called. "Eight DEA agents were at her house with a warrant for your arrest."

"Why would they be looking for me at her house?" I asked. "I haven't been there for years."

"I don't know, but Connie is very upset. She said that they made a big scene in the neighborhood." I could understand the Feds looking for me, but I couldn't understand why they were looking in a place that I hadn't even visited for years.

The paperwork read: United States v. Kevin Shird. It was me against the entire United States of America. Even with the best lawyers money could buy, this had all the ingredients of the beginning of the end. What would happen now? Would I be going down the tubes, like all of the other hustlers before me? Was this what this thing we call "the life" is all about? One minute you're on top, and then suddenly the rug is pulled from underneath you, like a Saturday morning cartoon. Anthony used to always say, "The cars, the houses, the money… Have fun now because you can't take this shit with you to prison."

From there my attorney took over the case and what he found out was a big surprise to both of us. The federal case against me had nothing to do with Diamond in the Raw or anything involving Fayette and Mount Streets. Several months before my indictment, a crew that I was doing business with about a year and a half earlier was indicted for heroin trafficking in connection with some Nigerians in Queens, New York. Shortly after they got nabbed, many of those defendants began providing information to the government about their past deals with me. That's when two other guys and I became the target of the government's fury, prompting additional indictments against us. The guys that provided information to the Feds had a close relationship with one of the most well known kingpins to ever walk the streets of West Baltimore. Ironically, this was the exact same manner in which Anthony was indicted a few years earlier. After a few months of fighting with the Feds, my attorney and I realized that the U.S. Attorney was holding four aces against my pair of twos. If it had gone to trial, it wouldn't have been a case, it would have been suicide. So I threw in my chips, pled guilty to the charges, and headed off to federal prison.

INSIDE THE JOINT

The yellow lettering on the back of the tall, white, middle-aged man's blue windbreaker read: **UNITED STATES MARSHAL**. I had just received a free ride to an undisclosed location, courtesy of federal law enforcement officials. From the federal courthouse, I was transported to the Princess George's County Detention Center. It had finally happened. I thought I had escaped it, but now, I had met the fate so many of my compadres had met.

The van was driven into an empty loading dock big enough to hold a cargo container, but in this case, the freight was convicted felons. The "packages" were swiftly unloaded and taken inside for inspection. Walking with shackles around my legs and hands took some getting used. I could easily fall on my face and injured myself badly, aggravating the already unpleasant day. The U. S. Marshals that transported us were courteous and respectful, unlike the storm troopers that we would shortly be subjected to. I realized that this had to be part of the marshals' training. They weren't at all like the county officers, who used every opportunity to throw a verbal jab or two. The marshals rarely ever made a disparaging remark and didn't show any distain towards us.

157

The detention center was only temporary housing. I would only be there until the Federal Bureau of Prisons found space in their prison system for me. This could take about three to four weeks. Until that day, I would be stuck here in this hellhole.

"The county officers here don't have a lot of patience, and they especially don't like federal prisoners." I was appreciative to the marshal who said that to me. I thought it could potentially end up being valuable information. He also told me that getting into an argument with the officers here could mean big trouble.

At that time, the county sheriff's department was under investigation by the FBI for wrongful deaths and for shootings involving their officers and unarmed suspects. The detention center was under investigation for an inmate's death and some serious inmate beatings. The allegation was that the officers there had beaten an inmate to death. I learned very fast that there are a lot of ways you can get killed in prison.

I had been to jail before, but only for a very short time, never more than two or three days. This time there wouldn't be a bail hearing to spring me loose. This wouldn't be just a few hours or days out of my life. When you're in prison and you know you won't be going home any time soon, you develop a completely different mentality.

I soon discovered that I had a mild case of claustrophobia. As I lay there on my bunk, I had the feeling that the walls were closing in. The tiny cell was shrinking with every hour that passed. It felt like someone had his hands gripped around my throat and was squeezing. Being locked down for eighteen hours a day took some getting use to. Not being able to come and go as you please is a hard pill to swallow. Only being allowed out of the cell for a shower and three meals a day was tough, early on.

Every chance I got to come out of the dark hole, I took advantage of it. The relief would only be short lived.

The smell that loomed through the air inside the prison was horrific. The entire place had the smell of moldy flesh as it rots away over time. After a few days, you become accustomed to the unthinkable fragrance. The food being served to the guests here at this motel for the accused and convicted was appalling. The dishes didn't bear any resemblance to what I remembered food to look like or taste like. During the first couple of days, I wouldn't eat it. But then I realized there wouldn't be anything better coming along any time soon. The hunger pains were a sign that my body was upset with my decision. After a few days of dissatisfaction, the meals eventually became more palatable.

The first inmate that I shared the cell with turned out to be an addict who was coming down from a night of smoking crack cocaine. Now he was fighting the demons that were stealing his sanity. When the guards first placed him in the cell with me, he was still hallucinating. The entire night, this guy was jumping all over the place and driving me crazy, so I couldn't have slept even if the mattresses weren't so uncomfortable. He told me that he thought someone was trying to kill him and that person who wanted him dead was inside of the two-man cell with us. I kept trying to reassure the guy that the only people inside the locked cell were him and me. I told him this over and over, but he was convinced that he was under attack. The next thing I knew, he began crawling around on the floor and attempting to hide behind the toilet. Can you imagine a grown man trying to hide behind a two-foot tall toilet inside a prison cell? This really brought home for me the reality of what my life now was. The entire night, I was yelling to the guards to remove the guy from the cell and take him to the infirmary.

"Yo, this man needs some fucking help!" I yelled. "Somebody needs to get this guy some help!"

He was going to seriously injured himself if something wasn't done soon. I could remember when I was a teenager, seeing a guy high on cocaine trying to hang himself at the police precinct lockup. He tied a bed sheet around a pipe running across the ceiling, looped the other end around his neck, and jumped. The cops ran in and got him down before he did any permanent damage, but the scene was really ugly. I definitely didn't want to see that happen here. Finally, they transferred the guy to the psychiatric unit. Even though I had been around people like this for years in the streets as they fought the demons associated with drug addiction, this was a crazy scene to me. I had seen addicts, frantically searching for a vein, inject needles into their necks. I had seen the heart of a crack addict stop beating from an overdose. I have seen grown men defecate in their pants because they couldn't get a fix. I thought I had seen it all. But this was different. It's one thing to see people in bad condition in the streets; it's another thing when you're locked in a ten foot by ten foot jail cell with him.

A couple of weeks later, I was transferred to Petersburg Federal Correctional Institute in southern Virginia. Petersburg was one of the Federal Bureau of Prison's oldest prisons and on the outside, looked like a castle from the medieval times. There were stories of legendary prisoners who were once housed there, dating back to the 1940s. This renowned institution once housed the notorious 1990s crack dealer, Rayful Edmund, from Washington, D.C. For his own safety and for security reasons, he had to be transported to the courthouse in Washington in a military helicopter. Once upon a time, this was home to an impressive array of crooks, from CIA spies who sold secret information to the Russians to Colombian drug overlords who murdered foreign dignitaries. Petersburg's reputation was a mighty one, as far as correctional institutions went. And now this place was my home.

When I first arrived there I was intimidated by the nostalgic history of the well-known federal prison. It was a surreal moment for the one-time leader of the pack, who was now known more commonly as prisoner number 28878-037. In a way, incarceration in the federal system was somewhat of a badge of honor, only worn by those who gave orders. Watching the Italian mobsters and international drug traffickers as they sashayed their way around the track inside the prison yard thrilled me. I began to think that prison wasn't so bad after all. Ridiculously, I started to think that it was a small price to pay to be the boss.

As time went on, I began to understand that these former bosses of the streets were struggling just as hard as everyone else to reconcile themselves to the pain of incarceration. The absence from the game had taken its toll on these deflated men, who were once honored by the streets. Sadness, despair, and melancholy pierced their lonely souls. The most difficult thing for me to deal with was being away from my family. I missed them very much, and I had a brand new daughter! Even though I was selling drugs, I did everything that I could to help my family. With that in mind, I made a deal with the devil before I left the streets, with the hope that my child would have financial support.

Harvey, who was part of the Diamond in the Raw crew, asked me to jump-start his rise to the top before I was sent off on my journey. I was going away to prison and I had a young daughter that needed to be taken care of. My plan was to make sure my child had the support she required, but plans don't always work out.

"Okay, this is what we're going to do, alright?" I told Harvey. "Since you want me to make this hookup for you, I want you to give $10,000 a month to my people to make sure that my daughter is good. You got it?"

"Yo, that's cool, man; I don't have a problem with that," he answered. "Man, don't worry about anything. I'll make sure that's taken care of."

One of my connections in New York wanted to continue doing business, even after I went away to prison, so making the connection for Harvey was easy. Jude was his name and he was originally from Nigeria. The way these guys looked at it, they didn't care that you're going to jail. Their main focus is to continue the revenue stream they had with you, even if they continue it with your grandmother. Stuffy and Smith were getting ready to go to jail, Ronnie was already in Jessup doing time for a handgun charge, Nate was too inexperienced, and Dave was still smoking crack. The only guy left standing was Harvey, so he'd have to do, even if I didn't completely trust him.

Before my sentencing, Harvey and I took a trip to New York to introduce him to Jude. Jude was a businessman, but he was a snake in the grass as well. In hindsight, everyone in the game has to be considered a snake. If you turn your back on them, it could be the last time you turn your back at all.

Jude's operation smuggled heroin from Bangkok, Thailand into Nigeria where they would store it there. He then sent prostitutes from the States as mules, flying them from New York to London and then connecting to flights to Nigeria to pick up the drugs. After a week or two in Nigeria the mules would then return to New York with the merchandise.

The heroin was broken down into seven gram pieces, which made them easy to swallow. These objects were called "eggs," but they are actually shaped more like large bullets. Each individual egg was wrapped tightly in plastic to keep it dry. The mules used an over-the-counter medication to numb their throats to help them swallow the "eggs". The body weight of the carrier dictated how much dope they could carry in their stomachs. The larger the women, the larger their stomachs were, the more dope they could ingest. If one of the packages had burst in their stomachs they would have died instantly from a massive overdosed. Once the heroin was safely ingested, the mule was ready to return to the United States.

This was a very dangerous exercise for obvious reasons. A person's body naturally begins to digest whatever is in the stomach on its own after a period of time. That's one reason the eggs were wrapped in so many layers of plastic. The mule had to be back into the States within thirty-six hours to safely use the bathroom. If not, they might have to use the toilet on the airplane or in the airport. They'd lose their valuable cargo and possibly get arrested.

I had worked through this process with Jude a few times before, and now Harvey would be doing it. He didn't have to do much but other than sit on the sidelines and wait on the package to arrive to him from New York, but he didn't waste any time putting in the double cross. In a matter of two months, Harvey disappeared with a kilo of Jude's heroin. It didn't take Jude long to begin making plans to kill Harvey and everyone he knew. When I got word of this unfortunate turn of events, I was stunned at Harvey's lack of concern for anyone but himself. But I have to admit, I wasn't totally shocked, either.

Several people had warned me not to trust him my former business associate. So, as angry as I was at Harvey, I realized the entire situation was my fault for going against my instincts. Harvey had promised to take care of my daughter, but Harvey didn't do anything he promised, and probably never had any intentions of doing so. It wasn't a surprised that Jude began to question whether or not I was involved in Harvey betraying him, but it was distressing to me because it put me in a tough spot. If Jude had believed that I helped Harvey, he could have retaliated against my family. He could have killed them all and there wouldn't have been anything I could have done about it.

During my incarceration, it seemed like my entire world was falling apart around me. I became extremely bitter about the way many people that I had helped in the past were now treating me. Slowly, I began to realize that nobody in the game gives a damn what happens to anybody else. Most of them might tell you, "Yo, I got your back," and they may think they mean it. But things change and when you're out of sight, you're out of mind. There were people who I had really gone out of my way to help, and they were now refusing to even accept my telephone calls. Some of them even began to treat my family like outcasts since I had been away, almost like they were happy with my circumstance. Even Mike gave me the cold shoulder. I had instructed my daughter's mother to ask Mike to return thousands of dollars I had loaned him to get on his feet after he was shot.

"I've been calling you and leaving messages because Kevin needs the money you owe him," my child's mother said to Mike.

"Tell him I said he's not calling the shots and I don't have shit for him", was Mike's rude reply.

My girlfriend was understandably upset.

"What kind of friends do you have?" she asked. "You helped all of them and now their turning their backs on you. We're in a bind right now, Kevin, and I needed that money for your child." I had flown all the way back to Baltimore from Florida to see Mike on his deathbed and this was how he repaid me.

The only thing that I had left at the time was my daughter and her mother, but even that began to slip away. It's very difficult to maintain a relationship with a woman while you're in prison. No matter how much you may love her or how much she may love you, it's a struggle. If you're only going to be away for one month, you can handle that. But to ask a woman to wait around for you for two years while you're doing time is a really tough request to make. Some women can handle it and some women can't. Most women can't. By no means is that a slight to women, because if the woman was in jail, most men couldn't, or wouldn't, wait around for her.

It's not normal for any person to be without affection and love for an extended period of time. Have you ever been in love with someone and then had to take a long trip for a couple of days, or maybe even weeks without that person? Now multiply that by one thousand and that's the way you feel when your mate is away in prison. You sometimes hear about a woman feeling obligated to wait around for her man while he's away because he was good to her before he left. I think that's a noble thing to do, if you have the will power. The reality is that it's a tough situation to be in. You both have physical and psychological needs. And then there is the distance; the guy may be housed in a prison in Virginia and his mate lives in Maryland. Just a simple visit could be difficult to arrange, especially with an infant daughter.

Going away to prison eventually destroyed every decent relationship I had with women. Suddenly leaving out of a woman's life can be devastating to her. Prior to your abrupt departure, most mornings, she's use to waking up next to the man she loves then, in the blink of an eye, he's gone. And more often than not, he's left a mess that she has to clean up. When you're away from the person you care about the most for long periods of time, it drains the love and compassion that you and that person once shared. The relationship begins to deteriorate because you're just not in that person's space. That's the reality.

In Petersburg I spent a lot of time planning to revitalize my once-bustling drug operation. Even though I made an attempt at a legitimate business when I bought the flower shop, I was never rehabilitated and never fully committed to changing. The money was just too good. Most days were spent developing my business plan. I was attempting to cultivate new drug distribution connections. Federal prison was like a smorgasbord of illegal networking. Everything from Peruvian cocaine to No. 4 heroin refined in the jungles of Burma was available for a lucrative distribution contract on the streets. Counterfeit money and illegal firearm contacts were also available, as international crime syndicates sought American partners to do business with. Many guys were making deals over the phone directly from the prison in clear view of the big sign on the wall that read: ALL CONVERSATIONS ON THIS PHONE ARE MONITORED AND RECORDED.

By the time I was released from prison in the winter of 1995, I was on a mission to prove to the world that my previous success wasn't just a fluke. The flower shop that I owned was close to bankruptcy. A bad deal to start with, the situation had turned very sour in my absence. The real estate investments that I made weren't doing well, either. The term "property taxes" was unfamiliar to my ears, until the city government seized those properties for failure to pay. My source of cash was depleted and I used that as motivation to ignite my engine. In no time at all, I was back in "go" mode and back on the streets. I was bitter because of the way people I thought respected me, treated my family while I was in prison. Bitterness can be a very powerful motivation. You have to be careful what direction it moves you in because it may be luring you onto a path of self-destruction. Prison had done nothing to change my irrational thinking process, because I never really tried to change.

The Mexican contacts I was able to solidify while in Petersburg made good partners for my new business. I flew out to Los Angeles where I could to seal the deal with a handshake. A few months of shipping cocaine coast to coast was profitable, but the relationship was short lived. During the following summer, my rise to the top was halted dead in its tracks once more by an arrest in Los Angeles. Delayed again like the four o'clock train at Penn Station which never seems to make it on time, I had been arrested for paying a mule to smuggle cocaine onto a plane at the Los Angeles International Airport.

The orange jumpsuit worn inside the L.A. County Jail by the inmates didn't fit me very well. Neither did the war that raged on a daily basis inside this urban penal institute. The Crips, the Bloods, and every other gang that laid claim to the sidewalks of this City of Angels, rampaged from dusk to dawn. Jailhouse murders were a common occurrence, as the everlasting beef continued with no sign of slowing down. I had been inducted into chaos and turmoil, where one guy's blood on another man's shank was just a mere bump in the road.

I was finally sentenced in the late summer of 1995 and I was transferred to a state prison located in the middle of the desert of Kern County, California. There I began to serve my three-year sentence. The landscape was desert, valley, and mountain terrain, giving me three for the price of one. There was no human life beyond the fence for miles and miles. This rugged land was intimidating; it was almost like I had been exiled to another planet, far from Earth. There would be no escape; there was nowhere to run.

The gun tower was manned by a sniper every single minute of the day. The shooter stood ready and waiting; death was just a millimeter away. One wrong move and some mother's child would be going home in a body bag. As the natives roamed the prison yard, you could feel the tension in the air. Every knife in the penitentiary had been sharpened and shaved. Every inch of these steel bone-cutters was ready for damage, ready for war. Most of the inmates, including me, wanted to make it home alive to see their families once again.

The two Mexican gangs that controlled this California correctional facility had a deadly beef that could only be resolved through a show of force. The rumor in the prison yard was that it was going down today, so watch your back. This rumor had been making its way around the penal for several days now, as every ear listened intently.

Here in this California prison controlled by gangs, wearing the wrong color wasn't just lack of style; it could get you killed. With the enemy on the prowl, I prayed the Lord my soul to keep. Suddenly, out of the corner of my eye, I spotted the Mexican gangs squaring off. The rumble was going down, now! Armageddon had arrived for the two Mexican gangs as they fought in the center of the prison yard with a vengeance.

Every black and white man in the yard stood back as the two Latin rival's waged war against one another. The neutral stance by the other races was important; it meant that the agreement had been reached to allow the Mexicans to slug it out. Using both hands, one fully tattooed man fiercely jabbed a knife through someone's torso. The victim, who was engaged in another brawl at the time, never saw it coming as the blade separated him from life. At a distance, I could see the blood oozing from the wound as he fell to the ground. One gang member was down and there were fifty more to go. Suddenly, a sound rang out from above as three shots were fired in the direction of the ruckus. I threw myself down because the guards up in the tower were on it and I needed to live another day. I needed to get back home to Baltimore.

Silence prevailed as all four hundred inmates in the prison yard lay flat on the ground, including me. Everyone was hoping to survive because the prison guards were known for their bad aim.

"Down! Down! Down!" the storm troopers repeated, as they responded to the scene in full riot gear. In a matter of seconds, they had encircled the yard and restored order. The shields, batons, and riot helmets made them a force to reckon with. Several of the Mexican inmates had bruises, some had more serious wounds. As calm returned to the yard, the bodies that stayed down were the bodies that stayed down forever. But the talk skinny kid from Edmonson Avenue was still alive.

❋ ❋ ❋ ❋ ❋

The daytime temperatures there normally reached one hundred and ten degrees in the summer, which was unbelievably hot for this East Coast native. Even at midnight, ninety degrees was customary. Back in Baltimore it was a big news story when temperatures reached just ninety-five degrees, so this was unprecedented to me.

One afternoon while I was sitting in my cell, the prison staff told me that I had a visitor, which was a huge surprise. *Who was it that journeyed this far to see me?* I wondered to myself. Other than my Mexican partners down in Los Angeles, I didn't know anyone in California. Maybe those guys had sent some beautiful Mexican señorita over to entertain me. I got dressed and splashed cold water on my face, because I knew a shower at that time wasn't an option. Showers there in the housing unit were designated for a specific time of the day only. In prison, everything moved on a schedule, even washing your rear-end. I brushed my teeth and glanced into the mirror, hoping to look somewhat presentable in my orange jumpsuit. Two guards escorted me down the long hallway to the visiting center, where contact with the outside world was conducted. I was directed to a small room only used for visits from attorney's and law enforcement officials. I asked the guards what was going on. When the door to the small room opened, the once-fuzzy picture became clear.

The two guys standing there wearing cheap suits were either cops or lawyers, neither of whom I had any interest in having a conversation with. As the prison guards began to remove the handcuffs and leg irons, I felt a small sense of freedom returning. I no longer felt bound like cattle and I could now concentrate on the matter at hand. Sitting down at the small steel table, I was uncertain about the situation. The two guys wearing the cheap suits were middle-aged white guys. One of them was very tall and the other was very short. The tall slender man began with, "Hello, Mr. Shird." Yes, they were Baltimore City Police homicide detectives. Their heavy Baltimore accents were a clear giveaway.

The detectives said that they were assigned to the Cold Case Squad, investigating an unsolved murder. In Baltimore, they had gained national recognition for their effectiveness. I was surprised to see them here in California, interested in having a conversation with me. What reason did these guys have to fly all the way here from Baltimore?

The file with photos of Anthony's body was lying in the center of the table. In one of the photos, I could see his blood-soaked clothing clinging to his lifeless body. He was wearing his black full-length leather coat that his mother had given to him as a gift. The sight of my old friend lying dead in a pool of blood was unsettling. These two unwelcome visitors from back east peeled back the scab on wounds that still had not healed.

The short guy chimed in with, "We want to talk to you about the murder of your old friend."

In all the years that had gone by, I never expected this to happen. How much did they know?

"Well, amongst other things, we have an anonymous letter from someone stating that you were Mike's accomplice in the murder of Anthony," one of the men explained. "We don't know who wrote it, but from the handwriting analysis, we know the writer was a female." It was obvious they already had some pieces to the puzzle and it was obvious they were just fishing for the others.

Leaning over the table, I said, very slowly and clearly, "I didn't have anything to do with that. I don't care how many phony letters you got." I was highly agitated by the assertion that I was involved in my friends' death. Regardless of whether they had a letter from someone or not I knew I had nothing to do with Anthony being killed. Were they trying to pin this thing entirely on me, just to close the case? Did a letter exist at all? And if it did, who was the mysterious female who wrote it?

I had been carrying this burden around with me for a couple of years. Even after so much time had passed, I still felt terrible about it because of concealing the truth from Ms. Alternease. She deserved to have closure in the death of her only son. I still felt like I should've stepped to the plate some kind of way. She was a good woman and she deserved an answer. Every moment that I was in her company riddled my soul with guilt. And now the police wanted to talk about it.

The cops said that back in Baltimore, Mike had been arrested for Anthony's murder, but the case was thrown out of court because of lack of evidence. And Anthony wasn't exactly an upstanding citizen, so the state's attorney office was reluctant to pursue the case any further. If he had been a retired schoolteacher from the suburbs, I wondered if his killer would have been pursued to the ends of the earth.

"Look, we know you were close to both Anthony and Mike at one point," said the tall detective. "We also know that Mike killed Anthony for revenge." These guys had been doing their homework. They were close to the truth. "We know Mike did it, but we also know that it will be extremely difficult for us to ever prove this in court." This was my opportunity for me to get this off my conscience and close the book on the entire situation. So I came clean. I confirmed what they already knew.

Mike must have been shaken to his core after being exposed and arrested for the murder of Anthony. I can imagine that the Baltimore City Correctional Center wasn't such a nice place to be for him. Suddenly, his life had been turned upside down; the way Ms. Alternease's life was turned upside down on the night she found out her son was murdered. Anthony never got a second chance, but Mike did. The case against him was dismissed by the court. Shortly afterwards, Mike became an ordained minister at a local church, preaching the gospel to those who would listen. Mike's mother, who was a very religious person herself, was probably very influential in him moving in that direction. What a leap that was! From a cold-blooded murderer to a man of God in a matter of a few years. It seemed as though Mike had decided to clean up his act. There's no doubt in my mind that he came to regret his former murderous ways.

The mysterious hit man who was trying to kill Mike was never discovered, either. And guess what, the doctors in the trauma unit at the hospital who told Mike he would never have a child were wrong. He did have another child giving real meaning to the adage, "God works in mysterious ways."

THE UNDERCOVER BROTHER

My frequent flier mileage between prison systems continued to pile up as I made a trip from the West Coast back to the East Coast in handcuffs and leg irons. After I finished my prison sentence in California in 1997, I was transported to a federal prison in New Jersey to complete a sentence for a probation violation. At the time I was arrested in California, I was still on federal probation, so that arrest was a violation of my terms of release.

There at Fairton, the federal correctional institution in the southern part of Jersey, I met a man named Jesús. His full name was Jesús Flores. Jesús was Mexican and he was from Puebla, which is the fifth largest city in central Mexico. He was a rather short guy, standing around 5 feet 7 inches. He was about forty-nine years old, with slight streaks of gray running through his hair. Jesús had a rather extensive background in the Mexican army, where he was once a high-ranking officer. Taking an odd turn in his career path, he later became a highly sought-after member of a Mexican drug cartel. Jesús and his cartel compadres imported heroin and cocaine into Mexico by way of the Guatemalan border. The heroin had been shipped to Guatemala directly from China, using contacts Jesús had established there. It would later be smuggled into the United States by this crew at the

Arizona and Texas border crossings. This guy wasn't your average drug dealer who packed a pistol to protect bags of weed from the neighborhood stickup kid. He was an international drug importer who moved thousands of pounds of illegal drugs from country to country with a telephone call. Jesús was the type of guy that you only read about in books or saw on the evening news, but would never meet in person. If you were to meet him in public, you wouldn't have any idea what a ruthless man he really was. He was always mild mannered, until he became upset. That was when you would see the fire in his eyes as he erupted like a volcano.

Jesús had been in prison for five years already when we met. He was my cellmate for an entire year and we became friends. When you have to live in a ten-foot-by-ten-foot jail cell with a guy for months on end, there's bound to be some type of camaraderie established.

Jesús was well respected around the prison by everyone, but especially by the Mexican prisoners. Whenever there was a problem among the Spanish-speaking brothers, he would often intervene and resolve the matter. His people looked upon him as a leader, even when he didn't want to assume the role. He preferred to keep a low profile because he was expecting to be released shortly. He figured that he had more important things waiting for him on the outside than squelching a jailhouse beef.

There are some very talented guys behind the fence and Jesús was one of them. He considered himself an expert jailhouse cook who could whip up almost any dish in the penitentiary. Many of his buddies worked in the prison kitchen, so we had access to all types of foods and spices. They'd smuggle tomatoes, green peppers, beef, lamb and chicken out of the kitchen, like mules crossing the border, back into the housing units, where he would cook them. Jesús prepared delicious meals only available to those who lived behind the wall. This was probably nothing you'd want to eat in the streets, but for jail, it was considered gourmet. My only complaint about living with my short Mexican friend was that he snored like crazy. In the prison environment I was a light sleeper, because you never knew when the war could erupt. This guy drove me bananas as he snored the night away, like an out-of-control washing machine. He seemed awfully small to be making so much noise. The ear plugs that we smuggled out of the prison factory helped to silence the noise, but it was still tough getting to sleep some nights. Most of the time, going to sleep before him was the only way I could get a decent night's sleep.

Often, we sat up talking about our families and how we couldn't wait to spend time with them once we returned home. Jesús had three daughters that he adored. When you're in prison and away from your family for so long, you begin to appreciate them much more. The things that you once took for granted are missed beyond description. Jesús and I would often discuss what we were going to do when we were released. He would always describe to me how beautiful México was, with its picturesque settings. I promised him that one day I would make the trip there to visit him.

We'd also discussed our plans of getting back into the business of illegal pharmaceutical sales. Jesús was still well connected with the cartels in Mexico, so he could still get his hands on anything he wanted. That was all I needed to hear before I decided to place all of my chips on the table with him. The Feds had taken almost $2 million cash from Jesús at the time of his arrest, so he was eager to get all of it back. Even after serving years in the pen, he still wasn't finished with the "game", and neither was I.

That was my biggest problem that I still wasn't ready to walk away from the game. The lure of the wealth and the material possessions I could acquire was strong. It wasn't like I was in love with the streets or like I enjoyed being shot at by an unknown assailant. But I felt that I still had one more chance to dance with the devil. But this time, I would have a better plan, so things would be different. My success was assured, I thought. My connection was all the way down in Mexico, so there was no way I could get caught. Jesús and I had our plan together and there was nothing left for us to do but put it into action.

In the late fall of 1998, I was released from prison in New Jersey. My travels around the country secured in shackles were now complete. My daughter's mother was there to pick me up for the ride back home to Baltimore. By this time, our relationship had really taken a serious turn for the worse. I had never thought it would happen, but the years that I had been away had deteriorated the bond we once had. She began dating other men, which really didn't sit well with me. Should she have been faithful to me during all the years I had been imprisoned? Who knows? I wasn't exactly a great boyfriend, either. The fact that she decided to move on with her life shouldn't have been a shock. But it was, and it was painful.

Looking out of the window during the two-hour ride home, my thoughts were calm and calculated. I had discovered patience during my years behind the steel bars, but I still hadn't been rehabilitated. I was determined not to be defined by the time I had spent behind bars, but by my ability to climb to the top once again. The Candy Man was back and just waiting to pitch more goodies to the dysfunctional customers who would pay cash. I was just buying time until Jesús was out of the joint, and at that moment, we would unleash havoc in my bid to once again rule the streets.

In the spring of 1999, Jesús was released from prison and immediately deported to Mexico. He wasn't a U.S. citizen, so it was the normal procedure.

For me, the cycle of criminal activities continued. I was like a drug addict itching to get high, but my addiction was the scent of dirty money. I scheduled an early morning flight to Houston, Texas. Houston International Airport was the largest airport that I can ever remember traveling through. This place was like a small city, featuring every character imaginable. It took me several minutes to get from one side of the airport to the other, maneuvering my way through the cowboy-boot-wearing travelers. When I finally arrived at the gate, I realized that there was a small commuter plane waiting, which turned my stomach. I hated commuter planes because the flights were so bumpy, almost like riding on a roller coaster. This flight to Laredo was probably the most uncomfortable flight I had ever been on. On this warm afternoon, the air turbulence across the Texas skies was unmerciful.

Laredo is located in southern Texas; it borders the famous Rio Grande River, featured in many old Westerns. Just across the Rio Grande was a small Mexican town named Nuevo Laredo, which means New Laredo. In that area was a huge concentration of Spanish-speaking residents. Just about every human being within eyesight was wearing a cowboy hat to shield them from the hot Texas sun. Jesús had suggested that I make reservations at the La Posada Hotel. He told me that I would probably be comfortable there and he was exactly right. When I arrived, I was very impressed with the pink-colored Caribbean-style hideaway. It was upscale, but in a very different, Texas kind of way. I immediately called Jesús, who was down in Mexico in an area called Juarez.

"Buenos dias, Senor Jesús," I said, in my best impression of Spanish.

"Buenos dias, Senor Kevin," he responded, when he answered the phone. He knew it was me. What other black American guy would be calling him in Juarez with such a ridiculous accent?

"Where are you?" he asked.

"I am here in Laredo."

"Do you still have the directions that I gave you?" he asked.

"I do, and I will meet you in Nuevo Laredo, alright?"

"No problem, Kevin. I'll see you tomorrow."

I was drained by the long day of traveling. All I wanted to do now was get a good night's sleep so I would be rejuvenated. I would be going across the border to Mexico early that morning and I really didn't know what to expect there. But I was having a difficult time sleeping. I actually woke up in the middle of the night from a terrible dream that I had been arrested in Mexico.

Morning came very quickly, and the sun was rising high and bright up in the Texas sky. I took advantage of the continental breakfast downstairs in the hotel lobby. The smell of freshly cooked cinnamon buns and fruit was a pleasant way to start my unpredictable trip.

Before I began the journey, I noticed that my directions weren't as clear as I had thought, so I tried to ask for help from the many pedestrians walking past the front of the hotel. My other problem was that I had to first find someone who spoke English. I had difficulty doing that, even though I was still inside the borders of the United States. This was a first for me.

I finally found my way to the river crossing that Jesús told me to take. Off in the distance, I could see the signs marking the way. To my left was a sign that read "Bridge #6;" to my right, a sign labeled "Bridge #5." That bridge went directly across the Rio Grande River and into Mexico. My view of the bridge was clear and I could see pedestrian and car traffic slowly traveling back and forth. I continued walking in the direction of Bridge #5, just as the small piece of paper I was carrying instructed me to do.

Getting across the border into Nuevo Laredo was a snap. It was almost like entering a deserted subway station in New York City at three o'clock in the morning, when virtually no one is around. I had to almost force the Mexican authorities to view my passport upon entry. They had no interest in the black gringo who was hoping to introduce himself to their country.

Nuevo Laredo looked like a snapshot of the Old West in its heyday, when the border towns still hosted gunfights and saloon brawls. There was an open air market selling DVDs and cell phones and other modern electronic devices, but they were not creating much buzz. The sale of Coors Light and apple pie assured me that we weren't far from the USA. The look of the day in this town must have been the cowboy hat, where these Spanish-speaking conquistadors had good fashion sense. The salesmen were standing next to their merchandise in the open-air market shadowing their products. They had the marketing skills of their American compadres from the North, and could really seal the deal, selling their three-dollar Nike T-shirts.

The first law enforcement official I saw in this new frontier looked like a character from an old Western. The revolver that hung low from his holster looked less intimidating than a cigarette lighter. In my mind, I commended this guy for his courage to carry such a laughable weapon to protect the town. If he was able to shoot just one bullet from this tiny contraption, I would've been surprised.

Jesús was sitting at a small café, drinking a Mexican-style cappuccino as he waited.

"What's up, my man?" he greeted me.

"What's up?" I replied. This was the first time that we had seen each other outside of the penitentiary.

"How do you like Mexico so far?" he asked.

"I love it."

"Well, this is nothing, man," he assured me. "After we make a lot of money, I'll take you over to the coast to see Acapulco. The place is beautiful… You'll love it."

He said that he had fifty kilos of cocaine that he wanted to bring across the border.

"I'll send ten to you in Baltimore to get you started, but the rest has to go to Phoenix for my people there." He said the cartel had customs agents that he was paying off to get the drugs through the border. The agents that he had in his pocket were the key to the success of his operation. He and his crew used a red four-door sedan with Texas license plates, to blend in with the weary travelers. Jesús explained to me that a hidden compartment was underneath the rear seats to conceal the stash. The compartment was welded shut with the drugs inside. If the car was ever searched, it wouldn't be found because the only way into the compartment was to cut it open with a blowtorch. There was also the possibility that the drugs would be detected by drug-sniffing police dogs – which were plentiful at the border – so the compartment would also be packed with coffee and perfume to conceal the scent of the cocaine. Jesús and his crew had all of their bases covered.

Once our meet-and-greet was done, I wasted no time getting back to the border. I still couldn't believe I was in Mexico, setting up drug deals. Going back over to the other side of the Rio Grande wasn't as easy as coming into Mexico because the border guards were American. They were a lot more focused than their Mexican counterparts. They had no choice. The United States is the haven of the world, where every Tom, Dick, and Diaz wanted his slice of the American pie.

I was on my way back to Baltimore and the complicated – but potentially prosperous – plan was now in play. The package would be delivered shortly. Instantly, I was in gangster mode, gathering the troops for action. The Diamond in the Raw leader was back to play the game one more time. The self-destructive mentality that led to my downfall in the past had reared its ugly head once again.

Then, out of nowhere, Jesús wanted to change the financial arrangements of the deal. Instead of complete consignment for the drugs, Jesús said he needed money for the down payment. I wondered why he suddenly needed that. It was odd to me that he would change the rules in the middle of the game, but it definitely wasn't unheard of. As I did the math, I concluded that even with money down, ten kilos would easily put me on the map and this deal would pay for itself. In the back of my mind, I still wondered why Jesús had made the change, but I didn't worry because he was my man. We had been in the trenches together, behind the fence. If you could trust anyone, it would be your former cellmate.

Early in the morning of October 28, 1999, I received a call from Jesús on my cell phone.

"What's up, my man, you ready?"

"Yo, what's up, Jesús?"

"The cocaine will be there today. Do you have the money?"

The Jesús that I knew would never use that kind of language over the phone, because of the possibilities that someone was listening.

"I'm good, man, I'm good." I almost hung up the phone on him, but I didn't.

"My people will call you later today when they get to Baltimore, okay? His name is Tony, okay?" Jesús said.

Later on that day, I received a call from a guy named Tony, who said he was working with Jesús. We arranged a meeting at a restaurant near the airport, where we could exchange the money for the drugs. The behavior of Jesús while on the phone made me feel somewhat uncomfortable. I wasn't sure if I smelled a rat or if I was just nervous from being out of the game for a while.

When I walked into the restaurant, the scene had all of the indications that something wasn't right; I could feel it. Something was odd and the Game Gods were trying to give me a hint. But for some reason I didn't respond to the subtle signs that had kept me alive for so many years. I wanted the money and I wanted this deal to go down so much that greed blinded my common sense. Choices.

I walked up to the bar to order a small glass of Pepsi and cognac. Rarely did I ever drink alcohol, especially when I conducted business. This was a testament to my state of mind at the time. I had played this scene out a hundred times before, but something was different this time.

Hurricane's was the name of the bar, next to the Sheraton Hotel by the airport. The place was filled with people from everywhere, enjoying themselves. The social drinkers were putting in their orders with the bartender as others were out on the dance floor. Tony had described himself on the phone as a middle-aged Hispanic man who would be wearing a black jacket. He was supposed to be the guy that helped smuggle the cocaine from out west inside the sedan with the hidden compartment. He said he would be there to collect the cash and drop off the package. I spotted a guy sitting in a booth fitting his description.

"How you doing, man. I'm Kevin," I introduced myself.

"What's up, Kevin? How's everything?"

The uneasy feeling wouldn't go away, yet I pushed on.

"Here's the money me and Jesús talked about," I said, handing Tony the backpack containing $60,000 in cash.

"Give me a minute. Everything's in the car, I'll be right back." Tony got up from the table with the bag of money in his hand, to retrieve the cocaine. This was when all hell broke loose.

Tony hadn't stepped five feet away from the table when someone grabbed my left arm from behind.

"What the fuck!" I shouted. While the person behind me was pulling my left arm backward, another assailant stuck an automatic handgun in the middle of my chest, freezing me. I knew that it was a nine-millimeter because I had been on the other side of that weapon many times before. A third person grabbed me by my neck, placing me in a chokehold while dragging me out of the booth I was seated in. I could hear people yelling, but I couldn't understand what they were saying. Their words were garbled by the fear which seemed to deafen me. That's what happens when you think that you're going to die. The first thing to go is your hearing. At least, it was for me.

With the muzzle of the handgun still firmly planted against my sternum, there wasn't much I could do. If I moved an inch, this guy could have easily blown my heart right out of my body. The plot had been executed perfectly and I was a goner. These guys had clearly gotten the jump on me. Every patron in the watering hole was watching as the killers made their move.

Then, out of the corner of my eye, I could see the face of my assailant. He was a red-faced white guy, screaming at the top of his lungs. *Why would a white guy want to assassinate me?* I thought to myself. The person that was holding my left arm was now twisting very hard. The yelling was escalating, but the voices began to sound clearer. My assailants were actually yelling: POLICE! GET DOWN! DOWN ON THE FLOOR!

What an ingenious plan this is, was my first thought. The killers were pretending to be cops so that patrons inside the bar wouldn't interfere or call for help. This was like something out of an old gangster movie.

Slowly, I began to realize that it wasn't a ruse at all. As this wave of fury subsided, I was able to regain my senses. There seemed to be nine or ten of them. Some of my attackers were dressed in camouflage and wearing bulletproof vests. They all had identification badges hanging from their necks and the badges which read "DEA." That was the moment when I realized I was in big trouble. After the melee ended, the handcuffs were placed on me and I was escorted out of *Hurricane's,* off to another hurricane of sorts.

It wasn't until I arrived at the U.S. District Courthouse in Baltimore from the detention center two days later for my bail hearing that I realized the true scope of my arrest. Sitting there in the courtroom in front of the judge, I began reading the court documents that had been filed against me by the federal prosecutor. Upon reading the truth, all the life was sucked out of me. Tony, whom Jesús had introduced me to, was actually an undercover DEA agent. My main man Jesús, who had shared a prison cell with me, had set me up. My heart dropped and my soul was broken. I was physically in pain. I glanced back at the agents who had arrested me, as they sat in the front row. If it wasn't for the paralyzing effect the situation was having on me, I would have given them thumbs up for a job well done; they had played the player.

The case took some time to work its way through the court system. After tossing every argument from entrapment to insanity up against the wall to see if any of it stuck, my attorney realized he had run out of options. There wasn't much he could do. The case was seemingly cut and dried, as the hard evidence against me continued to mount. Jesús had tape recorded all of the telephone conversations between us. Tony, the undercover agent, had been wearing a wire when he entered the restaurant. And there were pictures of me sitting in Mexico with Jesús, putting together the plan.

I was sentenced to ninety-two months – more than seven and a half years – in federal prison. Once again, I was abandoning my responsibilities as a father to my child. I never found out why Jesús decided to set me up with the Feds. This was the same man who was supposed to be a stand-up guy in prison and an international drug trafficker. The feds must have had something big on him. In the game, you never know who may decide to flip on you or when the dreaded double cross may come.

STEEL HOUSE ON
THE MOUNTAINTOP

My first stop inside the federal prison system this time around was the Federal Correctional Institute Allenwood in Allenwood, Pennsylvania. Allenwood was situated right in the middle of the Susquehanna Valley. During the ride there, the sight of the snow-capped mountains was oddly settling. It was a picture postcard you might see during the holiday season. The mountain walls were so high; they seemed to hang from the sky. This was the coldest place I had ever been, but the view was spectacular; I just would've preferred to see it under much different circumstances.

Allenwood was a fortress of solitude guarded by men of steel. With its layers upon layers of barbed wire fencing, this place was impenetrable. The inner fence was electrified, just in case you were lucky enough to make it that far. There was a forty-foot tower on both sides of the compound, always manned by a sharp shooter with an M-16 rifle, locked, loaded, and ready. Alcatraz had nothing on this place. If there had ever been a prison that was escape-proof, this was it.

Allenwood had been one of the more recently built penitentiaries in the federal system at the time. It wasn't built like some of the older ones, like Lewisburg, Petersburg, or Leavenworth. It was more prisoner-friendly, meaning there was less metal exposed that a prisoner could use to make a weapon. Although Allenwood wasn't a "gladiator school," like many other penitentiaries were, jailhouse murders still occurred. A few weeks before I arrived, another prisoner threw an inmate off of the top tier during a brawl. His fall was about fifteen feet down to the hard concrete floor. The medical helicopter landed in the prison yard to airlift the poor soul to the nearest hospital, but they were not able to save him.

There really is no equilibrium in prison, no real balance. You either belong there or you don't; there is no middle ground. I have met many despicable characters that truly belonged in jail with the key thrown away forever. These guys are the ones that I would never want my mother, my sister, or my daughter to encounter in a dark alley at night. I've also met many guys in prison that have no business being there for the length of time they have been. They could've easily been productive citizens, if not for that one, or even two, bad decisions they made. I've met more guys with 20-, 30-, 40-, and 50-year prison sentences for more non-violent crimes than I care to remember. They had messed up, but were forced to endure punishment far more severe than their crimes warranted. Most of them weren't murderers or kidnappers or child molesters. The majority of them were in prison because of selling illegal drugs. Do I think that if you are found guilty of a drug crime you should not go to jail? No, I do believe you should be punished for your violations. On the other hand, do I think that the system is broken and needs a major overhauling? I absolutely do. In my case, though, I deserved every minute I spent in jail because of my relentlessness. I had no plans of stopping until I was stopped.

There are drug dealers in prison with sentences longer than guys that have been convicted of raping children and elderly women. There is something extremely wrong with our criminal justice system with respect to sentencing. Lengthier sentences for drug convictions are not the answers to fighting illegal drugs. With African-Americans making up only 13% of the population in the United States, but 41.3% of the prison population in America, something is wrong with this picture. The war on drugs doesn't produce any winners, it only produces losers. The biggest losers are the children growing up with no father.

The law library at Allenwood was a place where an inmate could stimulate the intellect. The inmates were in charge of maintaining the law library, with limited input from the prison staff. Here in prison were some of the most intelligent guys I have ever met in my life. There were guys there more versed in federal statutes and the U.S. Sentencing Guidelines than some practicing criminal attorneys I've met. They had to be well-versed, because they were fighting for their lives. Some of the inmates there had cases that went all the way to the United States Supreme Court. Inside the library, you could truly understand how serious things actually are. There were guys that had been fighting their cases for twenty years and more, with nothing to show for it. That was a lot of time invested in trying to have your freedom returned to you. When you're sitting in a prison cell, serving a life sentence, what else do you have to do but fight for your life? I can remember meeting a guy there who had been appealing his case to the appellate courts for seventeen years. He was serving a fifty-five-year sentence for drug trafficking, so the way the laws were when he was sentenced, he had to serve more than thirty-five years before ever being considered for release. He told me that he wouldn't stop fighting for his freedom until the day he died.

Prison is one of the most depressing and dispiriting places on the face of the earth. Upon awakening in the morning, you could find that the guy you were having a conversation with the night before died in his sleep or was killed at the hands of another inmate. The old-timers use to tell stories of how the dead prisoners were treated. They said that when inmates died in prison, their bodies were transported to the local hospital still handcuffed and shackled until a doctor officially certified them dead. Only then were the handcuffs and shackles removed. That really gave you something to think about. I never wanted to be the handcuffed dead guy lying on the stretcher on his way out the front gate of the prison.

There is a huge AIDS and HIV population behind bars, much larger than the national average and in need of serious help. Most of these guys have a really tough time getting the proper medical care they need to survive. As sad as this may seem, most of them are just waiting for the clock to run out because the burden is too great. The healthcare in prisons is very poor. Inmates die all the time from health complications that could have easily been avoided or treated. Even though guys in prison have been convicted and sentenced for violating laws, that doesn't mean that they are not human and shouldn't be treated as such.

Behind the fence, I attended college classes to broaden my horizons. Instructors came in from the local community college a few days a week to conduct the courses. The curriculum was the same taught out at the college campus, so if you didn't study hard, you had no way of receiving a passing grade. This was a good opportunity for me grow intellectually, because education is always a plus, especially in prison. Some guys were even able to receive a master's degree in prison. That was a hell of an accomplishment. A man has to be commended for managing to stay focused while dealing with the anguish of incarceration.

Our biggest sources of information coming in from the outside world were cable news channels and newspapers. There was a small group of us that watched CNN religiously to see what the top news stories in the world were. Unfortunately, most of the other inmates had no interest in world news and could care less what was happening on the outside. Some were just genuinely not interested, but others were desperately trying to block out what was happening on the outside. The pain of thinking about life out in the free world was too much to bear.

Even though we were in prison, we still understood how our current situation and the lives of our families could be affected by events. Plus, the evening news was something that I had always lived for. My father had instilled that habit in me a long time ago. A few weeks after I arrived at Allenwood, the United States invaded Iraq. Many of the inmates, like people all over the globe, had an interest in the matter.

There was one inmate who I actually met earlier, when we were both in the county jail, awaiting sentencing on federal charges. His name was Steve and he was originally from Trinidad. He often stayed glued to the television for information regarding the progress of the war. He was there serving a twelve-year sentence for selling crack cocaine in Baltimore. This guy hated America in a way that I could never understand. I don't know if it was because he wasn't happy with his treatment in the court system or if it was because he was mad at the fact the he got arrested, but he was very bitter. With some guys, you just don't know the exact source of their fury; all I knew was that he had a powerful disdain for the United States.

"Man, I hate this country, I hate this country," he'd mumble repeatedly. "These people here are no good, man, these people are no good." He was a very smart guy, so the way I looked at it, he just had a different opinion than others. If that was what he thought about this country, then so be it. I learned that if you haven't walked in other people's shoes, you should never judge them. His time in the States may have been a terrible experience for him and maybe that was why he hated this country; I had no idea. Nevertheless, the guy had a really strong opinion about why the war in Iraq was started in the first place.

"The United States is no good, man," he said, "the United States is no good. There are no weapons over there, man; there are no weapons over there." He was referring to weapons of mass destruction that the U.S. claimed were in Iraq. This guy would argue with anyone and everyone about this subject. The information that Iraq had missiles was all over the news every day and everyone believed it, except Steve. But in the end, it turned out that he was right. He was just a prisoner confined to a federal penitentiary in the mountains of Pennsylvania, but he could see the trees through the forest.

In 2003 there was a horrible flu outbreak all over the United States, so the evening news began referring to it as the "super bug." People were dying from this flu virus in numbers not seen in the United States in decades. Elderly people and infants were the most vulnerable and were being hit the hardest. The prison population at Allenwood was not spared; the flu outbreak behind the fence was at almost epidemic proportions. The flu vaccine was being rationed there because of a nationwide shortage. Behind the fence it was being saved for the inmates with diseases that weakened their immune systems, which made them more vulnerable to contracting the flu. Because of the small confines of prison, I contracted the flu; I had never been this sick before in my entire life. I'd been sick with the flu before, in prison, but those instances were nothing like this one. The symptoms were unreal, as the sickness attacked every inch of my body. I was aching from head to toe. I felt so weak that I was out of breath by the time I walked from my cell to the inmate showers that were just a few yards away. The congestion in my chest was so heavy I was struggling to breathe. Around the fourth night with the dreaded illness, my situation became worse and I actually didn't think that I was going to wake up the next morning. Because of my high fever, I thought that I was going to die in my sleep. My head was spinning and I was completely discombobulated. I had on several layers of clothing, but I was still freezing cold. Fortunately, I did wake up the next morning. The clothes I wore to bed were soaked because I was sweating profusely all through the night.

In Allenwood, there was a serious gang environment that had to be navigated with caution if you wanted to live to see another day. Gangs had been in prisons longer than I had been going to jail, but this was like none that I had ever seen in a federal prison before. It seemed like there were more gang members on the compound than individuals like myself, who preferred neutrality. I never wanted to be in someone else's gang because I was always my own boss. Anyway, most of the gangs were Hispanic. Even though there were some Crips and Bloods gang members there, the Honduras and Guatemala gangs were feuding with each other almost every day. These guys had no problem cutting each other to shreds over anything from a card game to a bad batch of cocaine smuggled into the prison. Their knives were as sharp as the blades of ninja warriors, and they used them often to skillfully slice and dice their gang rivals.

When the wars were declared among the rival tribes, the prison officials had no choice but to lock the entire institution down. This meant that every inmate in the prison was confined to his cell, sometimes for days, weeks, or even months. This was a sort of solitary confinement for the entire jail until tempers cooled. This tactic usually worked, but only until the next war was on again, only until the competing gangs were back in conflict.

Another inmate at Allenwood I grew fond of was Leonard Rollack, but everyone in the prison called him Pete. Pete was serving a sixty-year sentence for distribution of heroin, for which he was convicted in 1987. He was the co-defendant of New York mob boss, Gene Gotti, the brother of deceased Gambino crime family boss, John Gotti. Pete was one of the biggest heroin traffickers to ever come out of notorious Harlem, New York. I met Pete in the prison yard early one morning while doing pull-ups, when I first arrived at Allenwood. He knew that I was new to this steel house on the mountaintop. You can always tell when a guy is new in the joint, because for the first couple of days there's always this look on his face like, *where the hell am I?*

Pete and I hit it off right away. He was one of the coolest guys I had ever met, in or out of prison. He also was one of the smartest guys you would ever want to come in contact with. Pete was what some people would refer to as a "jailhouse lawyer." Because of the vast amount of knowledge Pete had pertaining to federal law, many of the inmates turned to him for help and advice. He was much-sought-after in a place where men could only dream of things as simple as walking down the street.

Because there were no weights at Allenwood to workout with Pete organized a yoga class, and I used to wake-up at 5 a.m. in the morning to attend. We'd walk down to the gym in the blistering cold of the unforgiving mountain winds. The guards usually had the doors of the gym unlocked and waiting, as the heaters in the building battled the early morning chill. This wasn't exactly a yoga class like those you would attend in the regular world. It was actually a DVD we viewed on the television set inside the gym. This was the first time I had ever done yoga before. I thought this was a feminine workout or for soft guys who couldn't handle the strain of lifting weights. This workout quickly made a believer out of me, as the muscles in my arms in legs burned with every movement.

Later on in the day, I'd walk around the prison yard with Pete, as we loosened up a bit from the earlier morning exercise. The conversations we had were enlightening, as I sought direction for a better life. The pressure of being imprisoned in these mountains was weighing heavily on my thoughts and mind as I wondered what to do next. Listening to Pete gave me a better understanding of life and where I fit into it. Pete used to say, "Everyone has a place in this world, but the tricky part is to figure out where your place is."

I remember saying to him, "Pete, do you ever get tired of this shit?"

"Man, I got tired a long time ago," Pete answered. "Now I am just numb. I have been behind this fence for almost twenty years now. I keep on fighting my case because I have a kid to get back out there to. That's why I keep on fighting."

"Do you ever feel like giving up?" I asked.

"I feel like giving up all the time, but I won't. My son is a lawyer now and I promised him that I would be home one day to see him defend one of his cases in court. I told him that he better not lose." We both laughed.

The snow, the rain, and the hail: all the elements began to feel exactly the same, as the pressure numbed my body from head to toe. As I roamed around the prison yard, the rain unleashed from the clouds above rolled down my face, but I couldn't feel it anymore. My heart and soul were stale, almost inhuman. I was like a zombie, but inside, I was fighting to stay alive. I could've easily given up and succumbed to the negativity around me, but that one last ounce of hope was saying, "You got to stay focused."

Life in this lonely mountainous region of central Pennsylvania behind the fence was a struggle. The environment was brutal and could eat a man alive. The only way to survive here was to watch your front and watch your back, all at the same time. But you also had to be thinking about what was next for you. If you were fortunate enough to avoid having a sixty-year sentence, like Pete had, one day you would be back in the streets. It could be sooner or it could be later, but one day you were walking out of the prison gate. Unfortunately, some guys would go to their deaths behind the wall, handcuffed and shackled, until the coroner gives the thumbs down. Not one day went by where I wasn't thinking about what was next for me. If I was still alive, what was I going to do when I hit the streets? I was sick of doing time behind the barbed-wire fence. The bottom line for me was this: I was never coerced into selling drugs. I made a conscious decision to get involved in something that I knew was wrong from the very beginning. At some point, I had to take responsibility for my actions. The obstacles I now had to overcome were the price I had to pay for my decisions. Taking responsibility is the only way that I could turn the page and move on. Regardless of roadblocks, the ultimate decision to do the right thing rested with me.

MAKING THE CHANGE

In the winter of 2004 I was transferred from Pennsylvania to the Federal Correctional Institute Fairton in New Jersey to serve the remaining portion of my sentence. The prison was located in rural south central part of New Jersey, about fifty miles southeast of Philadelphia and forty miles west of Atlantic City. With federal incarceration, you never know when you're going to be transferred to another prison. Sometimes an inmate is transferred in order to have him housed closer to his home, but oftentimes, it is done for disciplinary reasons. It's a form of punishment, transferring a prisoner to a Colorado prison when his family lives in Boston. In some cases, you could be transferred from Maryland to Texas without any explanation at all, leaving you scratching your head. Luckily for me I landed in New Jersey, which wasn't far from my home, with exactly two years remaining before my release.

At Fairton I was reunited with Abdul Hakim Ali, whom I met several years earlier while serving a parole violation at the same prison. Actually, we met around the same time that Jesús was my cellmate. Back then I didn't know much about Ali other than the fact that he was Muslim and he was a very good handball player. Actually he was a great handball player. But later

I discovered that he was an even better human being. Back in those days I was still focusing on doing the wrong thing, so we didn't have much in common, other than an occasional game of handball.

Ali was a native of the tough streets of Brooklyn, New York. He was serving a life sentence for a jailhouse murder he committed in California in 1974. He had previously been an Army soldier, stationed in North Carolina. Ali was originally convicted of stealing Army equipment from the base and selling it to civilians. He was sentenced to seven years in prison for those crimes, but while serving his sentence, he became involved in a prison gang. He was very young at the time and made a very devastating decision. There was a fight between him and another inmate from a competing gang. Ali stabbed the guy and killed him. He was convicted and sentenced to life in prison for the murder. Some of the same gang members who had sworn their allegiance to Ali testified against him at his trial, helping the prosecutors send him away with a life sentence.

Ali was the leader of the Islamic community inside the prison. He would always greet me with, "As-Salaam-Alaikum," which in Arabic, means "peace be upon you." At the time I wasn't involved in Islam, but I always showed respect for the religious beliefs of others.

"How have you been, man? It's been years," I greeted him.

"I've been okay," Ali answered. "How's that handball game?" We both laughed. "Well, I'm still the champ on the compound, so whenever you're ready, we can get a game in." Other than in a competitive sports challenge, Ali was a very mild-mannered and humble man.

"How's your family been?" he asked. "Is everything okay at home?"

"They've been doing well."

Ali and I began to talk a lot during this second tour for me at FCI Fairton. He could tell that I was in a different place in my life; I wasn't the same kid he met on the handball court a few years earlier. I wasn't looking for a drug connection to make a move with once I hit the streets. I had grown weary of the game. I realized I had to do something different. I knew that my life needed to be in a different place, I just wasn't sure how to get there.

It was Ali who helped me open my mind to spirituality, and recognize that I needed to involve a Higher Power in my transformation. He enlightened me about the religion of Islam, which I never truly understood. When I was growing up, I attended Christian churches with my family. I always prayed, but I never really felt connected with the religion. I attended Bible study and church services, but I never quite got it. While sitting in the church on Sunday, listening to the preacher deliver his sermon, I was never moved by his words. I never really felt like I had a place in the religion, although I believed there was a God.

With Islam, things were different for me in that I could feel the spirit and I felt attached to the religion. My understanding of God was clear, giving me the sense that I belonged there. Internally I struggled with my conversion and how I would explain this to my family. I had to do something to help me find the God that I always knew existed, but had so far been unable to find. I had to do what I thought was best for my own growth. Islam helped me see the world through a more humbling lens. I truly believe that Islam helped me become a better man. I remember one day asking Ali what was he before he converted to Islam and he replied, "I was nothing before Islam."

As head of the Muslim community, Ali led all of the prayer services, including Jumu'ah, every Friday around noon in the prison chapel. The sense of brotherhood there was something that I had never experienced before. Rarely in prison did I ever get the feeling that someone actually cared about my well being, but this was different. Because FCI Fairton was located so close to Philadelphia – which is twenty to thirty percent Muslim – the Muslim population there was larger than any other prison in the federal system. Prison officials were very sensitive to needs of Muslim inmates because religious services in prison help the inmates find a common ground. Prison officials also realized that the majority of the Muslim prisoners stayed out of trouble for the most part. The first time I observed Ramadan was a real challenge. Ramadan is the ninth month of the Islamic lunar calendar and during that month, Muslims around the world are required to spend the daylight hours fasting. You're not allowed to eat or drink until sunset. Not only is fasting done in the Islam religion, but there are many other religions that incorporate fasting into some part of their religious observance.

In Fairton I had a job in the education department as a GED tutor; I helped prisoners prepare to take the GED test. Most of these prisoners were genuinely looking for a better life for themselves once they were released. My salary was only fifty cents a day, and that is not a misprint. 50¢. I could have made more money working in a rice field in Korea. But the job was very gratifying to for many reasons. For one thing, I had access to all of the books and educational material that I wanted. I also was able to help other guys who really needed assistance. For the first time in my life, I met grown men who didn't know how to read or write. This was a real humbling experience for me. How in the world could anyone release a man from prison who doesn't know how to read, and expect him to be successful on the outside? How could he or she ever find a decent job to support themselves?

I had become obsessed with running when I was in Fairton. For about two straight years, every morning I'd wake up, eat a bowl of oatmeal, pray, and be in the recreation yard by the time the sun was up. I'd run about three to four miles, through rain, sleet, snow, or even the heat of the summer sun. The iPod was still a far off possibility, but I had my Walkman and it worked like a charm. Tunes from Jay-Z's *The Black Album* were my theme songs, as I ran for miles to alleviate the stresses of incarceration. I was in good shape physically and my health was the greatest it had been in my life. I knew I had a lot of work to do when I hit the streets to put my life back together and I wanted to be up to the task.

I had a pretty good grade point average in the college classes I was taking at Fairton. Just as in Allenwood, instructors came in from the local community college. I was getting closer to my release date and realized that I had a lot of ground to make up. Business law, marketing, and business management were the only courses that I took during that final semester. I loved going to college classes and getting ready for the outside world. I realized that I would still be behind, regardless of what I was able to do on the inside, so every little bit of knowledge I could get was important. Continuing to educate myself was also good for self-confidence. Knowing that you're doing everything you possibly can to help yourself is always a plus.

One day I was walking down the compound on my way to my housing unit when I heard Ali calling my name. "At seven o'clock, meet me out in the yard, I've got some good news," Ali said, as he proceeded down the walkway. I wasn't sure what he wanted to talk about, but it was no big deal. We regularly met in the yard at night to walk the track and talk about current events, sports and family. Ali and me had become good friends and a viewed him as if he was a real brother.

At seven o'clock, I was in the yard, waiting for Ali, when I saw him running through the recreation yard gate. "I went to see the parole board today," Ali informed me. I knew that he had met with the board several times before and was denied parole. For years the parole board hadn't felt that he was ready for release, even though his crime was committed thirty years earlier. "Today the parole board granted my release," Ali said with a big smile. "They gave me a date for this November."

"That's great news, man," I told him. He had been in prison a very long time and now he was going home to be with his family. He had been going back and forth with the parole board for years, trying to convince them that he was a changed man. Convincing someone that you've changed can be a difficult task when you've committed a murder, but anyone can turn their life around. This man was finally going home, after thirty-one years in prison. That had almost been as long as I had been living on the earth.

The evening before Ali went home, we spent some time together walking the track in the prison yard for the very last time. He was anxious to leave, but he was also uneasy. He hadn't been in the streets for three whole decades.

"Man, I'm really nervous," Ali told me, as we walked around the track for the final time. "I'm nervous, but I can't wait to get my life back." I couldn't even imagine what he was feeling because I hadn't been in a situation like that before. I had been released from prison before, but not after spending three decades inside.

"One thing I do know is that you're going to be okay," I told him. "With all of the work you've done here to turn things around for yourself, I can't see things going any other way."

"Thanks, man. I hope you're right. I've been gone for over thirty years. I got a lot of catching up to do. Ford was the president when I first came to jail." Over the thirty years that he had been in prison, Ali had done everything under the sun to become a better person. There was no doubt in my mind that his adjustment back into society would be successful. If anyone could make it, Ali could.

The next morning, it seemed like the entire prison wanted to greet him on his way out of the gate. I had never seen anything like it before, where everyone – from the good guys to the bad guys and down to the guards – was hoping for one man's success. So many inmates were stopping him on his way out to wish him good luck that someone had to tell him to stop talking and start walking. After serving thirty years, no one wanted him to miss his ride to the bus station. It was really inspiring for me to see Ali walk out of the prison gate. It really gave me something to look forward to.

I knew that my day was coming soon and I spent a lot of time putting together a plan for myself. What would happen if I used that same energy I had used in illegal activities to now build something positive? How would I fare? I was tired of playing this same old game. I needed something new. There are millions of successful people out in the world enjoying life, and most of them aren't involved in illegal activities. Most of them will never spend a day in prison, so why did I have to continue doing so? The majority of people in this country that are in prison have done something wrong to get there. That isn't to say that there is no one in prison that is innocent, but the majority of the people have done something wrong.

What if, just what if, I went out there and worked my but off and did the right thing? That's not to say that I had to get a job at McDonald's flipping burgers for the rest of my life or get a job sweeping streets forever. But what if I was willing to be patient and build a life for myself from the ground up, legally? As I contemplated the idea, there really was no down side. The way I looked at it, I could only see a huge upside. The biggest and brightest part of the upside was that I would never have to see the inside of a prison cell again.

When I was at Fairton, I worked hard to stay involved in everything I could that was positive, things that aided in my personal growth. Because that's what change is all about, right? Associating with people who want to do the right thing is always a good thing. I enrolled myself in a prisoner re-entry program there named the Choice Program. The Choice Program dealt with every issue imaginable, from criminal behavior and gambling to drug and alcohol addiction.

The guys in my class wanted me to write and present our speech for the class graduation. Most of the guys were going home the following day, so for many of us, this would have been our final day as a group. Most of us were hoping that our classmates would have success once they hit the streets. At first I was reluctant to deliver the speech, but in the end I decided that this would be a good opportunity for me. Public speaking was something I had dreaded, so this was a good chance to start getting used to doing things differently. And this is exactly what I said on that day to my graduating class and the prison staff who listened in:

"Good afternoon ladies, gentlemen, and invited guests. On behalf of my classmates, I would like to welcome you to another Choice Program graduation. When I first decided to write this speech, I wasn't sure what topic to begin with. We all have a story to tell. Before I started the Choice Program, I realized that I might have had a few issues to deal with. By the time I completed the program, I uncovered more issues with myself than I could count, even with the help of your fingers. Now I realize I have many, many stories to tell.

"One of the many benefits of this program is that it forces you to take a very in-depth look at yourself. That is exactly what this program has done, amongst other things, for me and for my fellow classmates. At some point in a man's life, he has to do some soul searching. Gentlemen, for most of us, IT'S TIME TO TAKE THE MASK OFF.

"A man that truly wants to change his life is faced with some very difficult challenges. One of those challenges will be for him to recognize that at some point, he can become his own worst enemy. The biggest obstacle between himself and a new life is that little voice inside of his head, that same little voice that may have brought him here to this institution. You know the one that I am referring to. The one that says 'he's lame' or 'that guy's a bird' or 'only a sucker would learn something from this program.' How about when that little voice says, 'I'm a real man' or 'this is just part of the game'? Maybe that little voice is right; this is part of the game. And guess what. We've all just been played. The 15-minute telephone calls, the lonely mothers, wives and children that we left behind, and the strip searches after a visit, where we have to stand naked in front of some strange man, no longer seem like an even trade. Again, IT'S TIME TO TAKE THE MASK OFF.

"When I make reference to taking the mask off, I am referring to the image, or façade, that several of us feel we have to portray. Many do this to be accepted by their peers. Many others use the mask as a form of security blanket. Some of us have spent many years of your lives trying to be the best gangsters, thugs, and G's that we could be; we've lost our own identities. Some of us don't know who we are or who we'd like to become. I'd like to suggest a small experiment. For one day, try being the best you that you can be. Who knows? You may just like yourself.

"One of the most profound and righteous things a man can do in his lifetime is to leave a legacy behind, a legacy that others can duplicate in an effort to enrich their own lives, socially, spiritually as well as economically. Four months ago, a man respected and admired by many died of cancer. This man's name was Johnnie Cochran. He was one of the most successful and prosperous attorneys in American history. This man routinely drew many comparisons to former Supreme Court Justice Thurgood Marshall. Prior to his death, Mr. Cochran was asked the question, what are the keys to his success? He answered that question by stating that there are three keys to success: Preparation… Preparation…Preparation.

"If a man is not prepared to take full advantage of an opportunity when it appears, how can he expect any real success? Every man in this room has an opportunity to be successful. It is up to him as an individual. The man who decides to enrich himself with knowledge and education, that man enriches himself forever. Suddenly, many doors that were once closed become open; increasingly, many barriers that once stood in his way begin to fall down.

"CHARACTER, gentlemen. One of the most underrated and under-emphasized human traits afforded mankind. Look at the man sitting next to you. Go ahead, take a look at him. Is this the man that you would allow to sit at the dinner table with your family? Is this the man that you would allow your daughter to marry? Or for that matter, your mother to marry? At some point, we have to analyze our own character. Not the character that many of us masqueraded as in the life, but the true character that exists within all of us. A great historian once said, "Show me a man with character and I will show you a man," making reference to the man that supports his children. The man that is loyal to his wife and family. The man who can be trusted; the man that can hold the door open for a woman to walk through, only as a genuine courtesy. As we attempt to re-enter society, this is an issue that should not, and must not, be overlooked. 'Character' is a word that needs redefining within all of us.

"In the mid-eighties there was a popular saying that went 'What have you done for me lately?' With that in mind, I would like to pose a few questions to you. What have you done for your rehabilitation lately? What have you done to increase your chances of success once you are released back into society? What have you done to prevent yourself from returning to Fairton's fine dining facilities? Each man in this room is eventually going home. That is almost guaranteed. What is not guaranteed is our ability to stay home. That is where the really hard work begins. We now have the skills to recognize faulty thinking. We now understand what 'mollification' means. The words 'cognition' and 'entitlement' are no longer foreign to us. With the correct rational thinking skills being applied, there is no doubt in my mind if I can be successful. With the proper rational thinking skills applied, there is no doubt in my mind that every man in this room can be successful. Gentlemen, again, IT'S TIME TO TAKE THE MASK OFF!

"I have been incarcerated for several years at this point. I have seen just about any and every situation imaginable in the prison environment. But yet and still I remain astonished by the huge amounts of talented men that exist behind these fences. There are enough tradesmen, academics, philosophers, and genuinely intelligent men here on this compound to run a small country. There are thousands, if not millions, of people in the world today with the potential to become leaders or successful in some capacity. Many of those individuals, possibly unbeknownst to them, are seated amongst us in this room as we speak. Ask yourself this question: 'Am I one of them?' Thank you."

I wasn't sure how my speech would be received, but I just went for it. The worst thing that could have happened was that some sociopath who didn't like something that I said would walk up and stab me. Fortunately, that didn't happen. I was extremely surprised to receive an ovation from the prisoners and staff who attended this ceremony. It was almost like a going home celebration. Guys were clapping and whistling, showing their appreciation for the words that I had just spoken to them. Everyone in the room could feel the message that I was trying to convey. They could feel that I had meant every single word that I had said. Even the associate warden, who I had issues with, pulled me aside to congratulate me on a well-delivered speech. This was one of the very few times I ever felt appreciated while in prison. I was actually holding back tears; prison is definitely not the place for a man to show that type of emotion.

I wanted to get a good night's sleep but I couldn't. I was going home the next day and my mind was racing like cars on a NASCAR speedway. I believe that I only slept for three short hours that night. The only reason that I even slept at all was the complete exhaustion of being so wired up. Mr. Cool had finally come undone. I was so anxious that I couldn't relax for one second. I was pacing back and forth around the cell throughout the night, anticipating ten o'clock the next morning, when the gates would open up for me to enter the new, exciting world that awaited me on the other side.

The first thing I did that morning when I woke up was pray. God had gotten me to a place where I would be seeing my family shortly and I prayed that he would continue with me on my journey. My daughter was 13 now and the second thing that I did was to call to tell her that I was coming home. When I called her, it was very early and she was barely awake. I only spoke to her briefly and I wasn't even sure if she could understand what I was saying. I wasn't sure if she could understand that I would be home in a few hours.

This was finally my day to join the Free World Club, whose membership was open to anyone who appreciated it. I was excited, but I was trying to stay subdued about the fact that I was finally walking out of this prison. All the days and nights when I had dreamed about this moment were finally coming to reality.

Zegory and Brandon, my nephews, had sent clothes to the prison for me to wear home. I could still remember the years when they were younger and I'd take them shopping at the mall. But now they were taking care of me. It felt strange when I put those new clothes on because I hadn't worn street clothes for many years. I realized that from here on out, almost everything that I did would feel strange because I would be doing it all as a free man. Walking down the street would feel strange. Getting a snack out of the refrigerator in the middle of the night would feel strange. Being able to hug my child when she's had a nightmare would seem strange. All of the simple things in life that I had taken for granted would now be returning to me, but this time I would appreciate them.

I was glad to be leaving, but I had to stay focused on everything that I had learned while I was inside. As easy as it would be to walk out of the gate on that day, it could be just as easy to walk right back in the next week. Far too often a guy leaves prison to only forget all the valuable lessons he learned, or should have learned, on the inside. For some guys, as soon as they hit the streets, they forget that they were ever incarcerated. The behavior that sent them to prison in the first place unveils itself at their welcome home celebration. They're sucked right back in, like through a straw, to this poisonous milkshake of malice and misbehavior.

GAME OVER

The rain had just ended and the skies were still gray on this early morning in the winter of 2006, as I stepped outside of the prison gate. The south Jersey winds were blowing hard and Mother Nature seemed tired on this discomforting day. The air was cold enough to chill my face, but I didn't care, because it was time to go home. When I first stepped outside, I still wasn't certain that it was real. There was one guard standing inside the final checkpoint, holding a shotgun, to protect the perimeter. For the right reasons, he wouldn't hesitate to shoot, so as I walked past him, I was still feeling nervous. Not until I was at least one hundred miles from the place would I be sure this bad dream was over. The shuttle was waiting on the other side of the front gate. The ride from Fairton to the public bus stop was about ten very long minutes. Even in the dead winter in southern New Jersey, my palms were sweating from the anxiety. Once we finally made it to the bus stop, I started to relax. Finally, I thought to myself that maybe it wasn't just a dream and maybe I was a free man after all. It took about forty-five minutes for the bus to arrive. I would take the public bus to Philadelphia and then from there, I would take a Greyhound bus down to Baltimore.

There inside the bus terminal in Philadelphia, the usual suspects paraded past the stage. Everything from the very bizarre to the very crazy was on display on this overcast morning. One unfortunate fellow standing over in the corner was having a heated argument with himself that he was sure to win. The bus station hustlers were patrolling the depot, as they sought to make a quick buck. Eventually, "All aboard to Baltimore," sounded over the intercom. It was in the middle of midday rush hour when the bus finally pulled away from the City of Brotherly Love. The ride to Baltimore would take four long hours.

Navigating through the horrendous traffic straight down I-95 was a difficult task in the beginning, as the Greyhound bus inched its way south. The view from the interstate was nothing new to me, although it had been some time since I last traveled the corridor. The older gentleman sitting next to me seemed very relaxed and comfortable. He didn't have a problem leaning his head over to my side of the seat every couple of miles as he slept. I wasn't in the least bit pleased with that, but I didn't think that he meant any harm. The baby that was crying in the back of the bus wasn't a big deal, although I could see some of the other passengers beginning to get annoyed. The U.S. Army soldier who seems to be on every commercial bus that I've ever been a passenger on was sitting at attention. I couldn't tell if he was on his way home from Afghanistan or slowly making his way there to the battlefield. The grandmother who is on every single one of these long rides was still knitting her yarn. The baby socks she was carefully crafting were almost finished.

Looking out of the window off into the landscape seemed like a dream that I hoped I would never awaken from. The feeling of euphoria was overwhelming for the man who had just been released from the penitentiary. I can remember how I used to count the days remaining on my prison sentence. As each day went by, I would put a large "**X**" over the date on my calendar, just like in the movies. I had made my way through the eye of the storm and now I was standing on the other side of the ocean, where the sun was shining bright. The small tear that I had fought off for most of the morning began to make its way to the surface. This droplet was a result of the many years of pain I had inflicted on myself. I had made it, I knew that now. I understood that I had been rewarded with another chance.

Off in the distance I could see a highway sign, but my 20/40 vision began to cheat on me. As the bus got closer, I could now see the sign that read, "WELCOME TO DELAWARE." For many years I had traveled up and down this East Coast corridor, usually on my way to or from New York City while involved in crime. On each of those trips, a swift tour through the state of Delaware was almost mandatory because of the way the small state bordered Maryland. Once I reached it, depending on the traffic, I was about an hour and a half from Baltimore. Just then, I realized that I wasn't far from the place I once called home. Soon, the Greyhound was making its way out of the Harbor Tunnel toward exit 53. From I-95, this view looked very familiar to the man who was now returning home.

"Are you getting off here in Baltimore?" a voice asked me. The older man sitting next to me was now awake and attempting to strike up a conversation.

"Yes, sir," I replied. "This is my stop."

"Are you from here, from Baltimore?"

"Yes, this is where I am from and I am glad to be home," I replied.

"Where are you coming from?" the gentleman asked.

I was reluctant to give him a truthful answer, but under the circumstances, a vague one would do. "I've been in New Jersey for a couple of years, working." I stumbled a little, hoping that my deception wasn't obvious. "I'm just glad to be back."

"What kind of work were you doing there?" the man inquired.

"I was a teacher," I said, stretching the truth by at least a light year. I couldn't tell the man that I had just been released from the penitentiary; I just didn't feel comfortable talking about that to a stranger.

"I haven't been to Baltimore since the 1970s," the older man said. "I had a girlfriend here that I used to visit before I went to Vietnam. She once lived near a street named Pennsylvania Avenue. Do you know where that street is located?"

"Yes, I know exactly where that is," I answered. "Is your friend still living there?"

Suddenly, I could see that I touched a nerve with the gentleman.

"No, she's not around anymore," he replied in a sad voice. "She was stabbed and killed by a drug addict who broke into her house to get money for drugs. Baltimore is a really tough place, young man." I could tell that the memory of the deceased woman was still a hole in his heart.

Minutes later, the Greyhound pulled up in front of the downtown station.

"Okay, sir, this is where I get off," I said to the man, as I stood up to leave. "Are you going inside?"

"No," the man replied, "I'm not getting off until we reach Richmond, Virginia."

"Okay, well, take care of yourself. This is my stop." I reached up on the rack over my seat to grab the small backpack

I had been carrying. As I reached the aisle, the older man smiled.

"You take care of yourself, too, young man, wherever you're coming from." I was off the bus when it finally dawned on me what the man had just said. Did he somehow know that I had just been released from prison? Was it that obvious? Suddenly, I realized that he probably knew all along.

It was a swift taxi ride to my new residence at the half-way house, as the cold began to settle in on the early evening. The halfway house was once a hotel; it had been converted into a place where people newly released from prison could stay during their transition back to the streets. During the daytime, you would be allowed to go out to work a normal job, and then return in the evening. This transitional period would usually last from one to six months, giving the newly-released person time to adjust to the real world. For guys who had been incarcerated for years, or even decades, this re-entry process can be vital to their success.

"This is 4601 East Monument Street," the taxi driver with the heavy West African accent said to me as we pulled in. "Is this the place you were looking for?"

"This is it," I said to the driver, as I paid him with some of the exit money a prisoner is given when he is released. It was very strange to me to feel cash in the palm of my hand. Just about everything felt strange in my newfound world of freedom. I grabbed my belongings and stepped out of the cab. Inside the halfway house, there were guys standing all over the place, chatting with one another. Surveying the landscape, I realized that there was no barbed wire or gun tower in sight. If you wanted to just pack up and leave, you were free to do so. Slowly, reality began to settle in: I was really free after all.

"Hello. What's your name?" the woman standing at the desk inside the main lobby said with a smile.

"My name is Kevin Shird."

"Okay, Mr. Shird, we were expecting you. I have some paperwork for you to fill out so that we can get you settled in, okay? If you have any questions, don't hesitate to ask. Oh, yeah, Mr. Shird, just to let you know, we don't refer to you guys as inmates here. You're no longer behind the fence. Here we refer to you guys as residents."

That sounded very good to me.

My new surroundings still seemed strange, as I began taking baby steps in the direction of a normal life. I walked down to the lower level of the building, where several pay phones were located. They were all outside, where the temperature dropped as the sun began to set, but I didn't care. It felt strange putting quarters into the phone now to make calls; I hadn't done that in a few years. I felt awkward not hearing that stupid recording on the line saying, "THIS IS A PREPAID CALL FROM A FEDERAL CORRECTIONAL FACILITY." The first call I made was to my daughter, who would have just gotten home from school.

"Hello, Brooke, this is your father. I'm home. I'm over in East Baltimore, in a place on Monument Street." For the first time in years, I was able to talk to my daughter longer than fifteen minutes. After speaking with her, I called my mother.

The first few hours after arriving at the halfway house, I began making an inventory of personal things I would need, like a toothbrush and deodorant. Then suddenly, something dawned on me. I realized that I only owned one pair of underwear. More than anything else so far, this thought bought things into perspective for me. I needed to make a phone call to ask someone to bring the former hustler and leader of the pack a few pairs of underwear. Everything that I once owned was gone: the cars, the houses, and the cash, all gone. I would now have to rebuild my life from the ground up, one brick at a time. The best thing I had going for me now was that my head was clear and my mind was focused. I knew exactly what I needed to do to continue on the path of redemption. One thing I was sure of was that I couldn't go back to prison; I didn't have it in me.

In the halfway house, where many are running wild, it's easy to fall prey to the evils that dwell there. A man recently released from prison is a vulnerable creature to begin with. He can easily become mesmerized by all the attractions and distractions around him. The same temptations that sent him on his original journey await him with a vengeance. Even in the halfway house, the level of mischief and game can rise above common sense very easily. With access to the world right at your fingertips, bad decisions are just a phone call away—crafty women, drugs, guns, and pushers. This smorgasbord of relapse is constantly blinking its illegal eye at the gentleman who may really want to change his life.

Even with the portable breathalyzer sitting at the front desk as you entered the building, Mr. Jack Daniels becomes a close friend to many of the residents. The mandatory weekly urinalysis was not a deterrent for those anxious for a bag of heroin and the occasional blast from the past. Not every single man or woman released from prison is necessarily trying to do the right thing. Some have no intentions of moving in the direction of the straight and narrow. Just as I was making plans to turn away from crime, others had made plans to embrace the game with open arms, just as I had the last time I was released.

Nowadays, I began to wonder who the hell would go through all of the things you have to go through to get out of prison, just too immediately return. This seems to me like the man who enjoys pain and suffering in the worse way; the man who would ignite a cigarette lighter and observe the flame as he holds his hand over it, burning his flesh. Walking out from behind the barbed wire was no easy task to begin with, and walking right back in was not on my agenda.

Early on, I was intimidated by my new world, as I continued to make the adjustment to it. Everything had changed and the streets no longer looked familiar to me. Where there was once a street, there was now a park, with trees lining the landscape. Where there was once a park, there was now a street, filled with cars and pedestrians. Many of the buildings and structures that fill the skyline now weren't there in the past.

The time that I spent away had definitely taken its toll on me. Physically, I was in the best shape of my life. I could have easily run a marathon. Psychologically, I noticed some side effects from the many years of anguish I had endured. My first thought was that the mental wounds would heal over time. But one day, I wasn't so sure.

I had only been in the halfway house for about three weeks. I was in the Towson Town Center, window-shopping, with little money in my pockets, just like many people do. Walking past The Gap store was interesting because I could remember shopping there many years ago; now styles had changed. The Apple Store was intriguing as well, even though I dared not walk into the place. As boggled as my mind already was by everything new and unfamiliar, I wasn't ready to take on the latest iphone. Walking past the Victoria's Secret store was very interesting, for obvious reasons. Then I caught the unmistakable scent of freshly-cooked pizza coming from the food court. So I dug deep down inside of my pockets in search of currency to of course purchase a slice.

Eating pizza in the mall is an American ritual that is enjoyed by many. It's like eating popcorn at the movies or having a latte in the morning at the local Starbucks. Pizza becomes a temporary, but satisfactory, reward for the forty-hour work week well done.

I walked away out of the food court while eating my slice pizza, when I suddenly experienced a mental lapse that scared the hell out of me. I stopped cold. Was it okay to walk through the mall while eating? For a split second, I didn't know. I had to ponder whether or not I would be penalized for my enjoyment. This was the weirdest thing in the world.

Back when I was inside the fence, it was a violation of the prison rules for an inmate to take food out of the dining area. More often than not, your punishment would be light, but it was still a punishment for breaking the rules. When it dawned on me that I was even pondering this situation, it completely freaked me out. This was when it became very clear that the many years I had been in prison had taken their toll on me. This was when I realized that I needed to take things slow.

The severity of the negative mental effects of being incarcerated varies from person to person. Some guys, once they are finally released, can experience what I can only describe as a form of post-traumatic stress disorder. The symptoms can sometimes be subtle and barely noticeable to the inexperienced eye. Other individuals fall into a deep state of depression after their incarceration, which often launches them into a spiral of dysfunction. I can remember speaking to a psychologist in prison about some problems I was having with my daughter's mother and how difficult my incarceration had been on our relationship. She told me point blank she wasn't really there to help the prisoners adjust to life behind bars, but to protect the officers and staff.

"How could that be?" I asked. She told me that the psychologist's primary function inside the wall was to identify prisoners who could be a threat to the staff and guards, individuals with a mental imbalance who might act out in a violent way because of that imbalance. Prison life alone has the ability to turn a man into a walking canceled ticket if he is not careful.

Life behind the wall can be a collection all things miserable and depressing, topped off with a scoop of absolute gloom. Closer to the end of my sentence I remember nights that I cried a tear or two while lying on that hard bunk, struggling to fall asleep. My heart was aching because of the bad Choices I had made in my life. Most men who have been in prison for an extended period of time have cried as well. Definitely not in plain view of others, but in the darkness of their cold dark concrete cell. The male ego temporarily puts itself to rest as the human being takes control. I cried because I expected a better life for myself. I cried because I left my child basically fatherless. I cried because I missed my family. I cried because I knew deep down inside that I could do better.

There is no one in prison who loves you; no wife there to cuddle with on those rainy days; no girlfriend to caress in the early morning when it's cold; no son to toss a football to in the backyard; no daughter to cheer up when her goldfish dies. The relationship that you once had with your loved ones on the outside becomes dysfunctional at best. The many months and years that you're out of their lives take their toll.

One of the few benefits of being incarcerated is that you finally have the time and opportunity to quiet the mind. Once you can quiet the mind, then, and only then, can you get to know who you really are. That is when you finally get the chance to figure out what makes you tick. You can then get a better understanding of what your strengths and weaknesses are. Suddenly, the man in the mirror isn't just a guy who looks familiar and for some strange reason you can't remember his name. Now, the man in the mirror becomes a guy you know very well.

I'm quite sure I dealt with some level of depression during my incarceration, but at some point, I became numb, or immune to the existence of those emotions. I had to do my best to thwart the most painful thoughts and feelings from bubbling to the surface. I developed tunnel vision just to make it through the days, the months, and the years. That was the only way I could handle the misery. That was the only way I could assure myself that I would have some level of reason and common sense once I returned to the streets.

I had spent a total of eleven years behind the gray wall, which now seems purely a waste of time. Once I did the math, a realized that I had spent over 4500 days in prison. Numbers never lie! Like sand in the palm of my hand, the grains of life had slowly begun to slip away. I had missed out on a lot of opportunities which I will never have a chance to experience again. The things every man experiences, like being married and raising kids, and having a work history; I had never really thought about these things much in the past, but now I was wondering how I could have ever let them pass me by.

WORKING HARD FOR
THE MONEY

Doing the right thing can be easy for most of the humanoids that roam the planet earth. For the others, it can be a complicated maze of indecisiveness and lack of determination, where the heart and mind struggle to walk the straight and narrow. It may take a lot more energy to do the right thing; more than it does to do the wrong thing. But once you've done the wrong thing, trying to shortcut life, you'll need triple the energy to clean up the mess you've made when it doesn't work out. There are millions of people in the world today that will never see the inside of a prison cell in their entire lives. Those same people have legitimate employment and work hard to support themselves and their families. They're doing the right thing to make ends meet, even when times get tough. So why couldn't I do the same?

I had been out of prison for about two weeks when I began looking to purchase one of the most important pieces of clothing needed for a man to gain advancement in life. I hit the stores in search of a simple men's suit to solidify my new image. Many years ago, Anthony had taught me that a suit and tie alone could dramatically change how others perceived a man. You could whisk almost any guy off the street corner and place him in a suit, and he might pass for a Washington diplomat. Anthony wore suits regularly and from a distance, you would never know he was a drug dealer.

"Kevin, do you know why I wear this suit?" Anthony said to the young street kid. "Because a suit and tie make a man look professional. They make a man look intelligent, focused, and businesslike. When you look like a businessman, people treat you like a businessman."

Now that I was older and more mature, I could understand his words to that seventeen-year-old kid. I could understand how important one's appearance is. Now that I was an ex-felon seeking employment, a suit and a tie was even more important for me. A suit and tie helps to make an ex-felon appear non-threatening to his potential employer. This is very important because regardless of what most people might say, they already have this preconceived notion regarding individuals who have been in prison. Some people have already decided in their mind how an ex-felon will act and what he will look like. Unfortunately, the burden of proof is on the person with the criminal background to overcome that prejudice.

Before I was released, I created a long-term and a short-term plan for myself in my quest to rebuild my life. Evaluating my situation, I realized that one of the many reasons I wasn't attracted to working a legal job in the past was the fact that I didn't like manual labor. Operating machines and lifting heavy boxes weren't the kinds of jobs I received satisfaction in doing. I don't think that I was lazy, but I just didn't feel comfortable in those environments. In reality, there's nothing wrong with manual labor; it just wasn't something I enjoyed.

I began preparing myself for a new career long before I was released from prison. My desire was to work in an office setting, so I needed to upgrade my knowledge of computers and my overall office administrative skills. At the time, there were no computers available at the prison, so the next best thing was to read as many books and magazines as I could get my hands on regarding computer literacy. I also read books on how to look for a job. Even seemingly inconsequential things – like how to greet a potential employer properly, with a smile and a handshake – I had to learn.

While I was in the halfway house, I was attending class at Baltimore City Community College. My class was early Saturday morning and even just that one class helped to keep the bright light bulb in my head from turning dim. It was a computer literacy class, which was a huge help in re-introducing me to technology. Up until then, I thought that PowerPoint was an exciting new video game with lasers, made by Sony for their PlayStation.

In the beginning, it felt awkward, strolling through the college building with all of those beautiful intelligent women. My instructor, with a heavy Somali accent, was a very nice guy who had plenty of patience. Computer technology can advance rapidly in just one year, so imagine how overwhelmed I was after over ten years of absence! The last time that I had regular use of a computer was when DOS was the operating system of choice. But to my surprise, many of the other students in my class were struggling as much as I was.

Having a job is mandatory while assigned to a halfway house, and finding something to satisfy that requirement wasn't as hard as I thought it would. I had received some placement assistance before I was released from prison. Early in the morning, most times before dawn, I would jump on the bus and then transfer to the subway to get to work. I hadn't been on a public bus or subway for years, so this was a weird experience, especially just prior to the bus stopping. You'd hear, "Next stop, Monument and Broadway Streets," in the proper-English-speaking voice coming from the audio system. To me, this was something straight out of a sci-fi movie. What I remembered from the last time I was on a public bus in Baltimore was the driver yelling out the stop. You just had to hope you could understand what he was saying and you wouldn't miss your stop.

Riding the subway, I familiarized myself with the city folks, who were hustling and bustling their way to and from school and work. Most of them were focused on improving their situation. I was absolutely excited to again be in the middle of all the action. Like most metropolitan cities, Baltimore definitely has its share of subway weirdoes, who provide a laugh or two for the other concerned commuters. I was ecstatic to be in the company of Baltimoreans again, even the insanely smiling ones who were losing their minds. It was great to be home!

My very first job during this quest to redeem my life was at a telemarketing firm, inside a small call center out in the suburbs. My task was to contact residences to request donations for firefighter and law enforcement non-profit organizations around the country. This job was tougher than I had thought it would be. In a very short time I hated the job, but I realized that I was extremely blessed to have a job at all. Having employment allowed me to leave the halfway house every single day, mingle with the public and to see my family. After being away for so long, this was something that I very much valued and appreciated.

But I regularly browsed the want ads for a better opportunity. About a month later, I was able to find another job, working in the telemarketing section of a local mortgage company. There I also contacted residences, but this time I was calling to invite the homeowners to refinance their mortgages. This was where I got my first taste of the mortgage industry, learning the ins and outs of interest rates and closing costs. After working there for only a brief period, I gained a lot of valuable knowledge pertaining to the real estate industry. But calling people at their homes was a tough job because they were sometimes abusive. As much as I used to hate being called by telemarketers myself, this was a very odd position for me to be in. I remember one evening calling this older woman in Wichita, Kansas. I started out by telling her about the services my company offered and I asked if she would be interested in refinancing her home. She told me she was trying to eat dinner and that I was interrupting her. I told her that I was sorry and that I could call back later. I thought I was being respectful, but she became even more upset.

"Call me back later?" the older woman repeated back to me. "What the hell are you going to call me later for? By then I will be sleep and you still will be bothering me." She called me every disgusting word in the book and some not yet in the book. There wasn't much I could say; all I could do was continue to be polite and hang up the phone. I didn't like this job much either, but again, I loved the fact that I had a job at all, because others in my situation weren't as fortunate. There were still a few guys in the halfway house struggling to find any employment.

Because of the crazy bunch of co-workers I had there, I began calling this place Loco Mortgage Company. Over half of the people working in my department got high. During lunch breaks, many would journey outside and smoke marijuana in the parking lot, like it was legal, then return to the office and continue working. The place sometimes smelled like a Jamaican nightclub, and to make matters even more bizarre, my supervisor often puffed on the illegal vegetation with the others. This was one of the funniest things I had ever seen in the workplace.

Some of them were getting intoxicated from something besides the green stuff, and they were always getting into arguments in the office. Once a month the police were summoned. This was just like being back in the streets. This was when I realized there could be madness happening anywhere that you go. There could be madness in the supermarket and madness in the subway, there's madness in the school or even madness at your church. Anywhere you go, there will be people doing things they have no business doing, and in a situation like that you have two choices. You can get *out* of the way or you can get *in* the way. In the case of the Loco Mortgage Company, I chose to get out of the way. Throughout my employment there I continued looking for other jobs, because I knew this wasn't the place for me. With all of the drama going on and the fact that the hourly wages were little to nothing, I thought it would be smart to make preparations for a brighter tomorrow. I needed stability and most of all, a drug-free environment, so I definitely couldn't stay where I was. I also needed to be able to support myself financially, because money wasn't exactly falling out of the trees. Choices.

A friend of mine named Tia suggested I create a resume to use when I went on job interviews. I informed her that I had no experience preparing a resume because I never needed one. On my way to purchase a kilo or two of something special, the Colombians never asked to see my resume. For the type of administrative jobs that I was looking for now, I would need an impressive one. But when Tia and I began to create one for me, we realized that I had years of missing employment information in my work record. How would I explain this to a potential employer?

"Uh, I've been in a coma for over eleven years and I just woke up."

Tia had a lot of experience preparing resumes for ex-felons. She had worked in a workforce development program called the Center for Urban Families, where she did this all the time for men re-entering the workforce after their release from prison. Tia did a great job helping me fill in the gaps. She used the jobs I had in prison, like GED tutor or teachers assistant. She didn't exactly state on the resume that these jobs were in prison, but she did say that whatever I did, I should be honest with the prospective employer about my past. These days it's difficult to hide your background, thanks to the Internet, plus court records are public information. So with all these things in mind, we created a resume and I began pounding the pavements looking for a new job.

I was confident that I could do the job if I was given the opportunity. But the problem was I had to convince someone else to believe this. Once I was in the interview with my potential employer, I would proceed through the entire process and it seemed like the interviewer loved me. But at the very end, he or she would say, "I would like to bring you into our company. But first, is there anything "else" you would like to tell us?"

This was usually the point where I'd get nervous, but I would trudge on, saying, "I made some really big mistakes in the past, for which I am sorry for and now I'm ready to move on." I'd tell them that I served time in prison and their eyes would cloud over like they had just interviewed one of America's Most Wanted. Many companies have policies prohibiting individuals convicted of a felony from working there. Once the company policy itself blocks you, there isn't much you can do about it. Regardless of your capacity to do the job, no human resources person is going to jeopardize their job just to give you a chance. Oftentimes I would leave the interview feeling dejected. It was painful, but I had to keep going. I had to work to support myself and I couldn't go back to the streets.

While still working at Loco Mortgage Company, I had to leave the office one day to see my car insurance agent. I had managed to save enough money to purchase a very used vehicle. The agent that I was using was a longtime family friend named Bill. While in his office, he began asking me some routine questions like, "Where are you working now?" I told him that I was working at a mortgage company. He asked me what type of job I was doing there and I said I was a loan officer. I wasn't exactly a loan officer, although I had aspirations of moving up the ladder and becoming one very soon. The title "loan officer" just had a Louisiana hot sauce-type of twang that sounded cool to me.

Suddenly Bill yelled for his partner Red. Bill told him, "We got a loan officer here." Upon receiving this piece of information, Red got excited.

"Oh, he's a loan officer," Red said. "Wait here, I'll be right back." I didn't understand what was going on with these two guys.

Red returned to the office in a matter of seconds with a telephone in his hand, talking with someone on the other end. "Yes, the guy is right here," I heard him say, referring to me. "Yes, he's a loan officer and he's here," Red told the mystery man on the other end of the line. Then he handed me the phone.

Who is this guy on the other end of the phone and what does he want to talk to me about? I wondered to myself. I took the phone and said, "Hello. How are you doing?"

"How are you doing?" he replied. "My name is Xavier and my office is about two blocks from where you are now. Do you have a minute to come up to see me?"

The mystery man gave me directions and hung up. I saw that Bill and Red were standing there with these humungous smiles on their faces, but I didn't know why.

"Who was that guy?" I asked.

"He runs a mortgage company up the street," Bill replied, "and he's looking for new loan officers for the company." I ran outside, jumped into my old used car, and headed up the street to this new job opportunity, hoping that this would be the break I had been waiting for.

As I walked through the door to the office, I was impressed with the stylish decor. The office was very clean and professional looking, and the receptionist at the front desk greeted me with a smile. She was an older black woman with gray hair and a wonderful personality.

"Hello. How are you doing?" she said to the unknown visitor.

"I am doing fine," I replied. "How are you? I'm here to see Xavier."

"Have a seat and I'll let him know that you are here."

I sat on the Italian leather sofa, staring at all the licenses and plaques on the walls that acknowledged the company's achievements.

Xavier arrived to greet the new loan officer prospect waiting for him. He was a much larger man than I had expected, based on his voice in our telephone conversation. He was somewhere around fifty years old, African American and balding. He also had a slight country drawl that assured me he wasn't a Baltimore native.

"How are you doing, Kevin? Nice to meet you," he said, grasping my hand firmly. As I followed him down the long hallway, I got a glimpse of the elegant offices which were very stylish.

These guys had class and professionalism far beyond my current employer. We entered a large meeting room with a huge conference table that looked like it came right from the movie *Wall Street*.

When I sat down with Xavier at this huge table, I was nervous. This was a big deal for me because I needed the job, and I was not a loan officer. I hoped I knew enough to sound like one, but I really did not know. This wasn't actually an official interview; it was more like a meet-and-greet. As our conversation began, I felt more and more at ease with the laid-back personality of my potential supervisor.

"So, you're a loan officer," he began. Of course I told him I was. I had to stick to that story. But I knew very little about the mortgage business, other than the little bit I had learned about refinancing as a telemarketer.

"So, how long have you been a loan officer?" I knew that question was coming. This could have been the fatal blow, but I fought back with a dose of intellectual rhetoric, determined not to be exposed.

"Well, I have only been a loan officer for a couple of weeks actually. I'm in training now with my current employer, learning about adjustable rates and HUD regulations." It was the best I could think of to say without lying too much. Suddenly, I didn't think that he would go for it and I assumed that the gig was up, but his next statement surprised me.

"Well, you could easily continue your training here and I would train you myself."

I was floored. This felt great! It felt great that someone wanted me to work for them! This looked like it could be my new start.

The meeting went well and I left feeling upbeat. He had invited me back for an official interview on Monday. The only

WORKING HARD FOR THE MONEY

problem was that I had left out a very important piece of information. I hadn't said a word to him about my criminal background. He hadn't asked, but I knew it was bound to come up on Monday. I knew I would have no choice but to explain my situation to him. I was still in the halfway house and he would definitely find that out because the staff at the halfway house would be calling to verify my employment. There was no way of getting around it.

The next day, I called Bill to get his insight on the situation. I asked him if he or Red would call Xavier and have a discussion with him on my behalf, which, of course, Bill agreed to do. He knew that I was making a huge effort to stay employed and off of the streets.

The sun was shining high up in the sky early Monday morning on the day of my official interview with the mortgage company. This was a great day to be alive – especially for me, the ex-hustler-turned-good-guy who was just looking for a job. I arrived early for my nine o'clock meeting with Xavier. There was no way I was going to risk being even a second late for what could be the interview of my life. From the parking lot I could see some of the other employees as they began to pull in for work.

Finally, I made my way up to the second floor offices. Waiting to greet me was the same receptionist from the other day, still smiling graciously. And this time, she introduced herself as Mrs. Pearl. She still seemed to me the nicest woman in the world.

I sat in the lobby, waiting for Xavier to appear and of course I was nervous, but also confident that I could pull this off. I knew Bill had told Xavier about my situation and Xavier was still willing to give me a shot.

The interview went off without a hitch and I had my much sought-after second chance at a new life, a life that I could be proud to tell my family about. I thought the feeling I had when the meet-and-greet went so well was the best feeling I could ever experience, but I was wrong. This was *much* better!

Xavier advised me to keep the details of my criminal background to myself. He assured me that this would remain our secret. After leaving the office that day, I had the impression that Xavier may have once had some type of legal problems and someone may have given him a chance. Whatever his reason was for hiring me, I didn't care.

Once employed, I was always the first one there, waiting for Mrs. Pearl to arrive and open the office. Coming in early would allow me to finish up any leftover studying I was doing. I knew that Xavier would want to quiz me on the information and I didn't want to disappoint him. Learning all of the terminology in the mortgage business was a challenge, but I was up to the task and it got easier as I went along. I was determined to be the best loan officer I could be. I felt that my future depended on this job because I knew without it, I could possible be back in the streets.

After pounding the pavements for months looking for a gig I could be proud of, but at the same time a job that would support me financially, I found it. With some hard work, I could convert this into the career I desperately needed. The majority of the guys who get released from prison don't want to go back to the streets. There are some guys in prison who establish a plan of crime and grime even before they get released, like I did the last time, but most aren't thinking that way. The top priority for most of them is to find an opportunity to work and live with dignity.

One overcast morning I needed to get to the closest bank to make a withdrawal. I was a nine-to-five guy now, so direct deposit to my bank of choice had become a new convenience in my life. I was going through the regular routine of filling out that ridiculous withdrawal slip to access my currency—needing permission from the bank to get my hands on what I considered to be mine was still a new practice for the former dealer. For some reason I thought the ATM was still kind of weird. Go figure! My old ways of keeping a shoebox full of cash in the closet were long gone. I was just about finished filling out the withdrawal slip when I heard someone call my name. It was my old friend Taiwan walking through the door of the bank! I couldn't believe it!

"Wow, how have you been?" I said to her. She looked just as good as I remembered. I gave her the biggest hug that I could muster as I pondered whether or not to let her go.

I had been home from prison for several months now and still hadn't run into her, although she was always on my mind. You could live in Baltimore for years without ever running into someone that you're acquainted with. I heard through the proverbial grapevine that she was doing well.

"I've been doing great," she answered with a huge smile. "What about you? My mother told me that you stopped by the house. When she told me about you stopping by, I had no idea you were even back home."

"I've been back for almost three months," I said.

"What are you doing now?" Taiwan asked. I told her I was working in the mortgage business.

"That's good. I'm glad that you're back. How is Brooke doing?"

"Brooke is fine. She's getting tall. She's playing soccer in school now."

Back in the day, Taiwan and I were so close that when my daughter was born she was the very first person I called from the hospital. She was happy with the birth of my daughter because she knew that I was happy. I never sensed any type of jealousy or anything like that from her because she wasn't that type of person.

She opened her wallet and showed me some pictures of her two sons. By now she was a married woman with a family. I could see that life had been treating her well as she explained to me that she was now an entrepreneur.

"You really look good," I said, trying to maintain my composure. Her blush was similar to that which she displayed many years ago at the Shake and Bake Skating Rink when I first met her with her friend Melanie. Back then we all were just kids.

"Thanks," she said. By now we were both standing in the line with the other banking customers. Once the teller in front of me became available, I rushed up to the window to complete my transaction. I wanted to get that out of the way so that I could continue my conversation with Taiwan before she disappeared. I hadn't seen her for several years and there was a lot I wanted to say. I could tell that she was happy to see me, but this had been a tongue-tied moment for the both of us. Neither one of us were absolutely prepared for this day. I waited for her at the door as she completed her transaction with the teller. I just couldn't let her get away.

We continued our conversation out in the parking lot of the bank, where there was much more privacy. "I never thought that I would ever see you again," I told her. "When I was away I thought about you all the time."

"Wow, you really did?" she asked. She was actually surprised by the statement, but she could tell that I was being honest. In the past we had never played games regarding how we our felt about one another.

We continued chatting for a short time longer before Taiwan had to depart. I gave her one last hug just before telling her, "I'll always love you." I told her to take care of herself and that I would see her around, which I knew probably wouldn't happen. She was a businesswoman now, with places to go and people to see. Maybe she had to get to the supermarket to purchase groceries for the family. Maybe her husband was waiting to take her out to breakfast. Who knows? Her life had evolved and she was doing pretty well now. I was glad to see that, but at the same time I was a little envious. I was envious because I always wondered what our lives would have been like together. Now, I could only think and imagine.

For the first time in many years, I actually felt like a proud man again. I finally felt good about who I was. Over the course of the many years I had been incarcerated, my dignity and self-esteem had taken a beating, but now the winds had shifted. Finally, I felt like people were viewing me in an entirely different light and I felt whole again. I didn't feel like an inmate anymore; every day, I felt more and more like a human being. Now I just wanted to be an Average Joe – a guy who goes to work every day to secure a decent life for himself and his family. By ten o'clock in the evening, Average Joe is in the bed, getting rested for the next morning. Average Joe is content with his life and Average Joe never goes to prison. He's not selling dope on the street corner, he's not a hustler, nor does he have any desire to engage in that misguided love affair with the dark side. In my book, Average Joe is an okay guy.

The days of trying to be a star in the streets wasn't something that I yearned for any longer. The stars in the streets don't shine for very long before something or someone extinguishes their light. It's okay to be a star, as long as you're not destroying someone else's life in the process. Mothers and fathers are stars to their young children, and so are husbands and wives to one another. I wanted to be a star again, but only to my daughter.

INTERVENTION

"You don't want to die, do you, homeboy? You don't want to end up in the morgue waiting for someone to come to identify your body, do you? The game is over Kevin. Leave the streets alone, kid, while you still got a chance."

If Anthony was alive today, these are the words he would whisper to the former hustler who was now determined to fly straight. Anthony was a smart guy, and he would see the writing on the wall. He would see that it was time to cut my losses and move on; the game is over.

It's not rocket science!

Fading back into the days of yesteryear, I can remember one particular situation when I was about seventeen years old. And there again, my family was faced with financial hardship. My mother and father had already been separated for a while. My sister Wanda had moved out and she was living with her boyfriend. Me, my brother, and my sister Karen had moved into a small apartment with my mother. My mother was working three jobs just to make ends meet. She had a daytime job, where she commuted from Baltimore over to Washington, D.C. and then she would trek over to her night job in Baltimore. On top of that, she had a weekend job as a receptionist. It was tough on my mother, trying to feed three kids with no support, but she did the best that she could.

The bills were piling up rapidly and the bill collectors made their presence felt with every annoying phone call. There were several moments when big decisions had to be made to keep the house in order. On this particular occasion, the burden was to pay our rent to keep a roof over our heads. We often had eviction notices posted to the front door of our apartment. I remember walking down the street, and seeing clothes and furniture of evicted residents sitting on the corner. I would examine the items very closely to make sure that they weren't from our apartment. I'd breathe a sigh of relief once I realized the items weren't ours. For a young kid whose biggest worry should have been his first kiss, this was far too much anxiety.

There's nothing more embarrassing than to be thrown out of your home and your personal belongings are sitting on the corner when you return from work or school. I've even witnessed people evicted in the snow and rain, as the water droplets destroy everything that they own. That is one of the most humiliating feelings in the world. The entire neighborhood knows what has happened to you. I've even seen occasions where the neighbors see that someone has been evicted and they steal the personal belongings of the displaced individuals.

It was about 8:30 in the morning and my mother had already left home for work. She was usually up at the crack of dawn and out of the door before seven o'clock. There we were, the four of us, living in a two-bedroom apartment. It was small but it was clean, of course, because my mother wouldn't have it any other way. I was home with my brother and sister. Still in my room, I was half asleep because it was very early. Suddenly there was a hard knock on the door front. This was odd because no one usually came to our house this time of morning, but it seemed no big deal.

My sister got to the door before anyone else was able to rise out of their warm bed. Unfortunately for us, we had received a very unwelcome guest. It was the head maintenance guy from our apartment complex, along with a city sheriff. My sister quickly ran into the bedroom to alert my brother and myself. These guys were there to enforce an eviction notice by removing our belongings from the apartment. The rent had been a few months late and the landlord was fed up. My father was still unemployed and drinking heavily, so he wasn't providing my mother with any financial assistance.

The head maintenance guy and the sheriff were demanding that we produce a total of $1,650 for the late rent and late fees within the next hour or we would have to leave the apartment. My brother tried to call my mother at work, but he was having a difficult time reaching her. Her supervisor was telling him that she hadn't arrived in the office yet. Both my sister and my brother, who were older than me, began to panic. I was just thinking that I didn't want to be out in the street. I was thinking about how embarrassing it would be to have all of our things sitting on the corner.

When I looked out of the living room window, I could see five or six guys from the maintenance crew standing outside of our building. They reminded me of the way the cops surrounded the bad guys in the movies and for the moment, we were the bad guys. Our rent was late and these people wanted to be paid. In my mind, I could see all of our furniture and clothing sitting outside on the corner, as the neighbors rummaged through them.

My sister started making calls to my aunts and to my older sister Wanda for money. Wanda quickly responded to the distress call. She sent her boyfriend to our house with $400. We were still short, but suddenly my brother was able to reach my mother at work. There wasn't much she could do at the time because she simply didn't have all of the money.

My mother told my brother that she only had $850 in an envelope in her bedroom closet. Now we had $1,250 bucks, but we needed more, and the pressure was on. The sheriff was a black woman and I got the sense that she hated this part of the job. You have to have really thick skin to kick families out of their homes. But I got the impression that the head maintenance guy – who was a complete idiot – was enjoying every minute of this.

My brother began to cry, and my sister did as well. I kind of expected her to cry because she was a girl, but I was surprised to see my brother breaking down. Back then, I was of the mindset that boys didn't cry about anything, but I was wrong. I figured since he was older than me, he should be trying to keep things together for the rest of the family. Finally I realized that I had to do something stop this madness.

I had just begun selling weed around this time, mostly to my friends at the high school and some neighborhood weed-heads. I was only selling five-dollar bags and I wasn't making a large amount of money, but I was making enough to take care of myself. I had money when I needed to get sneakers and clothes or to pay for other small items. My mother had no idea that I was selling weed. I rarely saw her because she was so busy working. When I woke up in the morning, she was already off to work and by the time she got home at night, I was already asleep.

The sheriff had given us an hour to get the money together and that hour was up, but we were only able to collect $1,250, which still left us short by $400. I went into my bedroom and grabbed my Nike shoebox out of the top of the closet. Even though I had plans for this money, I had no intention of being thrown out on the street corner. I removed $400 from the box. We now had enough to pay the rent. When I got to the living room, the sheriff and the maintenance man were arguing with my sister's boyfriend. He was trying to persuade them to give us a little more time. Over all of the commotion, I yelled,

"I have the rest of the money here!"

Everyone in the room turn their attention to me. There wasn't a sound as I handed the money over to the sheriff.

The sheriff took the cash and gave us a receipt as she prepared to exit the apartment with a smile because she didn't have to evict another family from their home. My brother and sister were definitely relieved that we wouldn't be sleeping on the corner for the night.

Finally, my brother called my mother, who was still at work, to tell her that everything was okay. He also told her that I came up with the remaining money to thwart the eviction. She was glad that we hadn't been evicted, but concerned about the source of the additional funds.

"Where did Kevin get $400 from?" she asked my brother. He couldn't answer her because he didn't have a clue. At the moment, everyone was just pleased that we had a roof over our heads for another night.

Later on in the evening, when my mother returned home, she questioned me intensely as to where the "rent rescue" money came from. I told her that I saved it from doing odd jobs in the neighborhood. I'm not sure if she believed that, but I definitely don't think she thought it was from selling weed. But when the parent is working day and night and getting home late, exhausted from the day's grind, it's difficult to keep up with a teenager who's already on the other side of the fence.

A single parent trying to raise a child is tough, but trying to raise three can be an enormous challenge. My mother was faced with the difficult job of raising a teenage boy who had his eye on the streets. There are millions of teenagers growing up in the world today with only one parent, but still they thrive. Young people who have supervision, of course, have a better chance of emerging on the other side unscathed. When you're young, it's easy to do something stupid that you may have to pay for the rest of your life. But at some point in your life, you still have to take responsibility for your actions.

Now, I was a grown adult and I had to make better choices, regardless of the circumstances and regardless of whatever challenges I was facing. I could no longer justify bad behavior just for the sake of survival or for the sake of prospering financially. Dealing illegal drugs just didn't make sense anymore. I had done that in the past, making excuses for my actions, but now I could no longer brainwash myself into thinking that breaking the law was the only way.

It's not rocket science; it's just common sense.

Trying to survive and get ahead is a full-time job for nearly every Tom, Dick, and Harry. In these tough economic times, there are a lot of people living on the edge. But they keep going because they have this valuable commodity called freedom that they aren't willing to compromise.

My mind was made up: I would not go back. I was going to figure this thing out this time around because I had no other choice. I felt a sense of urgency every day, knowing that my life had to continue moving in a positive direction. I knew, deep down inside, that there was a better life awaiting the tall skinny kid from Edmondson Village, who no longer had an appetite for the streets.

Before I was released from prison, I forgot what it meant to struggle financially. Struggling wasn't something I had been accustomed to as an adult, even though I had grown up in a financially distressed household. My adult life had been just the opposite of my youth, because of my criminal lifestyle. When I was in the game, I didn't know what the word "struggle" meant because money came easily. While I was incarcerated, the Federal Bureau of Prisons clothed me, fed me, and housed me for years. The bureau had also provided free medical and dental care for me during that time. It may sound a little crazy, but a lot of guys who get released after being incarcerated for a very long time find it difficult making the transition back to being self-sufficient. Some of them end up returning to the dark side, just to get by. For a man who is returning to the streets, re-learning how to live, without dirty money, can be a challenge.

I realized that it was going to take a lot of hard work at the mortgage company, but I was up to the task because I had to be. I couldn't go back, so I had to do it right this time around. I had spent more than ten years behind the wall. In ten years, I could have been married, divorced, and remarried all over again. I could have received a bachelor's degree in almost any university, not to mention a master's, and doctorate to boot, if I had worked hard enough. I could have gone on to law school, passed the bar exam, and become a lawyer. In ten years, I could have gone to medical school, graduated, and become a doctor. I could have traveled around the world several times, maybe even on foot. I could have built the tallest building in the world, sold it to Donald Trump, and started construction of another one, just to do it all over again. I could have set many milestones in ten years to make myself a proud man, while making my family proud as well. Instead, I blackened the eye of the surname given to me at birth. Being the first one in my family to do time in prison wasn't what my mother expected from me when she first placed me in the Head Start Program.

Some days, the words spoken by Red, Morgan Freeman's character in *The Shawshank Redemption,* who was serving life in prison for murder, reverberated throughout my head. When asked by the chairman of the parole board whether or not he feels rehabilitated Red stated:

> "There's not a day goes by I don't feel regret. Not because I'm in here or because you think I should. I look back on the way I was then: a young, stupid kid who committed that terrible crime. I want to talk to him. I want to try and talk some sense to him, tell him the way things are. But I can't. That kid's long gone and this old man is all that's left. I got to live with that."

I could feel those words in my head every day. He was tired from spending so many years in prison and so was I.

I can never forget the first time I watched that movie. Red's mind was made up a long time before he ever spoke those memorable lines to the parole board. The movie went on to be nominated for seven Oscars. That fact says a lot about how the message of that movie grabbed hold of so many people's hearts and minds. I can almost guarantee you that none of the members of the Academy of Motion Picture Arts and Sciences who voted for this award ever spent any significant time in prison, but they obviously felt this character's pain.

One of my biggest struggles has been trying to convince people from my past that I'm a changed man. When I walk down the street, I run into people all the time who knew me many years ago. They don't have any idea who I am today. Most don't understand my journey.

As I look around the streets, I realize that I made the right choice by getting out the game. Things have changed dramatically inside the concrete jungle. The drug trade is no longer a viable business; it is on the brink of destruction. It's a business that offers no future, even though some young kids believe that the streets will be kind to them. Most of the people that I knew in the illegal business ten years ago are no longer in it. Many of them are in jail, dead, or confined to a wheelchair with old injuries sustained in the violence. Most of those that have retired haven't done so voluntarily; only a few made the conscious decision to exit the business.

Most of the former drug corners inside the concrete jungle now resemble ghost towns. The open-air drug market, which once stood on North and Pulaski streets, is empty, courtesy of a new crime-fighting strategy by the police department. Fayette and Mount Streets are free of the carnage resulting from Diamond in the Raw. North and Longwood Streets reflect a kinder, gentler West Baltimore these days. Harlem and Dukeland Streets no longer host some of the most violent shootouts the game has ever seen. Edmondson and Monroe Streets are eerily quiet compared to the history of this legendary drug distribution corner. Other than the occasional bag of weed bartered to the young hooligans on this turf, the war has subsided and the ceasefire is still in effect. Almost all of the high-rise housing projects that once encircled downtown Baltimore have been imploded to clear the land for green development. The powers that be are making accommodations for the two new biotech centers that are racing to become a visible part of the city skyline. The fact that the availability of low-income housing in the city has been slashed over the years, due in part to the expansion of Johns Hopkins, can arguably be considered an even exchange for the hundreds of jobs that have been created.

THE CORNER

The Corner... What an unpretentious title for such a dishonorable place, where human life is shredded and devoured without much thought. Back in 1997, Fayette and Mount Street and the surrounding territory became the backdrop for a book titled *The Corner: A Year in the Life of an Inner-City Neighborhood*, written by David Simon and Ed Burns (Broadway Books, 1997). The book spent a considerable amount of time on the *New York Times* bestseller list and received high praise for its compelling story. Many of the characters profiled throughout the pages of this award-winning piece of literature performed odd jobs from time to time for the Diamond in the Raw crew. Some of them were hardcore heroin addicts who had been injecting the drug for years on end. Others were lookouts, the ones that chanted "Five- O" when cruising patrolmen entered the block. Most of them didn't have prominent roles in our organization, but there was still a relationship that worked for all parties involved: we wanted the money, they wanted the drugs. It was a match made in hell.

I became aware of the book in the summer of 1997, when I was incarcerated in federal prison in the mountains of Schuylkill, Pennsylvania, serving out a sentence for a probation violation. Among Baltimoreans, the book was the talk of the town well before it became nationally acclaimed. To my knowledge, this was the first book of its kind, one that featured an inner city neighborhood in such blistering detail, details that would turn the stomachs of many readers.

It was close to 4 p.m., a few minutes before count time. That's the time when all federal prisons conduct a count of the inmates in their custody, which is then reported to the Federal Bureau of Prisons headquarters in Washington, D.C. I was standing on the top tier, staring down at the other inmates and wondering how the hell we all got to this place. I spotted a guy named Barksdale, waving and yelling up towards me to get my attention. I knew who Barksdale was, but he and I had not had much interaction so far. He was also a Baltimorean from the west side, and a former heroin addict serving a sentence for weapons violations.

"Yo, Kevin…. Yo, Kevin….what's up? Kev, I need to talk with you before we lock in for count, okay?"

During those days, I was pretty much a loner. I didn't have a lot of time remaining, so I kept to myself to avoid unnecessary problems. When I saw Barksdale waving at me, I walked down the metal stairs of the tier and met him where he was standing, at the bottom level. He had a book in his hand.

"Have you seen this shit yet? You guys are all over it." He was referring to me and the Diamond in the Raw crew, which I didn't completely understand at the time. He told me that his sister had sent the book to him.

One of the few luxuries available in prison is books sent in from the outside world. Prison officials make it relatively easy for families to send books in to prisoners. They have to be mailed by the bookstore, so no contraband can be placed inside the package. Reading was one of the things that kept a lot of inmates, including myself, from going off the deep end. Reading reminds you that there is still a life on the outside. The books are censored once they reach the prison, so not all subject matter is acceptable. But as long as you're not attempting to get books on how to construct a homemade bomb or how to escape from jail, there is usually no big issue.

I saw the title of the book, which really didn't intrigue me at all, although I was curious as to why Barksdale wanted so badly for me to see it. I took it from his burly hands – which were still slightly swollen from injecting heroin in the streets – and began browsing the pages.

"What is this about"?

"It's about Fayette Street, around your way," he said.

Now I was really baffled. *Why,* I wondered, *would someone write a book about Fayette and Mount Street?* Barksdale said that my former crew had been mentioned many times in it. He said that it was written by a Baltimore Sun newspaper reporter and a former Baltimore City police detective. He directed my attention to a passage in the book: *They're back in business on Mount Street, too, where Diamond in the Raw has the best package.*

My jaw fell down to the floor. I couldn't believe what I had just read. Barksdale turned a couple of pages and directed me to another passage: *Across the street, the Death Row and Diamond in the Raw Crews immediately reopened the Mount Street shop.* After further inspection of the book, I could see that it was riddled with references to Diamond in the Raw. Barksdale could see the surprise on my face.

"If you want to check it out, I can get it from you later," Barksdale said. "Actually, go ahead and keep it for a couple of days." I grabbed the book from him and sprinted back to my cell, eager to see what the hell this was all about. I climbed up into my bunk and buried myself in the pages. Scene by scene, this book described exactly what had been going on. The information on Fayette and Mount Streets was no longer classified, not that it truly ever was. But now the whole world would know. This was more than just a book; it was like a crime scene investigation.

As I pored through the pages, in my mind, I went right back to the streets. I was standing on the corner of Mount and Fayette all over again. It was a warm day in midsummer and some on the block had an attitude for inflicting pain. I could hear the ambulance siren blaring as paramedics sped their patients away to the University of Maryland Hospital. Their cargo in the back was wrapped, head to toe, in a white sheet, just another victim of circumstances. Little Stevo was still riding up the street on his stolen bike, undoubtedly with a bag or two of weed tucked away in his pocket. This kid was high all the time. In juvenile hall, they called him "Weed Head." With my sensory juices flowing, I could almost smell the cabbage and chicken cooking at Ms. Ethel's house on Fayette. She always left her kitchen window open and you could smell the food from blocks away. Her delectable dishes had a distinct fragrance and reading this book brought it back to me.

In my mind, I could see the heroin addicts lined up in the alley, from Bruce Street all the way down to Gilmor, waiting for the testers to be handed out. They heard the rumor that someone had a new package getting ready to hit the street. The rumor was correct; it was Diamond in the Raw. Nate was sitting on the front steps on Fayette, keeping a close eye on every human that moved. Beside him was his nine millimeter handgun, wrapped in a newspaper, just in case the stick-up boys got any crazy ideas. The entire scene played repeatedly in my head, just like I was there all over again.

It took about four days to read the more than five hundred pages, so for me, that was a serious read. My first thought was to destroy it, but when sanity returned, I realized that would be foolish because there were many copies all over the city and soon, all over the country. On the fifth day, I spotted Barksdale in the prison yard as I rounded the track.

"So, what did you think about it?" he asked. "Good shit, right?"

"It's a lot," I told him, adding that there was too much information in that book for my comfort. Barksdale looked at the book differently from the way I did. He was just excited that someone had taken that much interest in writing about his neighborhood. To him, West Baltimore had gained some long-overdue celebrity status. My view was nowhere as cheerful. From an entertainment prospective, the book was great because it had all of the excitement and intrigue that readers look for; but for me, this book was a big problem. This was a true story that could send a lot of people – especially me – to jail for a very long time. That was the part that I didn't find entertaining. *The Corner* scared the hell out of me because I was already sitting in jail and there was more than enough information in that book – including names of witnesses – to spark a federal investigation that could keep me there.

This was the point where I finally realized that no secret in the streets is ever really a secret. If you and one other person know about it, it could go public at any moment, and usually does. Eventually somebody is going to talk about it and when they do, you better pray to God. CONSPIRACY TO DISTRIBUTE HEROIN AND COCAINE. Not a light accusation to have leveled against you, especially if it's printed in a sealed federal indictment.

In 2000, the book became a miniseries on HBO, which was directed by native Baltimorean and famous Hollywood actor, Charles S. Dutton. It won three Emmys, including one for Outstanding Writing for a Miniseries or Movie.

Many people across America watching the miniseries had to be shocked. They probably couldn't believe that people were living this way inside the United States. People have no idea what it is like in the inner city. The way of life for the family at the center of the series was dysfunctional, to say the least. For many people watching, this had to be a hard concept to grasp. This wasn't reality TV, but it was the reality of life in this part of the world. This wasn't Hollywood at its best, but one section of an inner city inside of America at its very worst.

Even as the miniseries was airing, many of the same events were unfolding on the streets. The characters, the scenes, the drama, the deaths, and the misery: all true. For the life of me, I can't understand how these guys were able to get this story. I have to commend them for their work. They could have easily written *The Corner* using third-party information and accounts of events, but they didn't. They actually risked their lives to bring this story to print. They deserve all of the accolades that they received. The people of West Baltimore didn't usually show a lot of love to guys who infiltrate the hood to write about their dirty deeds.

Nowadays, when I drive up Fayette Street past "the Corner," I get this eerie feeling, like the war is still being waged. I can still remember the gun fights breaking out in the middle of the street, the New York boys battling a local crew. I still remember seeing bodies lying on Mount Street, riddled with bullets as the blood slowly drained from the wounds. They'd eventually become just more statistics on the evening news. I can still remember Officer

Peanut Head driving the tan unmarked police car down Mount Street, chasing the drug addicts and their dime bags.

Since those days, the neighborhood has transformed dramatically. Most of the old stash houses have been torn down and replaced with manicured landscaping. Some of them have been less fortunate, with their boarded-up windows and doors sealing the old entrances. The smell of gunpowder from discharged weapons is no longer in the air. The crime rate in the area has been reduced. The city officials have done a masterful job of cleaning up the place, but there is still much work to be done. The corners at Fayette and Mount Streets are empty and the heroin buyers are gone. They've moved on to greener pastures, where their demands for pleasure can still be met. There's no one standing there in the alley yelling, "Diamond in the Raw" any longer. And there were no competitors on the corners yelling "Killer Bee" or "Terminator," because those guys are long gone. Most of the members of those crews are now awaiting mail call in some federal prison somewhere in America.

Those old images are embedded in my mind, even though the neighborhood is nothing like it uses to be. Sometimes I think I'm dealing with what I can only describe as an acute post-traumatic stress disorder, except I have never been to Afghanistan; my war has been waged here on the streets of West Baltimore.

The only human in sight on this early summer morning, when I took my tour through the old neighborhood, was a kid who looked to be about four years old, riding his tricycle in the middle of the block. I could see no parent or guardian around to keep a watchful eye on the young boy. A few years ago, you could never leave a young child outside unattended because there was no telling what might happen. At any moment, the violence could erupt and gunfights could begin. Or the heroin heads could start a stampede up the block once Diamond in the Raw announced that testers were being given away.

Even Ms. Ethel had moved away from the "Corner". On every block in every hood, there's an elderly woman living there that everybody loves and Ms. Ethel was that elderly woman here on the "Corner". But now, you could no longer smell the cabbage and chicken cooking in her kitchen, because the kitchen was gone. In fact, the entire house was gone. The remaining neighbors told me that Ms. Ethel move out because there was too much excitement and too many gunfights, which was bad for her heart condition. A few years after she moved away, the city moved in with their bulldozers and demolished her old place. You would never smell her good cooking in the neighborhood again.

Little Stevo was no longer riding his red bike up and down the street with his stash of weed tucked away in his back pocket. Stevo is no longer little and he stopped smoking weed a long time ago. He graduated to bigger and dumber things, like smoking crack. He and another guy were trying to rob a local store for money to buy crack, when the cashier tripped the silent alarm. The cops were waiting for them outside and Stevo was shot several times. He's now a quadriplegic, confined to a wheelchair for the rest of his life. No more bicycle rides for him. And no more armed robberies as well. Nate was no longer sitting on the "Corner" with his nine millimeter, watching out for the stick-up boys. They're long gone, and Nate has traded in his nine millimeter for a tool belt. He is a mechanic now, working on commuter trains. Most of the Diamond in the Raw crew, and the other crews involved in the mayhem, are gone. Most of us had been sent to prison at some point or another for various crimes. A few of the other guys were killed after the original operation had been closed down, still trying to continue the game. They just wouldn't let it go.

Baltimore as a whole has gone through a miraculous transformation over the years. From the construction of multi-million dollar condominium developments located at Federal Hill to the rapid growth of luxury apartments. At Fells Point, change is abundant as well as the addition of more jobs continues. A rash of skyscrapers reaching up to the heavens has blossomed to create a different metropolitan skyline. Harbor East has literally created a new hub for the young Generation X crowd looking to wine and dine. Canton is still the place to be on Saturday night when jumbo lump crab cakes and scallops are weighing heavily on the mind. But while some areas of the city look immaculate and their progress is to be applauded, others parts of the city still need work.

Many people have lost their lives due to the violent drug trade that once overwhelmed some areas of the city. If I tried to write down all of their names, I would possibly run out of ink and paper. The senseless deaths of men isn't just life wasted, it's also a sin that can never be forgiven. Anthony, Tony, Glen, Fats, Lucky, Mooch, Dave, Tony, Alvin, Cecil, Maurice, Vincent, Gary, Apple, Marvin, Warren, Ervin, Smith, Wimpy, Sweet Pee, Sean, Donald, James, Darrius, Ears, Black. All of them have perished while in the game and *because* of the game, and the list goes on. Most residents who have lived in this town for a substantial amount of time are likely to know someone who was a victim of, or a witness to, the violence in the city. For far too many people, this had become a way of life.

Recently I met a woman named Joyce, who was the community leader of OROSW (Operation Reach Out Southwest). OROSW is the neighborhood association that encompasses the

Mount and Fayette Streets area as well as other neighborhoods throughout that portion of West Baltimore. Joyce was interviewed by the authors of *The Corner*, where according to her she provided insightful information to them about the neighborhood. She stated that their book did assist in raising the consciousness of the local officials, which caused them to provide additional resources. But early on Joyce had a concern about the writers' ability to report in an unbiased way. David Simon was a newspaper reporter and Ed Burns was a former Baltimore city cop, and in Joyce's view, their backgrounds could make them unable to be fair and unbiased. She was also concerned that their perspective of the community would be so horrifying to the outside world that it would hurt the community's efforts to fix its problems.

One day Joyce told me a story. Some years ago, she was working out of the offices of her former employer, located on Monroe Street. She was sitting at her desk, having a cup of coffee on a gorgeous morning, when out her window, she saw fifteen or so people running across the street, handing money to a guy. That guy was actually one of my drug runners. The runner had moved the location for the delivery of the heroin intended for his customers from Fayette Street, in an effort to evade the cops.

Joyce was infuriated by what she had witnessed. She opened up the window and began yelling to the crowd, "You better get the hell out of here before I call the police! This is why the neighborhood is in this condition now! It's because of this crap!" Neither the runner nor the addicts even flinched. It was like they never even heard her, but of course, they did.

"You," she continued, pointing to the runner. "I've seen your face around here before and I will remember you!" She couldn't believe the audacity of them, engaging in illegal activity right outside of the office of the community organizer!

I could remember the exact time period she was referring to. When Joyce told me this story, I thought to myself, *Wow, this was really ironic.* The folks that were dealing the drugs outside of her window were from my crew. Back then, we were relentless and determined to distribute our bags of poison. Now, looking back on those days, I can't believe what a really messed up and twisted mentality we had. We were destroying other people's lives, and all we cared about was the profit.

LETTER TO MY DAUGHTER

Hi dad

How are yo doing. I am doing fine. I have a pictures you wanted for 2000-2001. I hope you like them. I sorry the place that you are in. I think about you to. I sorry I can't write a long letter like you did I am not good with writeing letters. The pictures are in the envlope.

Love, Brooke shird

263

"You have a prepaid call from a Federal Correctional Facility. To accept this call, press one now. If you do not wish to accept this call, you may hang up."

This was the automated message on the other end of the prison phone as I waited patiently. This was always an anxiety-filled moment for me. As easy as it was for you to accept my call, it would have been just as easy for you to hang up. That was always a gut-wrenching moment for me, trying to communicate with the outside world.

"Hello? Hi, Dad," was the way you would always answer the telephone when I called. "How are you doing?"

It had been many years since I had actually talked with you in person. But, just to talk to you by phone was a really big deal for me. "Hi, Brooke. How are you doing?"

"I'm doing fine, Dad," you answered. "I have a soccer game this morning and Mom is getting ready to drive me to the field. The playoffs start today and we're the second seed." You had been playing soccer since you were three years old, and now, 10 years later, I still hadn't been to any of your games. I had a few pictures of you playing, but that was about it. I had been incarcerated the majority of your life, which was a terrible example for a father to set for his child.

"That's a good seed! You guys sound like you could win it all. How many goals have you scored?"

"Dad, I haven't scored any goals," you answered, slightly irritated. "I'm a defender. Defenders don't score goals, they defend." I was really into sports, but I didn't know anything about soccer other than when a goal is finally scored during the game, the crowd goes insane. When I was growing up, soccer was nowhere near as popular as it is today.

"Oh, I'm sorry," I responded. "I don't know a lot about soccer." I tried switching gears. Are you going to continue playing when you get into high school?"

Do you remember us having this conversation on the phone, in 2005? I remember it like it was yesterday. Actually, I remember many of our telephone calls, because they were very important to me. Even though we had limited communication, I thought about you every single day.

"Yes, the high school that I want to go to has a sorry team, but I do want to continue playing."

I said, "That's good, because that way, you can get a sports scholarship to help me and your mother pay your college."

"Yeah, I have already talked to Mom about that. I think I want to go to Spelman in Atlanta, just to get out of Baltimore."

"Spelman? That's a really good school."

I can remember you saying, "I have a friend whose mother and grandmother graduated from there."

I was really glad to hear that you want to go to college. A good education is always a plus for everyone. That would definitely increase your chances of having a better life. A much better life than the one I lived for so many years.

"Do you know what you want to major in when you go to college?" I asked.

"Yes," you answered quickly. "I think that I want to be a lawyer or a model." I was okay hearing the lawyer part of your career plans, but the model portion was another story altogether. I didn't have anything against you becoming a model, but I realized how tough a goal that is to accomplish. To hear that you wanted to be a lawyer was ironic for obvious reasons, but great news for the parent who never was much of a parent at all.

The inmate telephone calls from prison only last for fifteen minutes, maximum. That wasn't a lot of time to have a conversation, especially when I hadn't seen you for many years. After our call ended, the prison policy was that I had to wait an hour before I could make another call. There were usually several inmates standing in line to call their families, so that one-hour wait could sometimes turn into two or three hours.

My conversation with you continued: "Speaking of school, how have your grades been? Your mother told me that you weren't doing so well lately."

The phone went silent. "Yes, my last report card wasn't great, but I'm doing better this quarter. I just received my progress report a week ago and I am doing okay in every subject except gym."

"What's the problem with gym?" I asked. "You're playing soccer, so you shouldn't have a trouble with gym." For reasons guys won't ever understand, a lot of young girls despise gym class.

Talking on the telephone to you was always good. It gave me even more reason to look forward to going home. When a man is in a federal prison, he's usually hundreds of miles away from home, so visiting is very difficult. The next best way to communicate is the telephone. The problem with the telephone was that by the time we got into a really good conversation, my fifteen minutes had expired. Sometimes having to end the call generated a lot of stress.

"I have to ask you a question, Daddy," you said to me. I had no idea what was coming next. It could be a fastball or it could be a slow curve. "When will you be coming home?"

For years I avoided answering that question when you asked and it wasn't that I didn't think that you had the right to know. I was just trying to spare your feelings. I can remember you asking me this same question when I was first incarcerated. I lied and told you that I would be home in one year. You burst into tears. Back then, a year was like a lifetime to you. Hearing you crying was tough for me, especially since I knew that I actually had much more time remaining than one year. I felt like I couldn't tell you that I had seven more years to go before I would be back home on the playground with you. I thought that I was doing the right thing by hiding the truth, but I realize now that I was wrong; I made a big mistake.

During this particular telephone conversation, I told the truth: "I have a year to go before I'll by home."

You responded by saying, "You said the same thing about two years ago, that you would be home in a year."

"Yeah, I did say that, didn't I? But this time it is actually one year. This time I am telling you the truth."

On the other end of the phone, I could hear a listless, "All right." I could definitely tell that you didn't believe what your father had just said, but that was okay. You were right not to believe me until I earned your trust back.

There was so much pain associated with being away from you that it is still hard for me to put it into words. I never meant to leave you and I missed you every single day. I'm extremely sorry that I went away and hurt you. It definitely wasn't something I planned. When you're not living your life the right way, at some point, you have to suffer the consequences, and that was what happened to me. But your family suffers the consequences, too. I hadn't seen you in four years at one point and that was very difficult to deal with. That is a long time for a father to be away from his child. The few times your uncle brought you to see me, you didn't like to see me behind bars and I could easily understand that. No one would ever feel comfortable seeing someone they care about locked away in prison.

A lot of things happened in your life during the time that I was gone that I wasn't a part of. Those aspects of your life I will never be able to get back. Never in a million years did I ever think that our relationship would evolve this way, with me being away from you all those years. If I had it my way, there are a lot of things in my life I would change. Being away from you would be one of them. All of your soccer games that I wasn't able to attend, your birthday parties where I wasn't there, all of the times you had homework and I couldn't be there to help you complete it, all of the times that you cried and I wasn't there, I wish I could change all of that. Every single second that I had been away from you, I would like to change.

There aren't many children who want to be without a father in their life. I can remember many times that my father wasn't there for me. Even though physically my father was around up until the time I was in my early teenage years, mentally he wasn't there because he was drunk most of the time. For me, this was like growing up without any father at all. I definitely can relate to how you felt when I was gone.

I realize that it will be hard to regain the trust that you once had in me. I remember when I even lied to you about why I was in prison to begin with. I was actually ashamed of being there and I didn't want you to be ashamed of your father. I didn't want you to feel embarrassed that your father sold illegal drugs to other kids' parents. I told you that I had been in prison for not paying my taxes, but that was a lie and I am sorry.

I remember being there in the delivery room to see you enter the world. By the time you took your very first breath, our bond was sealed. From that moment, I was very protective of you. I still remember when the doctor turned you upside down to drain the mucus from your nose. My first instinct was to grab you away from him until I realized that he was just doing it to take care of you. Later that day, I can remember looking at you through the window of the nursery at Sinai Hospital. You were only a few hours old when the nurses had you dressed in all pink. One of the nurses picked you up and brought you closer to the window so that I could get a better look. By then, they had washed the birth gunk off of your little body. You were the cutest thing that I had ever seen. You had a full head of black hair, more hair than any of the other new arrivals to the nursery. You were struggling to open your little eyes, but once open, you were fighting to deal with the shining light. You were also crying a lot at the time, although the nurses assured me that was a good sign. To them, a newborn crying was a sign that their senses were beginning to work properly.

A few days later when we were driving you home from the hospital, the funniest thing happened. You were crying in the car all the way up until the time I turned the music on. As soon as the tunes began to play, you stopped crying. I wanted to see if you had actually stopped crying only because of the music, so I lowered the sound and you instantly began to weep. Once I turned the sound up again, you became quiet. Only then was I assured that you would probably fall in love with music one day.

The first couple of days you were home from the hospital, it was a big adjustment period for everyone. You would usually sleep all day and then sip on your baby martini all night long, keeping everyone in the house at attention. That was okay with me because I was just happy to have you in the world. You were my first and only child and the love of my life. You changed my world forever.

I am sorry that things didn't work out between your mother and me. We both made some really bad mistakes in our relationship. I still regret those mistakes, but there is nothing I can do about them now but learn from them. I was only twenty-one years old when I first met your mother. Early in our relationship, we both did things to erode the trust between us. I was young, inexperienced, and far too immature. Those traits are not exactly the proper mixture for a successful relationship. Your mother and I both wanted things to work out, but we simply didn't have the tools needed to fix the problems we were having. One of the big problems was that I spent so much time in prison. That kind of absence was a huge hurdle that we could not overcome.

Going away to prison is what happens when a person makes the foolish choice to do the wrong thing; there's a heavy price to pay. I hope and pray that you continue to do the right thing with your life. That is not to say that once in a while you won't make a bad choice because everyone does. If you continue on the right path, the path that you have been on for most of your life, there is no doubt in my mind that you will be successful.

Now that I am back in your life, I know that every now and then, we may have a difficult time reconnecting. I've been gone so long that I may seem like a stranger to you at times. We need to get to know each other all over again and I realize that will be a tough task. It's going to take a lot of patience for me to rebuild the bond that I broke, but all I'm asking for now is a chance to prove myself to you. I won't let you down ever again and I hope that you will accept me back into your life.

Love, Dad

PART OF THE PROBLEM

The drug dealers and the addiction are both part of this complicated problem that seems to have no solution. The hustlers who distribute the needles to the addicts to inject the deadly poison are part of the problem. The illegal sale of firearms on the street is also part of the problem. The boosters selling stolen flat screen televisions in exchange for cash to buy a fix, the guys on the street moving pirated DVD's of X-*Men*, the counterfeit twenty-dollar bills being circulated at a fast pace: all these things are part of the problem. The entire scene is one big conglomerate of dysfunction and mayhem.

This illegal smorgasbord of doom and gloom is venomous. In order to prosper in it, one man has to be prepared to turn another man's world upside down. It's the food chain of the concrete jungle, where these soldiers of misfortune struggle to survive. This vicious cycle serves no usefulness in a community already vulnerable and on the brink of destruction. The cycle may sometimes move to a different location in the city, maybe a different block, but it continues to turn.

You've got two choices here – you can be part of the solution or you can be part of the problem. I definitely wasn't part of the solution to the heroin and crime epidemic in Baltimore during the 1990s. Like many others, I was a part of the problem. I was actually helping to bleed the community dry, while others were desperately trying to apply a tourniquet. I never helped organize the community in a positive way. I sold havoc in a glassine bag, filled with the pain of a fire-breathing dragon.

There are zero benefits to using heroin. The addict suffers, the family of the addict suffers, and the community as a whole suffers. For many, this becomes an ongoing scenario that transcends generations. A father, who is a heroin addict, fathers a son that grows up to become an addict, who then has a child himself that grows up to become an addict. It's a vicious cycle of destruction and despair, sprinkled with a dash of mental anguish and served with a glass of complete dysfunction.

Even though the streets where Diamond in the Raw used to spread its poison are now cleaned up, Baltimore still has one of the largest populations of heroin addicts in the country, per capita. Baltimore is actually a great place to live, if you're not involved in the underworld or the street mayhem that sends a man off to a bad place. This city has two divided cultures that live side by side and not far away from one another. There are the majority of people, who obey most of the laws of the land on a daily basis, and then there are those who twist and turn each city ordinance into a useless piece of paper.

Back in the 1980s, former-Mayor Kurt Schmoke proposed a radical plan to fight illegal drug use in the Baltimore. The mayor wanted to decriminalize some illegal drugs at a time when legislators in Washington D.C. were spending millions, and even billions, to wage their infamous War on Drugs. For the hustler on the street corner, the former mayor's plan would have been devastating. Here was his plan: Who would pay cash for illegal drugs if they could get the stuff for free? That would be like fighting over water in the ocean. The dealers would be padlocking the doors to their stash houses faster than you could say OUT OF BUSINESS. And the crime related to drug activity would plummet instantly, along with the murder rate, giving the inner city the possibility of tranquility once again. At the time many thought that an idea such as the former Mayor's may have some validity, but would any government implement such an audacious course of action? Who would have believed that almost thirty years later state legislatures around the nation would be adopting initiatives similar to the former Mayor's proposal?

The monetary impact of crime on society has become staggering, but imagine this *hypothetical* scenario for a second. Someone burglarizes your home and steals a television valued at $600.00, then sells it on the street for money to buy illegal drugs. So, you call 911 and the police are dispatched to your location, which may cost the city at least $250.00. The cost to the police department to dispatch a crime lab technician to your home to lift a fingerprint sample and return it to the lab to be analyzed would cost over $1,000.00. The cost to the homeowners to have the door or window damaged during the break-in fixed may cost $400.00 (hopefully covered by homeowners insurance). This is an example of the costs to society for what could be perceived by many as a minor crime. When you look at more serious crimes like shootings or murder those costs multiply by thousands of dollars. The cost of transporting a shooting victim in an ambulance to the hospital, plus his or her emergency room treatment could start at $10,000. (Oftentimes guys in the streets don't have health insurance to cover medical costs). The additional cost to the police department to conduct a crime scene investigation to collect forensics and police detectives assigned to investigate the crime could start at around $10,000. What some people may not realize is that these costs for public services have to be paid by someone and that someone ultimately becomes the taxpayer, which means you and me and everyone else who pays taxes in the city.

These days, the violence in the streets seems more personal to me then years past. More mature now with a totally different perspective on life, I feel the pain of the young people crying out for help. Even though statistics indicate that violent crime in Baltimore has declined over the years, the harm to our young people doesn't seem to hurt less. When will the massacre end? The one which has engulfed many over the decades, lost at the hands of the game. To a degree, this has gone unnoticed, or maybe people have just become numb to it. After several years of hearing the same old news stories, it's no longer news; it's just another story. This massacre that I'm referring to doesn't just involve the people that succumb to drug-related violence in the streets. I'm also referring to the many people who have developed heart disease and died prematurely as a result of their illegal drug use. I'm referring to the people that have slowly damaged their liver and kidneys during their many years of abusing drugs. I'm talking about the people that have contracted HIV/AIDS as a result of sharing infected intravenous needles. What about the family members who become ill due to the stress of living with an addict, the one that steals from the household just to satisfy his or her addiction? There are no monuments for the many souls that have perished due to this vicious cycle. Many times, these deaths won't make the cut on the six o'clock news because the viewers have lost their appetites for these headlines.

The massacre going on now on the streets of not just Baltimore, but urban cities nationwide, does need to be addressed but in a different way then past years. So many individuals are affected by this complicated matter that it's impossible to count each casualty.

When I reminisce on my prison days in California, serving time for drug trafficking, I remember them being some hard times. There was one incident which still stands out in my mind. While speaking with my sister on the telephone one day, the conversation really turned disturbing. She reluctantly told me that our mother had been robbed. She had just gotten off of work one day and she was walking to her car. Some young crack addict literally jumped out of the bushes and snatched her pocketbook, terrifying her. My mother never put up a fight and all she could do was watch as the guy fled the scene with her belongings. Horrified by what had just happened, she went back inside the building where she worked to get help. The police were on the scene in minutes. He didn't make it far from the scene of the crime. Within minutes, the crack addicted purse-snatcher was arrested and booked for his troubles.

The irony to this is that this addict-turned-criminal was young, so he didn't realize how some African American women who lived in rough neighborhoods had learned to protect themselves. Back in the 60s and 70s, when my mother grew up, the wise thing for a woman who lived in a rough neighborhood to do was to carry a purse, but keep her cash in her pockets, or even in her bra. That is exactly what my mother did on this day. The cash was in her pockets, so the hapless purse-snatcher only got seven dollars. Once Mr. Genius finally did make it to court for sentencing, the judge showed him no mercy for his foul play and lack of good sense. He was sentenced to one year for each of the seven dollars he which stolen. So, he went to prison for seven years for stealing only seven bucks.

That incident really began to change my perception of the streets. At one point in time, I was the one providing the poison that helped turn these guys into addicts and from there, into criminals. I was dishing out pain, not just to these lost souls, but to their brothers, mothers, or fathers, who probably felt even more pain coping with an addicted family member.

The guy who robbed my mother could have killed her and the only thing that I could have done was helplessly feel the pain from behind a California prison wall. But who was I to complain? The guy who robbed my mother was undoubtedly an addict, so he could have been one of my customers or workers at one time or another. When I was out there selling drugs, I never thought for a minute about where the addicts were getting their money from or who they may have had to hurt to get it because at the time I didn't care.

But now I care. I care about a lot of things.

It's possible that some people reading this book may be saying to themselves, "This guy is full of it. He only wants to change now because he got caught." And others may be saying, "He's got some nerve to preach about this self-righteous bull. He was just a drug dealer himself. What does he know?" And guess what. I accept all of this as a fair assessment because at one point I was a big part of the problem and I was never wanted to be part of the solution.

At one of my recent jobs working in human services, I met some of the nicest people in the world. There I was reminded that there are still some very good people out on the planet today. On some days my office there could turn into the true-life version of the television show *The Office*, but for the most part, these were some very good-hearted individuals. There was this one particular situation that stood out to me. One of my co-workers was resigning to move to another organization. She had been there in this position for ten years, supporting the community. Ten years was just about the same amount of time that I had served in prison. Everyone knew that she was leaving, so my co-workers were giving her a farewell party.

The party was insightful for me, while at the same time, emotional for some of my co-workers. Many of them, including the woman who was leaving, began crying a waterfall of tears from the start of the ceremony to the end. This was the first time I had experienced such an emotional farewell party. She wasn't leaving like in leaving the country; she had just gotten another job across town. Everyone there was upset because of her impending departure. Suddenly I realized that my co-workers didn't want anything from this woman other than the love that she had given them over the years. To them, love was more valuable than any material items which could've been provided. A lot of the people that I had met in the game never really cared about me; the only thing that most of them cared about was what I could do to help them financially. I realized that the people at this party were the type of people I needed in my life. I needed people that would care about me.

This book isn't about me glorifying the game because the game is not pretty at all. This book speaks how a young kid should have made better decisions in his young life. This book is about the ugly side of the street life where many never live long enough to tell the story. When you're out there and you've got bullets whizzing within inches of your head, that's not fun. When you've got a person out there who wants to kill you for a fee, that's not fun. When there are federal agents working day and night to put you in prison for the rest of your life, that's not fun. When you have to live that way each and every day like I did, that's not fun.

When you're young and you have so much energy that you don't know what to do with it, you can be vulnerable. You can feel like you're hunting for the things that you want in life, without a clear understanding of the things you actually *need*. When you're twenty years old, you should be planning for the life you envision for yourself at age thirty. When you're thirty years old, you should be planning for the life you envision for yourself at age forty. The reason why so many young girls and guys in the community don't establish a twenty- or thirty-year plan for their lives is because they don't believe they'll even be alive that long. Many teenagers out in the community don't think that they'll be alive long enough to see twenty-five years old. That may sound kind of ridiculous, but it's reality for far too many. Some look at the kids standing next to them and see that many of them are dying or going to prison, so they develop this "I'm next" mentality. They don't feel the need to plan for the future because they don't think they have a future. I can relate to this irrational thinking because that was the scenario I faced at one time. When I was dealing drugs, I never thought that I would live to see the age of forty, but here I am. It was a long and tough road, mined with treachery and pain, much of which was self-inflicted; but with many scars and bruises, I made it.

For those that think that selling illegal drugs is the only way out, think twice, or even think three times before diving into this dark black hole filled with dead ends. You can roll the dice and hope the Game Gods will spare you, but if they don't, you're screwed. You can always take a shot at a dance with the devil. But I'm here to tell you that isn't the answer. As you have read, I wasn't the average guy in the drug business, but in the end, I turned out to be the average guy walking out of prison with nothing left but the huge task of rebuilding his life. Every drug dealer thinks he's got a better way to maneuver through the game. Every drug dealer thinks that he's got a better business plan than the guy before him. Every drug dealer thinks that he can tweak his blueprint just a bit differently than the other guy, so the ending will be different for him. That's the same thing that I thought.

That kind of thinking is part of the reason I served over ten years in prison, staring at the walls and wondering how the hell I got there. That kind of thinking is how I ended up leaving my daughter without a father in her life for over a decade.

Writing this book really took a toll on me mentally, as it should have. These pages contain the truth and very often the truth hurts. Having to relive all of the distasteful things that I have done in my lifetime was difficult. Many of the events mentioned here, I had completely forgotten about until I picked up the pen to write down my foul deeds. Most of the things I have written about here were buried deep inside the crevices of my psyche. Who wants to remember some of the worst times of his life, and then turn those nightmares over to print for the entire world to read? Who wants to remember the pain and suffering he's caused so many people? It's human nature to want to forget these things. Its human nature to want to delete these horrific data files from the computer of your mind. For many years I thought that I had rid myself of this pain, but I hadn't at all. I only covered up the laceration with a very thin bandage, just to slowdown the bleeding. As soon as I started writing, that bandage began to peel off, exposing those old wounds to the irritation of reality.

The pain of some of life's hardest lessons has a tendency to hang around for a very long time. For me, this book is the beginning of my healing process. This is my way of cleansing my soul and at the same time shedding some light in some very dark places. My hope is that this literature will inspire someone else to do the right thing when the wrong thing seems much easier. I hope my story can deter someone else from going down this unforgiving highway to nowhere. If a million people were to read this book and it only changed the life of one young soul, I could claim a small amount of success. But an enormous amount of work still has to be done. According to the calculations of the tall skinny kid from Edmondson Village who was good in math, there still would be many more lives to deliver from the lure of the streets.

THE END

ABOUT THE AUTHOR

KEVIN SHIRD

Kevin Shird is a former drug trafficker who has dedicated his life to preventing at-risk youth from going down a similar path. To that end, in 2007, he and childhood friend, Grammy-nominated R&B singer, songwriter, and actor Mario Barrett, partnered to co-found the Mario Do Right Foundation (MDRF). The mission of this unique non-profit is to educate, mentor, and support children living with substance-abusing parents and family members. His passion is driven by his own life growing up with an alcohol addicted father. As president of the foundation, Kevin has formed strategic partnerships with numerous organizations to bring resources to schools and communities, including a partnership with the National Institute on Drug Abuse. In 2011, the Mario Do Right Foundation and NIDA collaborated to present National Drug Facts Week, to forward its mission.

Kevin served in the human services arena prior to co-founding MDRF. At the Center for Urban Families, he helped ex-offenders looking for a better way of life to learn job skills to facilitate their reintegration into society. Before that, he worked at the Bon Secours Community Support Center, where he taught financial literacy to low-income residents in West Baltimore. A lifelong resident of Baltimore, Kevin firmly believes that supporting children living with substance-abusing parents and family members is crucial to reversing the city's drug problem and to protecting its youth.

In 2010, Kevin organized focus groups and consulted with officials at the University of Maryland Drug Treatment Center and the Center for Learning and Health at Johns Hopkins Bayview Medical Center before developing MDRF's prevention education program. The Live Right–Do Right program, launched in 2011, is a school-based substance abuse prevention program for adolescents and teens. The program was designed to educate and empower youth to make informed decisions, utilizing a holistic approach. The program contains a suite of wrap-around services, which include an evidence-based curriculum, family counseling and substance abuse treatment referrals, mental health evaluations, and mentoring. The evidence-based curriculum provides students with life skills training, using techniques proven to reduce the risk of alcohol, tobacco, and drug abuse.

In addition to his continuing work with MDRF, Kevin is a member of the Leadership Council for Open Society Institute-Baltimore, which focuses on testing the effectiveness of place-based philanthropy strategy on some of the biggest challenges facing Baltimore and other urban centers in the United States. In 2013, Kevin became a founding member of the National African American Drug Policy Coalition Baltimore Chapter.